T0324480

KERNELS FOR
STRUCTURED DATA

SERIES IN MACHINE PERCEPTION AND ARTIFICIAL INTELLIGENCE*

Editors: **H. Bunke** (Univ. Bern, Switzerland)
P. S. P. Wang (Northeastern Univ., USA)

*For the complete list of titles in this series, please write to the Publisher.

Series in Machine Perception and Artificial Intelligence – Vol. 72

KERNELS FOR STRUCTURED DATA

Thomas Gärtner

Fraunhofer Institute Intelligent Analysis and
Information Systems IAIS
Germany

 World Scientific

NEW JERSEY • LONDON • SINGAPORE • BEIJING • SHANGHAI • HONG KONG • TAIPEI • CHENNAI

Published by

World Scientific Publishing Co. Pte. Ltd.

5 Toh Tuck Link, Singapore 596224

USA office: 27 Warren Street, Suite 401-402, Hackensack, NJ 07601

UK office: 57 Shelton Street, Covent Garden, London WC2H 9HE

British Library Cataloguing-in-Publication Data
A catalogue record for this book is available from the British Library.

Series in Machine Perception and Artificial Intelligence — Vol. 72
KERNELS FOR STRUCTURED DATA

Copyright © 2008 by World Scientific Publishing Co. Pte. Ltd.

ISBN-13 978-981-281-455-5
ISBN-10 981-281-455-8

Printed in Singapore.

To my parents

Preface

All the interests of my reason, speculative as well as practical, combine in the three following questions: 1. What can I know? 2. What ought I to do? 3. What may I hope?

(Immanuel Kant, The Critique of Pure Reason)

Dear Reader,

my interest in what is now the topic of this book has begun during my studies at the University of Bristol, continued through my PhD in Bonn, and still lasts. Kernel for structured data are of interest to researchers in machine learning and data mining but also to practitioners in many other fields applying state-of-the-art machine learning techniques. Machine learning and data mining are two research fields concerned with automated learning that have demonstrated considerable success in a wide variety of applications and hence became key enabling technologies in many areas.

Kernel methods are currently one of the most popular class of machine learning algorithms. The best known kernel method is the support vector machine. Kernel methods are distinguished by their theoretically sound foundation in learning theory and their outstanding empirical results. These have first been achieved on domains where the objects of learning can easily be embedded in a Euclidean space.

Real-world machine learning problems, however, are often such that the objects that we want to learn about have no natural representation in attribute-value form. An example of such a problem is to estimate the activity of chemical compounds against an illness. In this application one very natural representation of such chemical compounds is their chemical structure graph. Kernel methods and other conventional machine learning algorithms can not directly be applied to this sort of problems.

This book is concerned with the extension of kernel methods to structured data. In particular we consider two different representation languages for structured data: logic and graphs. As a logic based representation we chose to use the basic terms of a typed higher-order logic. For graphs we will consider directed and undirected labelled graphs. The distinction between these representation languages is beneficial for the clarity of the description of the kernel function as well as from a computational perspective. Both formalisms, as we will see, lend themselves naturally to certain kinds of application domains. Together they cover most—if not all—kinds of structured data that might occur in real-world applications.

The natural way to extend kernel methods to logical and graph-based representations of structured data is to define a positive definite kernel function on the set of possible object representations. This book presents a systematic approach to define kernel functions for structured data and to apply these kernel functions to large scale real-world machine learning problems. We define and characterise suitable kernel functions for structured data and their computational properties. Our empirical evaluation shows that kernel methods with our kernel functions for structured data substantially outperform conventional methods on a variety of important application domains.

Life is just a long random walk

(Devroye, Györfi, and Lugosi. A Probabilistic Theory of Pattern Recognition)

Many thanks go to Peter Flach for introducing me to the world of machine learning and Colin Campbell for teaching me about support vector machines. Since then, Peter has helped me in an uncountable number of ways—Thanks!

Back to Germany I started my PhD thesis at the University of Bonn and at Fraunhofer IAIS which at the time was called GMD AIS. It goes without saying that my thesis supervisor, Stefan Wrobel, has had the largest impact on my thesis and thus this book. Thanks for your advice, support, help, comments, pleasant conversations, etc. I am also very grateful to the remaining members of my thesis committee and reviewers: Michael Clausen, Stefan Kramer, Wolfgang Alt, and Reinhard Klein. In particular, I want to thank Michael Clausen who read this thesis very carefully and gave many helpful comments.

Of course, fruitful research is only possible in friendly and pleasant working environments. Michael—thanks for providing such an environment. Tamás—thanks for your sense of humour and our scientific discussions. Hendrik and Francois—thanks for all our discussions and all the fun we had with many red wines and/or white beers. Myriam—thanks for all your help. Though I could easily continue this list of colleagues, I want to keep things short and just thank everybody who works or worked at IAIS (inside and outside the knowledge discovery group) who made my work time more pleasant and easier—Thanks!

One of the parts of my PhD I enjoyed most is travelling. Apart from meeting great people at various conferences, I had the honour of visiting different research labs for collaborations which always left me with some unforgettable experiences. Thanks to everybody in the Freiburg and Leuven machine learning groups—meeting you is always stimulating as well as a lot of fun (and extra thanks for Fluffy). During these travels and various conferences I met a number of people whom I had the pleasure of writing papers with that strongly influenced my thesis. Thanks go to Adam, Alex, Jan, John, Kristian, and Kurt. Just after submitting my thesis I had the opportunity of visiting the statistical machine learning program at the National ICT Australia. Thanks to everybody there for providing a great research environment. Since then, I have visited more groups—thanks to everyone in these groups—and co-authored more paper—thanks to Quoc, Vishy, Ulf, Tobias, Yasemin, Gemma, Hanna, and Jürgen. During the travel free time I enjoy most to work with the people that make up the CAML group: Gihad, Karim, Lana, Mario, and Shankar—Thanks!

The people most important to me must of course also be mentioned: My family and friends. The first and probably most significant influence to this book came, as might be expected, from my parents and sisters—Thanks! Throughout my life (scientific as well as real) I had the pleasure of meeting many more people than I can mention here from all over the world whom I now consider my friends. You know who you are—Thanks!

Thomas Gärtner   18th June 2008

Contents

xi

Notational Conventions

Where possible we will follow the notational conventions given below.

- Calligraphic letters $(\mathcal{A}, \mathcal{B} \ldots)$ denote sets (or particular spaces):
  - $\mathcal{X}$ an instance space,
  - $\mathcal{Y}$ a label set,
  - $\mathcal{V}$ the vertex set of a graph,
  - $\mathcal{E}$ the edge set of a graph, and
  - $\mathcal{H}$ a Hilbert space.

- Capital letters $(A, B, \ldots)$ denote matrices or subsets of some set:
  - E the adjacency matrix of a graph.

- Bold letters or numbers denote special matrices or vectors:
  - $\mathbf{I}$ the identity matrix, i.e., a diagonal matrix (of appropriate dimension) with all components on the diagonal equal to 1.
  - $\mathbf{0}$ the zero element of a vector space or a matrix with all components equal to 0. For the vector spaces $\mathbb{R}^n$ the zero element is the vector (of appropriate dimension) with all components equal to 0. In function spaces we will sometimes use $\mathbf{0}(\cdot)$.
  - $\mathbf{1}$ the matrix (in $\mathbb{R}^{n \times m}$) or the vector (in $\mathbb{R}^n$) with all elements equal t 1.

- Lowercase letters $(a, b, \ldots)$ denote vectors, numbers, elements of some set, or functions:

- n the number of training instances,
- x a single instance, and
- y a single label.

- Lowercase Greek letters $\alpha, \beta, \ldots$ denote real numbers.
- Bold lowercase Greek letters $\boldsymbol{\alpha}, \boldsymbol{\beta}, \ldots$ denote vectors of real numbers.
- Symbols:

  - $A \Rightarrow B$: if A then B.
  - $A \Leftarrow B$: A if B.
  - $A \Leftrightarrow B$: A if and only if B.
  - $f : \mathcal{X} \to \mathcal{Y}$ denotes a function from $\mathcal{X}$ to $\mathcal{Y}$.
  - $f(\cdot)$: to clearly distinguish a function $f(x)$ from a function value $f(x)$ we use $f(\cdot)$ for the function and $f(x)$ only for the value of the function $f(\cdot)$ applied to x. This is somewhat clearer than using f for the function as (out of context) f could be read as a number. In λ-notation we could denote $f(\cdot)$ as $\lambda x.f(x)$.
  - $\{x \in \mathcal{X} : p(x)\}$ denotes the set of elements of $\mathcal{X}$ for which the function $p : \mathcal{X} \to \Omega$ evaluates to true.
  - $\{f(\cdot) \mid f : \mathcal{X} \to \mathcal{Y}\}$: the set of functions from $\mathcal{X}$ to $\mathcal{Y}$ which are defined pointwise, that is, $\forall x \in \mathcal{X} : f(x) \in \mathcal{Y}$. Alternative notations are $\{f : \mathcal{X} \to \mathcal{Y}\}$ and $\mathcal{Y}^{\mathcal{X}}$ but we prefer $\{f(\cdot) \mid f : \mathcal{X} \to \mathcal{Y}\}$ for clarity.
  - $f : A \to B \to C$: As a shorthand for a function that maps every element of A to function from B to C that could be denoted by $f : A \to (B \to C)$ we use the notation $f : A \to B \to C$. If arguments $a \in A$ and $b \in B$ are given at the same time, the notation $f' : A \times B \to C$ could denote the same function.
  - $A^{\top}$ denotes the transpose of the matrix A.
  - $|\cdot|$ denotes the function returning the absolute value of a real number.

- Other notational conventions and exceptions:

  - A_{ij} denotes the component in the i-th row and j-th column of matrix A.
  - $A_{i\cdot}$ denotes the i-th row vector of matrix A.
  - $A_{\cdot j}$ denotes the j-th column vector of matrix A.
  - μ: a measure.

- P: a probability distribution.
- $\mathbb{R}$: the set of all real numbers.
- $\mathbb{N}$: the set of all natural numbers $1, 2, 3, \ldots$.
- Ω: the Booleans $\Omega = \{\top, \bot\}$.

Chapter 1

Why Kernels for Structured Data?

*Der äußere Eindruck auf die Sinne, samt der Stimmung, die er
allein und für sich in uns hervorruft, verschwindet mit der Ge-
genwart der Dinge. Jene beiden können daher nicht selbst die
eigentliche 'Erfahrung' ausmachen, deren Belehrung für die Zu-
kunft unser Handeln leiten soll. [...] mithin frei von der Gewalt
der Zeit ist nur Eines: der 'Begriff'.*

(Arthur Schopenhauer, Zur Lehre von der abstrakten oder
Vernunft-Erkenntnis)

Being able to learn from experience is what enables humans to adapt
to an ever changing environment. Be it the extraction of physical laws
from experimental data or be it the use of experience for decision making,
learning from examples is at the core of intelligent behaviour. Two strongly
connected types of learning are modelling of data and estimating a property
of some objects before it is observed. At a time where the amount of
data collected day by day far exceeds the human capabilities to extract the
knowledge hidden in it, it becomes more and more important to automate
the process of learning. Machine learning and data mining are two research
fields concerned with automated learning. In many business and scientific
applications the use of machine learning methods helped speed up and
reduce the cost of certain processes. For some example applications see
[Graettinger (1999); Fayyad *et al.* (1996)].

Within these research fields, recently a class of learning algorithms is
receiving an ever increasing amount of interest from researchers as well as
practitioners. The most popular learning algorithm in this class of so-called
kernel methods is the *support vector machine*. Its popularity stems from its
sound foundation in learning theory and its ability to provide superior em-

pirical results in many benchmark as well as real-world applications. For an overview over some of these applications we refer to [Bennett and Campbell (2000)]. A very prominent recent example is the superior performance of support vector machines in text classification [Joachims (2002)].

Support vector machines and other kernel methods can directly be applied to all kinds of data that are easily embedded in a Euclidean space. This is the case in the traditional setting of machine learning, which only considers examples represented in a single row of a table. However, there are many potential machine learning applications, where this is not the natural representation. Such an application is, for example, the classification of compounds given their chemical structure graph.

This book is therefore concerned with extending kernel methods in such a way that they can be applied to learning problems where the representation of objects in a single row of a table is not trivial. In particular, we will consider examples represented by terms in a typed higher-order logic, as well as examples represented by graphs. Both logic and graphs are two very common and general languages for representing structured objects. As we will see, they lend themselves naturally to certain kinds of application domains. Together they cover most — if not all — kinds of structured data that might occur in real-world applications. With a systematic extension of kernel methods to logic and graphs, we will be able to apply the whole range of available kernel methods to machine learning problems that involve structured data.

In the remainder of this chapter we will first introduce machine learning, kernel methods, and the particular issues of learning with structured data in some more detail. We will use a simple drug discovery problem to illustrate these concepts. After that, we summarise the goals and contributions of this book.

1.1 Supervised Machine Learning

We begin with an example application.

Example 1.1. The drugs we can buy today to fight a particular illness are probably better than the ones we could have bought a century ago and probably worse than the ones we could buy in a century. The difference between the drugs that fight the same illness are then properties like the effectiveness of the drug against the disease or the solubility of the drug in water. Researchers are working on improving these kind of properties of chemical compounds used as drugs. As an example, we will focus on the effectiveness of drugs in fighting some disease.

Suppose now we knew beforehand a way to estimate this effectiveness for any chemical compound. This knowledge could be used in many ways to speed up the design of new – improved – drugs as well as to reduce the costs of developing new drugs. A bit more formally, for each disease we would like to have a function that estimates the effectiveness of any chemical compound in fighting this disease.

There are different ways to obtain such a function given a disease. One possibility is to make use of chemical knowledge and knowledge about the details of the disease. A different possibility – the one we are interested in – is to look at drugs known to be effective in fighting this disease. Clearly, we can find functions that tell us that the known drugs are effective against the illness — the challenge is to find a function that generalises well over the given examples and thus is able to estimate well the effectiveness of other chemical compounds in fighting this disease.

This, exactly, is the type of problems *machine learning* is interested in. A bit more formally, we need to first introduce the representation space, the learning task, and the hypothesis space. The *representation space* is the set of all possible object descriptions that can occur in a given problem. Let $\mathcal{X}$ denote the representation space. In the example above, the representation space could be the set of all possible chemical structure graphs. The learning task we will mostly consider is *supervised learning*. There, we are interested in one particular (target) property of the objects and know the value of this property for some objects. Let $\mathcal{Y}$ denote the set of possible values of the property. In the example above, $\mathcal{Y}$ could be the set containing the values $+1$ indicating an active compound and -1 indicating an inactive compound. In this case, one speaks of *binary classification*. Alternatively, $\mathcal{Y}$ could be the set of real numbers representing some measure of the compound's activity. In this case, one speaks of *regression*. In supervised learning, we try to find a function that is able to estimate the value of the target property for all elements of the representation space. That is, we try to find a function from $\mathcal{X}$ to $\mathcal{Y}$ that has good predictive performance, or in other words, that generalises well over the objects with observed value of the property. We refer to Section 2.2.1 for a more precise definition of these terms.

It turns out that the difficulty of machine learning is not to find a function that reproduces exactly the known property values. There are many different such functions and unfortunately the function that has best predictive performance need not be among the functions that reproduce best the known property values. Indeed, machine learning algorithms usually prefer "smooth" functions that approximately reproduce the known property values over "non-smooth" functions that exactly reproduce these. This is called *regularisation* (see Section 2.3.2). Usually, also not even all possible functions are considered as solutions to the learning problem by every learning algorithm. The set of possible solutions considered by a learning algorithm is called its *hypothesis space*.

1.2 Kernel Methods

We will now have a fresh look at the machine learning problem introduced in the previous section.

Let us try to devise a simple method to find a function which estimates the effectiveness of chemical compounds against some illness. Recall that the way we want to find this function is to look at chemical compounds for which we know their effectiveness against this illness. Building on this 'experience' with other chemical compounds we want to construct an estimating function.

Suppose we knew how to compute a meaningful similarity between chemical compounds. We will now discuss how to predict the effectiveness of a chemical compound against some disease given that we know the effectiveness of other chemical compounds against this disease. 'Meaningful similarity' implies here that chemical compounds with high similarity have similar chemical properties and biological activity.

The machine learning method known as *radial basis function networks* works in two steps. The first step is a rather technical step in which some parameters (weights) of the estimating function are determined. We will skip this step here. In the second step we compute the similarity of the chemical compound we are interested in with all chemical compounds that are known to be effective and with all chemical compounds that are known not to be effective. Using the weights obtained in the previous step we can compute a weighted sum over the similarities to effective compounds as well as a weighted sum over the similarities to not effective compounds. Then we end up with two numbers. Comparing these two numbers we can estimate the effectiveness of the chemical compound we were originally interested in. The intuition behind this idea is that a chemical compound that is highly similar to many effective compounds but to few not effective compounds is likely to be effective itself and vice versa.

Kernel methods are a special kind of these radial basis function networks. By restricting the class of similarity measures that are considered to so called *positive definite kernel functions*, the parameters of the estimating function can be determined more efficiently and more reliably. The hypothesis space considered by kernel methods consists of all linear combinations of a given class of functions. More precisely, the hypothesis space of kernel methods is the set of linear combinations of positive definite kernel functions with one argument set to an element of the representation space. Mathematically, this space is a Hilbert space with a well-defined inner product and thus norm. For more details see Section 2.3.

The other important part of kernel methods is the algorithm that, given a kernel function and a set of objects with known value of the target property, chooses one function from the hypothesis space that is expected to have best predictive performance. In kernel methods it is common to formulate this as a convex optimisation problem. In order to avoid "non-smooth" solutions, the objective function of the optimisation problem is not just the deviation of the predicted values of the target property from their observed values (the so-called *loss*) but the sum of this deviation and a regularisation term. In fact, in most kernel methods, the Hilbert space norm of the hypothesis function is used as the regularisation term. Whenever the loss function, measuring the deviation between predicted and observed values, satisfies certain properties, this optimisation problem can be guaranteed to be convex as a result of only considering positive definite kernel functions.

The *support vector machine*, the most well known and most frequently used kernel method, is derived by choosing one particular loss function, i.e., one particular way of measuring the deviation of the predicted values from the true values of the target property. The convex optimisation problem can in this case be solved by quadratic programming methods. For this learning algorithm very good theoretical properties have been shown and very good empirical results have been achieved.

One of the features of kernel methods that we will exploit in this book is the independence between the learning algorithm and the kernel function. Different hypothesis spaces can be explored by simply using a different kernel function – without modifying the learning algorithm.

1.3   Representing Structured Data

This book is concerned with extending kernel methods such that they can be applied to machine learning problems where the representation of each object in a single row of a table is not trivial. In the context of the drug design problem introduced above, we consider the representation of chemical compounds by chemical structure graphs. That is, we represent a molecule by a set of atoms, a set of bonds connecting pairs of these atoms, and an assignment of element-types (carbon, oxygen, ...) to atoms and bond-types (single, double, aromatic, ...) to bonds. In this representation, for example, water is represented by a set of three atoms and a set of two bonds connecting the second atom to both other atoms. Furthermore, the element-type oxygen is assigned to the second atom and the element-type hydrogen to the first and third atoms.

Kernel methods have been applied to various real-world problems with very good empirical success. However, as pointed out above, kernel methods, just like other standard machine learning tools, can not directly be applied to problems like the one described in the example above. Why? Machine learning has traditionally focused on problems where each object can be represented in a single row of a table. In the drug design problem described above, however, describing each example in a single row of a table is difficult. Why is this difficult? Consider we had a function that maps every graph to a single row in a single table, such that "classical" machine learning algorithms can directly be applied to the images of the graphs under this map. Ideally, we would like to require three properties of this map: (i) Isomorphic graphs are mapped to the same image. (ii) The function can be computed efficiently, i.e., in time polynomial in the size of the graphs. (iii) Non-isomorphic graphs are mapped to different images. As the problem of deciding graph isomorphism is believed not to be efficiently solveable, i.e., it is believed not to be in P, we can not hope to find a function that satisfies all three properties. Without such a function we can not hope to apply standard machine learning algorithms to graphs represented in a table. Of course we could instead try to find a function that violates some of the conditions but is still good enough for most learning problems we consider or we could try to modify machine learning algorithms such that they interpret graphs represented in a table by one imperfect map in the correct way (respecting isomorphism, for example). Both approaches are not trivial and introduce various complications.

Fortunately, because of the modularity of kernel methods we also have a another option: We leave the learning algorithm unchanged, represent graphs in any meaningful way, and just adapt the kernel function to the chosen representation. This approach does not simplify the general problem but it allows a more systematic solution. Furthermore, considering that positive definite kernel functions themselves can be seen as inner products between the images of examples in a different space, it appears more natural to extend kernel methods to structured data by directly defining a positive definite kernel function on the data rather than first mapping it into a table and then mapping it (implicitly using the kernel function) into yet another space. Last but not least, mapping the data only once – implicitly using the kernel function – has computational advantages that we will explore later in this book.

1.4 Goals and Contributions

The central question this book focuses on is: How can kernel methods be applied in learning problems with structured data? The simplest answer to this question is that kernel methods can be applied to any kind of data as long as a meaningful kernel function is known. This gives rise to new questions like: How can we define what a meaningful kernel function is? Given some structured data — how can we define a meaningful kernel function in a systematic way? The second question is the central question of this book and we need to have an idea about the answer to the first question to answer the second. We will thus provide a categorisation of (more or less) meaningful kernel functions before defining kernel functions for specific kinds of data.

Based on these considerations, we develop two kernel functions for rather general data structures commonly used in computer science: logic and graphs. The logic we use is a higher-order logic with polymorphic types. For knowledge representation purposes we use only the ground terms in this logic and not, as frequently done in first-order logic, sets of predicates. The reason we can do this without losing much expressivity is that higher-order logics allow for the direct modelling of sets inside a term rather than by using a set of predicates only.[1] As a second representation language we

---

[1] The basic terms are powerful enough to even represent graphs in the usual way by introducing a set of identifiers (the vertices) and a set of edges, each consisting of a (ordered or unordered) pair these identifiers. However, the algorithmic and computational challenges of terms with and without identifiers are rather different. For example, without identifiers there are no convergence issues at all, while if we try to exploit the

consider directed and undirected labelled graphs. The distinction between basic terms and graphs is beneficial for the clarity of the description of the kernel functions as well as from a computational perspective. Both formalisms, as we will see, lend themselves naturally to certain kinds of application domains. Together they cover most — if not all — kinds of structured data that might occur in real-world applications.

Work on kernel functions for structured data has started with the influential work of Haussler (1999) and Watkins (1999b). Both proposed rather general frameworks that left several questions open to particular applications of these frameworks. This book is the first systematic approach to define kernel functions for structured data and to apply these kernel functions to large scale real-world machine learning problems. Our empirical evaluation shows that kernel methods with our kernels for structured data substantially outperform conventional methods on a variety of important application domains.

To sum up, the four main contributions of this book are:

- Characterisation of meaningful kernels for structured data and investigation of their computational implications.
- Definition of kernels for logic-based representations: Basic term kernels.
- Definition of kernels for graph-based representations: Walk-based kernels and cyclic pattern kernels.
- Empirical evaluation in a variety of application domains.

1.5   Outline

The outline of this book is as follows:

Chapter 1 gave a general introduction to this book and the areas in which it is located.

Chapter 2 first introduces the necessary mathematical tools needed for the further developments of this book. Then the general learning problem and the kernel based approach to solving learning problems are discussed. Afterwards a set of different kernel methods are described that will be used later in this book.

Chapter 3 develops the necessary basics needed for the kernel definitions

---

identifiers in a term in a meaningful way, convergence will be an issue. We thus consider basic terms (without such identifiers) and graphs, separately.

in the remainder of this book. First, some general remarks on kernels are given and examples of kernel functions often used for inner product spaces are given. Then it is described which combinations of kernels are again kernels. After that alternative kernels for sets are discussed and related work is described.

Chapter 4 describes how kernels for terms in a higher-order logic can be defined based on the type structure of the terms. First, an overview of the higher-order logic is given. Then the default kernel based on the type structure is defined and it is shown that it is positive definite. After that, the implications of using this kernel in a particular class of learning problems is analysed in more detail, before several applications are described.

Chapter 5 discusses kernels for instances that have a natural representation as a graph. First, graphs and some related concepts are introduced. Then, after the difficulty of defining computationally tractable graph kernels has been analysed, a number of effectively applicable graph kernels are proposed. Their application to relational reinforcement learning as well as molecule classification is described thereafter.

Chapter 6 concludes.

1.6 Bibliographical Notes

This book builds on the following published articles:

- Thomas Gärtner, Tamás Horváth, Quoc V. Le, Alex J. Smola, and Stefan Wrobel. Kernel methods for graphs. In L. B. Holder and D. J. Cook, editors, *Mining Graph Data*. John Wiley & Sons, Inc., New York, NY, USA, 2007. Copyright 2007 John Wiley & Sons, Inc. Reprinted with kind permission of John Wiley & Sons, Inc.
- Thomas Gärtner. Predictive graph mining with kernel methods. In S. Bandyopadhyay, U. Maulik, L. B. Holder, and D. J. Cook, editors, *Advanced Methods for Knowledge Discovery from Complex Data*, Advanced Information and Knowledge Processing, pages 95–121. Springer, Berlin/Heidelberg, Germany, 2005. Copyright Springer-Verlag Berlin Heidelberg 2005. Reprinted with kind permission of Springer Science and Business Media.
- Thomas Gärtner, John W. Lloyd, and Peter A. Flach. Kernels

and distances for structured data. *Machine Learning*, 57(3):205–232, 2004. Reprinted with kind permission of Springer Science and Business Media.

- Tamás Horváth, Thomas Gärtner, and Stefan Wrobel. Cyclic pattern kernels for predictive graph mining. In Ronny Kohan, Johannes Gehrke, William DuMouchel, and Joydeep Ghosh, editors, *Proceedings of the tenth ACM SIGKDD International Conference on Knowledge Discovery and Data Mining*, pages 158–167, New York, NY, USA, August 2004. ACM. Copyright 2004 ACM 1-58113-888-1/04/0008. Reprinted with kind permission of ACM.

- Thomas Gärtner. A survey of kernels for structured data. *SIGKDD Explorations*, 5(1):49–58, 2003. Reprinted with kind permission of ACM.

- Thomas Gärtner, Peter A. Flach, and Stefan Wrobel. On graph kernels: Hardness results and efficient alternatives. In Bernhard Schölkopf and Manfred K. Warmuth, editors, *Proceedings of the 16th Annual Conference on Computational Learning Theory and 7th Kernel Workshop*, volume 2777 of *Lecture Notes in Computer Science*, pages 129–143, Berlin/Heidelberg, Germany, August 2003. Springer. Copyright Springer-Verlag Berlin Heidelberg 2003. Reprinted with kind permission of Springer Science and Business Media.

- Kurt Driessens, Jan Ramon, and Thomas Gärtner. Graph kernels and Gaussian processes for relational reinforcement learning. *Machine Learning*, 64(1-3):91–119, 2006. Copyright 2004 Kluwer Academic Publishers. Reprinted with kind permission of Springer Science and Business Media.

- Thomas Gärtner, Kurt Driessens, and Jan Ramon. Graph kernels and Gaussian processes for relational reinforcement learning. In Tamás Horváth and Akihiro Yamamoto, editors, *The 13th International Conference on Inductive Logic Programming*, volume 2835 of *Lecture Notes in Computer Science*, pages 146–163, Berlin/Heidelberg, Germany, 2003. Springer. Copyright Springer-Verlag Berlin Heidelberg 2003. Reprinted with kind permission of Springer Science and Business Media.

- Thomas Gärtner, John Lloyd, and Peter Flach. Kernels for structured data. In Stan Matwin and Claude Sammut, editors, *The Twelfth International Conference on Inductive Logic Programming*, volume 2583 of *Lecture Notes in Computer Science*, pages 66–

83, Berlin/Heidelberg, Germany, July 2002. Springer. Copyright Springer-Verlag Berlin Heidelberg 2002. Reprinted with kind permission of Springer Science and Business Media.

- Thomas Gärtner, Peter A. Flach, Adam Kowalczyk, and Alex J. Smola. Multi-instance kernels. In Claude Sammut and Achim Hoffmann, editors, *Proceedings of the 19th International Conference on Machine Learning*, pages 179–186, San Fransisco, CA, USA, July 2002. Morgan Kaufmann. Copyright Morgan Kaufmann. Reprinted with kind permission of Elsevier.

Chapter 2

Kernel Methods in a Nutshell

The wub eased itself down in the corner with a sigh. "You must forgive me," it said. "I'm afraid I'm addicted to various forms of relaxation. When one is as large as I — "

(Philip K. Dick, Beyond Lies the Wub)

This dissertation is concerned with the application of kernel methods to structured data. Thus, obviously, concepts from both fields are relevant. As we will focus on different knowledge representations in different chapters, here we will mostly introduce preliminaries relevant to machine learning in general and kernel methods in particular.

We begin with a brief introduction of the necessary mathematical concepts. The range of relevant topics is rather broad and a fully self-contained summary is not possible here. The mathematical topics covered range from measurable sets, function integration, via linear and metric spaces, to inner product spaces, and reproducing kernel Hilbert Spaces. Another relevant topic is matrix computations such as eigenvalue decompositions and partitioned inverse equations.

The second section of this chapter is then concerned with the basic problem considered in machine learning. Particular issues are supervised learning, empirical risk minimisation, and performance evaluation methods.

The third section is concerned with the basics of kernel methods. Elements from statistical learning theory, model fitting, and regularisation are summarised and their impact on kernel methods is clarified.

Last but not least we present in this chapter a variety of different kernel methods that can be used to solve very different learning problems on data for which a meaningful positive definite kernel function has been defined.

13

2.1 Mathematical Foundations

This section introduces the mathematical background of kernel functions and of other tools used in this dissertation. The terminology and definitions follow in general along the lines of Kolmogorov and Fomins books on "Elements of the Theory of Functions and Functional Analysis" [Kolmogorov and Fomin (1960b,a)].

2.1.1 *From Sets to Functions*

A *set* is a collection of distinguishable things, each of which is called an *element* of the set [Cantor (1895)]. Two sets $\mathcal{A}, \mathcal{B}$ are equal ($\mathcal{A} = \mathcal{B}$) if they have the same elements. That a is an element of $\mathcal{A}$ is denoted by $a \in \mathcal{A}$. If all elements of $\mathcal{A}$ are also elements of another set $\mathcal{B}$, $\mathcal{A}$ is a *subset* of $\mathcal{B}$. If $\mathcal{A}$ is a subset of $\mathcal{B}$ and there is an element in $\mathcal{B}$ which is not in $\mathcal{A}$, $\mathcal{A}$ is called a *proper subset* of $\mathcal{B}$. The symbol $\emptyset$ is used to denote a set which has no element, the *empty set*. The empty set is a subset of every set. The *power set* of a set $\mathcal{A}$ is the set of its subsets, denoted $2^{\mathcal{A}}$.

Next we define the *union* ('$\cup$'), *intersection* ('$\cap$'), *difference* ('$\backslash$'), and *symmetric difference* ('$\triangle$') of two sets:

- $\mathcal{A} \cup \mathcal{B}$ consists of all elements of $\mathcal{A}$ and all elements of $\mathcal{B}$.
- $\mathcal{A} \cap \mathcal{B}$ consists of all elements belonging to both $\mathcal{A}$ and $\mathcal{B}$.
- $\mathcal{A} \backslash \mathcal{B}$ consists of all elements of $\mathcal{A}$ which are not in $\mathcal{B}$.
- $\mathcal{A} \triangle \mathcal{B} = (\mathcal{A} \backslash \mathcal{B}) \cup (\mathcal{B} \backslash \mathcal{A}) = (\mathcal{A} \cup \mathcal{B}) \backslash (\mathcal{A} \cap \mathcal{B})$.

The *Cartesian product* of two sets $\mathcal{A}, \mathcal{B}$ is the set of all possible pairs of elements from $\mathcal{A}$ and $\mathcal{B}$, i.e., $\mathcal{A} \times \mathcal{B} = \{(a, b) : a \in \mathcal{A} \wedge b \in \mathcal{B}\}$. Let $\mathcal{M}$ be a set. A subset of the Cartesian product $\mathcal{M} \times \mathcal{M}$ is called a *binary relation*. A binary relation φ is usually denoted infix, i.e., $a \varphi b$ means (a, b) is an element of the relation. A binary relation is

- *reflexive* if $a \varphi a$ for all $a \in \mathcal{M}$,
- *symmetric* if $a \varphi b \Leftrightarrow b \varphi a$ for all $a, b \in \mathcal{M}$, and
- *transitive* if $a \varphi b \wedge b \varphi c \Rightarrow a \varphi c$ for all $a, b, c \in \mathcal{M}$.

A binary relation that is reflexive, symmetric, and transitive is called an *equivalence relation*.

Let $\mathcal{M}, \mathcal{N}$ be two sets. A *mapping* $f : \mathcal{M} \rightarrow \mathcal{N}$ is an assignment of each element of $\mathcal{M}$ to one and only one element of $\mathcal{N}$. That a particular $m \in \mathcal{M}$ is mapped to a particular $n \in \mathcal{N}$ by a mapping f is denoted by $n = f(m)$.

Frequently the term *function* is used instead of mapping. For a set $\mathcal{A} \subseteq \mathcal{M}$, $f[\mathcal{A}] = \{f(a) : a \in \mathcal{A}\}$. Furthermore we define for every f the mapping $f^{-1} : 2^{\mathcal{N}} \to 2^{\mathcal{M}}$ such that for every $B \subseteq \mathcal{N}$: $f^{-1}[B] = \{a \in \mathcal{M} : f(a) \in B\}$.

A function $f : \mathcal{M} \to \mathcal{N}$ is

- *injective* if $f(x) = f(y) \Rightarrow x = y$ for all $x, y \in \mathcal{M}$,
- *surjective* if $f[\mathcal{M}] = \mathcal{N}$, and
- *bijective* if f is injective and surjective.

If a function $f : \mathcal{M} \to \mathcal{N}$ is bijective, the function $f^{-1} : \mathcal{N} \to \mathcal{M}$ is defined such that $f^{-1}(n) = m \Leftrightarrow n = f(m)$ for all $n \in \mathcal{N}, m \in \mathcal{M}$. This function f^{-1} is called the *inverse* of f.

A set for which we can denote the number of elements by a natural number is called a *finite set*, otherwise it is called an *infinite set*. Two sets between which we can establish a bijective function, are called *equivalent* and we say they have the same *cardinal number*. The Cardinal number of a finite set is simply the number of elements in the set. Infinite sets equivalent to the set of natural numbers are called *denumerable* and their cardinal number is denoted $\aleph_0$. Infinite sets equivalent to the set of real numbers between zero and one have the power of the continuum, denoted by $\mathfrak{c}$. For any set, its power set has higher cardinal number.

2.1.2 *Measures and Integrals*

A *system of sets* is a set whose elements are again sets. Usually all sets in a system of sets are subsets of some fixed set. The *unit* of a system of sets $\mathfrak{S}$ is the set $\mathcal{E}$ such that $\mathcal{A} \in \mathfrak{S} \Rightarrow \mathcal{A} \cap \mathcal{E} = \mathcal{A}$. A non-empty system of sets is called a *ring of sets* if it is closed under symmetric difference and intersection, i.e., if $\mathcal{A}, \mathcal{B}$ are in the ring then also $\mathcal{A} \triangle \mathcal{B}$ and $\mathcal{A} \cap \mathcal{B}$ are in the ring. This implies also that $\mathcal{A} \setminus \mathcal{B}$ and $\mathcal{A} \cup \mathcal{B}$ are in the ring. Furthermore, every union and intersection of a finite number of sets in the ring is also in the ring. Any ring of sets contains the empty set.

A *Borel algebra* is a ring of sets that, in addition to every sequence of sets $A_1, \ldots, A_n, \ldots$ that it contains, also contains their union. Every Borel Algebra has a unit. For any system of sets $\mathfrak{S}$ there is a Borel algebra containing $\mathfrak{S}$ and at the same time contained in any Borel algebra that contains $\mathfrak{S}$. This Borel algebra is called the *Borel closure* of $\mathfrak{S}$. A *Borel set* is a set that belongs to the Borel closure of the set of intervals $[a, b]$ of real numbers.

A system of pairwise non-intersecting sets $\mathcal{A}_1, \ldots \mathcal{A}_n$, is called a *finite decomposition* of $\mathcal{A}$ if $\mathcal{A} = \bigcup_{i=1}^{n} \mathcal{A}_i$. A system of sets $\mathfrak{S}$ that is closed under intersection is a *semiring* if for all $\mathcal{A} \in \mathfrak{S}$ and $\mathcal{A}_1 \subseteq \mathcal{A}, \mathcal{A}_1 \in \mathfrak{S}$ there is a finite decomposition of $\mathcal{A}$ containing $\mathcal{A}_1$ that is a subset of $\mathfrak{S}$.

A function $\mu : \mathcal{S}_\mu \to \mathbb{R} \cup \{\pm\infty\}$ is called a *measure* if

- $\mathcal{S}_\mu$ is a semiring of sets,
- $\mu(\mathcal{A}) \geq 0$ for all $\mathcal{A} \in \mathcal{S}_\mu$, and
- for any finite decomposition $\mathcal{A}_1, \ldots, \mathcal{A}_n$ of $\mathcal{A} \in \mathcal{S}_\mu$ it holds that $\mu(\mathcal{A}) = \sum_{i=1}^{n} \mu(\mathcal{A}_i)$.

The set $\mathcal{S}_\mu$ is then called the *domain of definition* of μ. It follows directly from the definition that $\mu(\emptyset) = 0$. A measure μ is *countably additive* if for any $\mathcal{A}, \mathcal{A}_1, \mathcal{A}_2, \ldots \in \mathcal{S}_\mu$ with $\mathcal{A} = \bigcup_{i=1}^{\infty} \mathcal{A}_i$ and $i \neq j \Rightarrow \mathcal{A}_i \cap \mathcal{A}_j = \emptyset$ it follows that $\mu(\mathcal{A}) = \sum_{i=1}^{\infty} \mu(\mathcal{A}_i)$.

We now consider countably additive measures whose domain of definition is a Borel algebra and real functions defined on a set $\mathcal{X}$ which we will assume to be the unit of the domain of definition of the measure. A function $f : \mathcal{X} \to \mathbb{R}$ is called μ–*measurable* if for any Borel set $\mathcal{A}$: $f^{-1}[\mathcal{A}] \in \mathcal{S}_\mu$. A function is called *simple* if it is μ–measurable and takes only a countable number of different values. A function satisfies a property *almost everywhere* if the property holds except for a subset of the domain which has measure zero. Two functions are *equivalent* if they take the same values *almost everywhere*.

A sequence $a_1, a_2, \ldots$ of real numbers *converges* to a real number a if and only if for every $\epsilon > 0$ there is an index N_ϵ such that $n \geq N_\epsilon \Rightarrow |a - a_n| < \epsilon$. The number a is then called the *limit* of the sequence and denoted by $a = \lim_{n\to\infty} a_n$. For brevity we sometimes write $a_n \to a$. A sequence for which there is no such number is said to *diverge*. The sequence is said to diverge to $\pm\infty$, denoted by $\lim_{n\to\infty} a_n = \pm\infty$ or short $a_n \to \pm\infty$, if for all $m \in \mathbb{R}$ there is an index $N \in \mathbb{N}$ such that $n > N \Rightarrow \pm a_n > m$. A series of real numbers $\sum_{i=1}^{\infty} b_i = b_1 + b_2 + \cdots$ converges to a if and only if the series $a_1, a_2, \ldots$ of partial sums $a_n = \sum_{i=1}^{n} b_i$ converges to a. A series of real numbers $\sum_{i=1}^{\infty} b_i$ *converges absolutely* if $\sum_{i=1}^{\infty} |b_i|$ converges. A sequence of functions $f_1, f_2, \ldots : \mathcal{X} \to \mathbb{R}$ is said to *converge pointwise* to a function $f : \mathcal{X} \to \mathbb{R}$ if for every $x \in \mathcal{X}, \epsilon > 0$ there is a $N_{\epsilon,x} \in \mathbb{N}$ such that $|f(x) - f_n(x)| < \epsilon$ for all $n \geq N_{\epsilon,x}$. A sequence of functions $f_1, f_2, \ldots : \mathcal{X} \to \mathbb{R}$ is said to *converge uniformly* to a function $f : \mathcal{X} \to \mathbb{R}$ if for every $\epsilon > 0$ there is a $N_\epsilon \in \mathbb{N}$ such that $|f(x) - f_n(x)| < \epsilon$ for all $n \geq N_\epsilon$ and $x \in \mathcal{X}$. Every uniformly convergent sequence of functions is pointwise convergent.

For a simple function that takes the values $y_1, y_2, \ldots; y_i = y_j \Leftrightarrow i = j$ the *Lebesgue integral* over the set $\mathcal{A}$ is defined by

$$\int_{\mathcal{A}} f(x)d\mu = \sum_{i=1}^{\infty} y_i \mu \left(\{x : x \in \mathcal{A}, f(x) = y_i\}\right) = \sum_{i=1}^{\infty} y_i \mu \left(f^{-1}\left[\{y_i\}\right]\right) .$$

A simple function f is called *integrable* if the above sum converges absolutely. An arbitrary function $f : \mathcal{X} \to \mathbb{R}$ is integrable over the set $\mathcal{A}$ if there is a sequence of integrable simple functions $f_1, f_2, \ldots : \mathcal{X} \to \mathbb{R}$ that converge uniformly to $f(x)$. The integral of f over the set $\mathcal{A}$ is then defined as

$$\int_{\mathcal{A}} f(x)d\mu = \lim_{i \to \infty} \int_{\mathcal{A}} f_i(x)d\mu .$$

2.1.3 *Metric Spaces*

A *metric space* is a set $\mathcal{R}$ along with a function $d : \mathcal{R} \times \mathcal{R} \to \mathbb{R}$ such that for all $x, x' \in \mathcal{R}$:

- $d(x, x') \geq 0$ (*positive*),
- $d(x, x') = 0 \Leftrightarrow x = x'$,
- $d(x, x') = d(x', x)$ (*symmetry*), and
- $d(x, z) + d(z, x') \geq d(x, x')$ (*triangle inequality*).

The function d is called a *metric*. If $d(x, x') = 0 \Leftrightarrow x = x'$ does not hold but the weaker condition $d(x, x) = 0$ holds, d is sometimes called a *pseudo-metric* and the space $(\mathcal{X}, d)$ a *pseudo-metric space*. Sometimes a metric is called a *distance*. The elements of $\mathcal{R}$ are sometimes called *points* in $\mathcal{R}$.

An arbitrary set, along with the function $d(x, x') = 1 \Leftrightarrow x \neq x'$ and $d(x, x') = 0 \Leftrightarrow x = x'$, is a metric space. Another important example of a metric space is the *Euclidean n-space*: The set of ordered n-tuples of real numbers $x = (x_1, x_2, \ldots, x_n)$ with $d(x, x') = \sqrt{\sum_{i=1}^{n}(x_i - x_i')^2}$.

Similar to the convergence of a sequence of real numbers, a sequence of points $x_1, x_2, \ldots$ in the metric space $(\mathcal{R}, d)$ is said to *converge* to a point $x \in \mathcal{R}$ if for every $\epsilon > 0$ there is a natural number N_ϵ such that $n > N_\epsilon \Rightarrow d(x, x_n) < \epsilon$ (or short: $\lim_{n \to \infty} d(x, x_n) = 0$). This corresponds to the sequence $d(x_1, x), d(x_2, x), \ldots$ of real numbers converging to 0. x is then called the *limit* of $x_1, x_2, \ldots$, denoted as $\lim_{n \to \infty} x_n = x$ or $x_n \to x$.

In a metric space $(\mathcal{R}, d)$, the set $B(x_0, r) = \{x \in \mathcal{R} : d(x_0, x) < r\}$ is called the *open ball* with centre $x_0 \in \mathcal{R}$ and radius $r \in \mathbb{R}$. The open ball $B(x, \epsilon)$ is often called the *ϵ-neighbourhood* of x. A point $x \in \mathcal{R}$ is called a *limit point* or a *contact point* of a set $X \subseteq \mathcal{R}$ if every ϵ-neighbourhood of x contains at least one point from X. The *closure* of a set $X \subseteq \mathcal{R}$ is the set of all contact points of X. A set is called *closed* if it is equal to its closure. A set $\mathcal{A}$ in a metric space $\mathcal{R}$ is *dense* in a set $\mathcal{B}$ if $\mathcal{B}$ is a subset of the closure of $\mathcal{A}$. $\mathcal{A}$ is *everywhere dense* in $\mathcal{R}$ if its closure is the entire space $\mathcal{R}$. A metric space is *separable* if it contains an everywhere dense denumerable subset.

A sequence of points $x_1, x_2, \ldots$ in the metric space $(\mathcal{R}, d)$ is called a *fundamental sequence* (or *Cauchy sequence*) in $\mathcal{R}$ if for every $\epsilon > 0$ there is a natural number N_ϵ such that $n, n' \geq N_\epsilon \Rightarrow d(x_{n'}, x_n) < \epsilon$. Every convergent sequence is thus fundamental. The metric space $\mathcal{R}$ is said to be *complete* if every fundamental sequence in $\mathcal{R}$ converges to an element in $\mathcal{R}$. A set $\mathcal{M}$ in a metric space is said to be *compact* if every sequence of elements in $\mathcal{M}$ has a subsequence that converges to a point x in $\mathcal{R}$. For an arbitrary set $\mathcal{N}$ in a metric space $(\mathcal{R}, d)$ it holds that: $\mathcal{N}$ is complete if it is compact and $\mathcal{N}$ is closed if it is complete. Furthermore, if $\mathcal{R}$ is complete and $\mathcal{N}$ is closed then $\mathcal{N}$ is complete.

2.1.4 *Linear Spaces and Banach Spaces*

A set $\mathcal{R}$ is a *linear space* (or *vector space*) over a field $\mathbb{K}$ if:

- Addition $+$ is defined such that $(\mathbb{K}, +)$ forms an *abelian group*, i.e.,
  - for any $x, y \in \mathcal{R}$ there is one and only one element $z \in \mathcal{R}$, called their sum $z = x + y$,
  - for any $x, y \in \mathcal{R}$: $x + y = y + x$,
  - for any $x, y, z \in \mathcal{R}$: $x + (y + z) = (x + y) + z$,
  - there is an element $\mathbf{0} \in \mathcal{R}$ with $x + \mathbf{0} = x$ for all $x \in \mathcal{R}$, and
  - for every $x \in \mathcal{R}$ there is a unique element $-x \in \mathcal{R}$ with $x + (-x) = \mathbf{0}$.

- Scalar multiplication $\times$ is defined such that
  - for any $\alpha, \beta \in \mathbb{K}$ and $x \in \mathcal{R}$: $\alpha \times (\beta \times x) = (\alpha\beta) \times x$,
  - for any $\alpha, \beta \in \mathbb{K}$ and $x \in \mathcal{R}$: $(\alpha + \beta) \times x = \alpha \times x + \beta \times x$,
  - for any $\alpha \in \mathbb{K}$ and $x, y \in \mathcal{R}$: $\alpha \times (x + y) = \alpha \times x + \alpha \times y$, and
  - there is an element $1 \in \mathbb{K}$ such that $1 \times x = x$ for all $x \in \mathcal{R}$.

As a convention, we often write αx instead of $\alpha \times x$. From now we will only consider vector spaces over the real numbers. Although many of the results in this and the following chapters carry over to vector spaces over other fields such as the complex numbers, practically relevant in machine learning are so far only vector spaces over the reals. This restriction will often simplify our discussion.

The elements of a linear space are called *vectors*. Given a linear space $\mathcal{R}$, elements $x_1, \ldots, x_n \in \mathcal{R}$, and scalars $\lambda_1, \ldots, \lambda_n \in \mathbb{R}$, $x = \sum_{i=1}^{n} \lambda_i x_i$ is a *linear combination* of $x_1, \ldots, x_n$. For $\lambda_1, \ldots, \lambda_n \geq 0$ and $\sum_{i=1}^{n} \lambda_i = 1$, $x = \sum_{i=1}^{n} \lambda_i x_i$ is a *convex combination* of $x_1, \ldots, x_n$. A set $\mathcal{X} \subseteq \mathcal{R}$ is *convex* if for any two $x, x' \in \mathcal{X}$, all convex combinations of x, x' are also in $\mathcal{X}$. The set of all linear combinations of $x_1, \ldots, x_n \in \mathcal{R}$ is called the *linear hull* (or *span*) of $x_1, \ldots, x_n$. The set of all convex combinations of $x_1, \ldots, x_n \in \mathcal{R}$ is called the *convex hull* of $x_1, \ldots, x_n$. The $x_1, \ldots, x_n$ are called *linearly independent* if and only if $\sum_{i=1}^{n} \lambda_i x_i = \mathbf{0} \Leftrightarrow \lambda_1 = \lambda_2 = \cdots = \lambda_n = 0$.

A set $\mathcal{X} \subseteq \mathcal{R}$ is linearly independent if and only if every finite subset of $\mathcal{X}$ is linearly independent. A linearly independent set $\mathcal{X} \subseteq \mathcal{R}$ is a *basis* of $\mathcal{R}$ if its linear hull is $\mathcal{R}$. If the basis of a vector space is a finite set, the space is called *finite-dimensional*, otherwise *infinite-dimensional*. The cardinal number of every basis of a linear space $\mathcal{R}$ is constant and called the *dimension* of $\mathcal{R}$. It can be shown that a space is *separable* if and only if it has a countable basis.

A function $f : \mathcal{M} \to \mathcal{N}$ mapping elements of one linear space $\mathcal{M}$ to another $\mathcal{N}$ is called a *linear transformation* (or *linear operator*) if $f(x+y) = f(x) + f(y)$ and $f(\alpha x) = \alpha f(x)$ for all $x, y \in \mathcal{M}$ and $\alpha \in \mathbb{R}$.

A linear space $\mathcal{R}$ is a *normed linear space* if for every $x \in \mathcal{R}$ there is a real number $\|x\|$ such that

- $\|x\| \geq 0$,
- $\|x\| = 0 \Leftrightarrow x = \mathbf{0}$,
- $\|\alpha x\| = |\alpha| \|x\|$, and
- $\|x + x'\| \leq \|x\| + \|x'\|$.

Every normed linear space is a metric space with the function $d(x, x') = \|x - x'\|$. A complete normed linear space is called a *Banach space*. A subspace of a normed linear space $\mathcal{R}$ is a closed non-empty subset $\mathcal{L}$ of $\mathcal{R}$ for which $x, x' \in \mathcal{L}$ implies $\alpha x + \beta x' \in \mathcal{L}$ for all $\alpha, \beta \in \mathbb{R}$.

A function mapping elements of a normed linear space $\mathcal{R}$ to a real number is often called a *functional*. A functional f is *linear* if $f(\alpha x + \beta x') = \alpha f(x) + \beta f(x')$ for all $x, x' \in \mathcal{R}$ and numbers $\alpha, \beta \in \mathbb{R}$. A functional $f : \mathcal{R} \to \mathbb{R}$ is *continuous* at a particular $x \in \mathbb{R}$ if for all $\epsilon > 0$ there is a $\delta > 0$ such that $\|x - x'\| < \delta \Rightarrow |f(x) - f(x')| < \epsilon$. A linear functional is a *continuous linear functional* if it is continuous for all $x \in \mathcal{R}$. Let f

be a linear functional continuous at $x \in \mathcal{R}$, that is short $f(x_n) \to f(x)$ as $x_n \to x$. This functional is also continuous at any other x' as with $x'_n \to x'$ we obtain

$$f(x'_n) = f(x'_n - x' + x) + f(x') - f(x) \ \to \ f(x) + f(x') - f(x) = f(x') \ .$$

A linear functional $f : \mathcal{R} \to \mathbb{R}$ is a *bounded linear functional* if there is a $b \in \mathbb{R}$ such that $|f(x)| \leq b\|x\|$ for all $x \in \mathcal{R}$. A linear functional is continuous if and only if it is bounded. Suppose $f(\cdot)$ is not bounded, that is for every $n \in \mathbb{N}$ there is a $x_n \in \mathcal{R}$ such that $|f(x_n)| > n\|x_n\|$. With $x'_n = \frac{x_n}{n\|x_n\|}$ we have $x'_n \to \mathbf{0}$ and $|f(x'_n)| = \frac{1}{n\|x_n\|}|f(x_n)| > 1$ which shows that $f(\cdot)$ is not continuous at $\mathbf{0}$. Conversely, choose b such that $|f(x)| \leq b\|x\|$ for all $x \in \mathcal{R}$. For an arbitrary sequence $x_n \to \mathbf{0}$ we have $|f(x)| \leq b\|x_n\| \to 0$ and $f(\cdot)$ is continuous at $\mathbf{0}$. Often 'functional' means 'continuous linear functional'. We will follow this convention.

Addition and scalar multiplication can be defined on functionals f, g as follows:

- For all $x \in \mathcal{R}$, $(f + g)(x) = f(x) + g(x)$.
- for all $x \in \mathcal{R}$ and $\alpha \in \mathbb{R}$, $(\alpha f)(x) = \alpha f(x)$.

The norm of a functional is defined as $\|f(\cdot)\| = \sup_{x \in \mathcal{R}}\{|f(x)|/\|x\| : x \neq \mathbf{0}\}$. The set of all functionals on a normed linear space $\mathcal{R}$ is called the *dual* (or *conjugate*) space $\mathcal{R}^*$. The conjugate space is always a complete normed linear space.

A set of points $x_1, x_2, \ldots$ in a normed linear space $\mathcal{R}$ *converges in norm* (*converges strongly*) to $x \in \mathcal{R}$ if the sequence $\|x_1 - x\|, \|x_2 - x\|, \ldots$ of real numbers converges to 0. This coincides with the convergence in the corresponding metric space. A set of points $x_1, x_2, \ldots$ in a normed linear space $\mathcal{R}$ *converges weakly* to $x \in \mathcal{R}$ if for every $f(\cdot) \in \mathcal{R}^*$ the sequence $f(x_1), f(x_2), \ldots$ of real numbers converges to the real number $f(x)$. Strong convergence implies weak convergence, as $|f(x_n) - f(x)| \leq \|f(\cdot)\|\|x_n - x\|$ for every functional $f(\cdot)$.

2.1.5 *Inner Product Spaces and Hilbert Spaces*

An *inner product space* is a linear space $\mathcal{R}$ along with a function $\langle \cdot, \cdot \rangle :$ $\mathcal{R} \times \mathcal{R} \to \mathbb{R}$ such that

- for all $x, y \in \mathcal{R}$: $\langle x, y \rangle = \langle y, x \rangle$ (*symmetry*),
- for all $x, y, z \in \mathcal{R}$ and $\alpha \in \mathbb{R}$: $\langle \alpha x, y \rangle = \alpha \langle x, y \rangle$ and $\langle x + z, y \rangle = \langle x, y \rangle + \langle z, y \rangle$ (*linearity*), and

- for all $x \in \mathcal{R}$: $x \neq \mathbf{0} \Rightarrow \langle x, x \rangle > 0$ *(positiveness)*.

The function $\langle \cdot, \cdot \rangle$ is called the inner product. Every inner product space is a normed linear space with the norm $\|x\| = \sqrt{\langle x, x \rangle}$ and thus (Section 2.1.4) a metric space with the metric $d(x, x') = \|x - x'\| = \sqrt{\langle x - x', x - x' \rangle}$. In every inner product space $\mathcal{R}$ the *Schwarz inequality* $|\langle x, x' \rangle| \leq \|x\| \|x'\|$ holds for all $x, x' \in \mathcal{R}$. Two elements $x, x' \in \mathcal{R}$ with $\langle x, x' \rangle = 0$ are called *orthogonal*. An *orthogonal basis* is a basis with pairwise orthogonal elements. The set of points $\{x \in \mathcal{R} : \langle w, x \rangle = 0\}$ is the *hyperplane* orthogonal to $w \in \mathcal{R}$. The vector $\frac{w}{\|w\|}$ is called the *normal vector* of the hyperplane. Two inner product spaces $(\mathcal{R}, \langle \cdot, \cdot \rangle), (\mathcal{R}', \langle \cdot, \cdot \rangle')$ are *isomorphic* if there is a linear operator $f : \mathcal{R} \to \mathcal{R}'$ such that for all $x, y \in \mathcal{R}$: $\langle x, y \rangle = \langle f(x), f(y) \rangle'$.

There are different definitions of the term Hilbert space. The most general definition used for example by Meschkowski (1960) calls an inner product space $\mathcal{H}$ a *Hilbert space* if

- $\mathcal{H}$ is complete with respect to the metric $d(x, y) = \|x - y\|$ (i.e., it is a Banach space).

Other definitions used for example by Kolmogorov and Fomin (1960a) require additionally that

- $\mathcal{H}$ is infinite-dimensional and separable.

The *Riesz theorem* states that for every (continuous linear) functional $f : \mathcal{H} \to \mathbb{R}$ defined on the Hilbert space $\mathcal{H}$, there is an $x_f \in \mathcal{H}$ such that $f(\cdot) = \langle x_f, \cdot \rangle$, that is $f(x) = \langle x_f, x \rangle$ for all $x \in \mathcal{X}$.

In the next section we will introduce a special class of Hilbert spaces important for the remainder of this book, so called reproducing kernel Hilbert spaces. It can be shown that every non-separable reproducing kernel Hilbert space must contain non-continuous functions. Still, the general theory of reproducing kernels which goes back to Aronszajn (1950) is also applicable to non-separable Hilbert spaces.

It is important to note that all finite-dimensional Hilbert spaces are separable and that all separable Hilbert spaces are isomorphic. It is often not necessary to distinguish between the different realisations of separable Hilbert spaces. An example of a finite dimensional Hilbert space is the n-dimensional Euclidean space. Examples of separable infinite dimensional Hilbert spaces are the spaces l_2 and $L_2(\mathcal{R}, \mu)$ for particular choices of $\mathcal{R}, \mu$. We next briefly introduce these spaces.

One important realisation of the Hilbert space is the space l_2 in which the points are all possible sequences $x = (x_1, x_2, \ldots)$ of real numbers such that $\sum_{i=1}^{\infty} x_i^2 < \infty$ (i.e., is finite) and the inner product is $\langle x, y \rangle = \sum_{i=1}^{\infty} x_i y_i$. This space can be seen as the infinite-dimensional analogue of the Euclidean n-space. It is separable as it has a countable basis and it is complete [for a proof see, e.g., Kolmogorov and Fomin (1960b)].

Another realisation of the Hilbert space is the space L_2 of square integrable functions on a set $\mathcal{R}$ on which a measure μ with $\mu(\mathcal{R}) < \infty$ has been defined. The functions $f(\cdot) \in L_2$ are assumed to be measurable and defined almost everywhere on $\mathcal{R}$. Functions equivalent on $\mathcal{R}$ are not distinguished[1]. A function is *square integrable* over $\mathcal{R}$ if the integral $\int_{\mathcal{R}} f^2(x) d\mu$ exists. The inner product in this space is given by

$$\langle f(\cdot), g(\cdot) \rangle = \int_{\mathcal{R}} f(x) g(x) d\mu . \tag{2.1}$$

It is readily verified that this integral is symmetric, linear, and positive, i.e., satisfies all properties of an inner product. Whether the space L_2 is separable depends on the measure μ and whenever more precision about its detailed properties is necessary, we denote it as $L_2(\mathcal{R}, \mu)$. Whenever $L_2(\mathcal{R}, \mu)$ is separable it is isomorphic to l_2.

2.1.6 *Reproducing Kernels and Positive-Definite Functions*

We begin by giving the definition of reproducing kernels and showing that they are inner products in the Hilbert space. We then show that the reproducing property is equivalent to positive definiteness of the function. For more details see [Meschkowski (1960)] and [Aronszajn (1950)].

Definition 2.1. Let $\mathcal{H}$ be a set of functions $\mathcal{X} \to \mathbb{R}$ that forms a Hilbert space. A function $k : \mathcal{X} \times \mathcal{X} \to \mathbb{R}$ is called a *reproducing kernel* if

- for every $x \in \mathcal{X}$ the function $k(x, \cdot) \in \mathcal{H}$ and
- for every $x \in \mathcal{X}$ and every function $f(\cdot) \in \mathcal{H}$ the reproducing property holds $\langle k(x, \cdot), f(\cdot) \rangle = f(x)$.

It follows directly from the definition that every reproducing kernel is symmetric and that for every reproducing kernel $k : \mathcal{X} \times \mathcal{X} \to \mathbb{R}$ there is a function $\phi : \mathcal{X} \to \mathcal{H}$ such that $k(x, x') = \langle \phi(x), \phi(x') \rangle$ for all $x, x' \in \mathcal{X}$. This function ϕ maps every element of $\mathcal{X}$ to a function in the Hilbert space of

---

[1] Otherwise, the condition $x \neq \mathbf{0} \Rightarrow \langle x, x \rangle > 0$ would be violated.

the definition $\phi(x) = k(x, \cdot)$. Then, by applying the reproducing property one obtains $\langle \phi(x), \phi(x') \rangle = \langle k(x, \cdot), k(x', \cdot) \rangle = k(x, x')$.

Every set of functions has only one reproducing kernel, as for two reproducing kernels k, k' we have

$$\| k(x, \cdot) - k'(x, \cdot) \|^2$$
$$= \langle k(x, \cdot) - k'(x, \cdot), k(x, \cdot) \rangle - \langle k(x, \cdot) - k'(x, \cdot), k'(x, \cdot) \rangle$$
$$= \langle k(x, \cdot), k(x, \cdot) \rangle - \langle k'(x, \cdot), k(x, \cdot) \rangle - \langle k(x, \cdot), k'(x, \cdot) \rangle + \langle k'(x, \cdot), k'(x, \cdot) \rangle$$
$$= k(x, x) - k'(x, x) - k(x, x) + k'(x, x)$$
$$= 0 .$$

In every Hilbert space that admits a reproducing kernel, weak convergence of a sequence of functions $f_1(\cdot), f_2(\cdot), \ldots \in \mathcal{H}$ to $f(\cdot) \in \mathcal{H}$ implies pointwise convergence: By weak convergence, the sequence $\langle f_1(\cdot), k(x, \cdot) \rangle, \langle f_2(\cdot), k(x, \cdot) \rangle, \ldots$ converges to $\langle f(\cdot), k(x, \cdot) \rangle$ and the reproducing property implies then the convergence of $f_1(x), f_2(x), \ldots$ to $f(x)$.

Let $\mathcal{H}$ be a Hilbert space of functions $\mathcal{X} \to \mathbb{R}$ and define for fixed $x \in \mathcal{X}$ the function $x' : \mathcal{H} \to \mathbb{R}$ by $x'(f(\cdot)) = f(x)$. The Hilbert space $\mathcal{H}$ has a reproducing kernel if and only if for every fixed $x \in \mathcal{X}$, $x'(\cdot)$ is a continuous linear functional. With the reproducing kernel $k : \mathcal{X} \times \mathcal{X} \to \mathbb{R}$ of $\mathcal{H}$ we can show that the functional $x'(\cdot)$ is bounded as

$$| x'(f(\cdot)) | = | f(x) | = | \langle k(x, \cdot), f(\cdot) \rangle | \leq \| k(x, \cdot) \| \| f(\cdot) \| = \| f(\cdot) \| \sqrt{k(x, x)} .$$

Conversely, if the functional $x'(\cdot)$ is bounded, according to Riesz' theorem, there is an $x_f(\cdot) \in \mathcal{H}$ such that $x'(\cdot) = \langle x_f(\cdot), \cdot \rangle$. Applying this function to $f(\cdot)$ we see that $k(x, \cdot) = x_f(\cdot)$ has the reproducting property $\langle k(x, \cdot), f(\cdot) \rangle = \langle x_f(\cdot), f(\cdot) \rangle = x'(f(\cdot)) = f(x)$.

This shows immediately that the Hilbert space l_2^* has a reproducing kernel, while L_2 has not. The Hilbert spaces of functions that we will later be interested in, are either viewed as l_2^* or as subspaces of L_2. Next we define what is meant by 'positive definite kernel' and show the equivalence of reproducing and positive definite kernels. This will provide us with a straightforward way of checking whether for a given function $k : \mathcal{X} \times \mathcal{X} \to \mathbb{R}$ there is a Hilbert space in which this function is the reproducing kernel.

Definition 2.2. Let $\mathcal{X}$ be a set. A symmetric function $k : \mathcal{X} \times \mathcal{X} \to \mathbb{R}$ is a *positive definite kernel* on $\mathcal{X}$ if, for all $n \in \mathbb{N}$, $x_1, \ldots, x_n \in \mathcal{X}$, and $c_1, \ldots, c_n \in \mathbb{R}$, it follows that

$$\sum_{i,j \in \{1, \ldots, n\}} c_i \, c_j \, k(x_i, x_j) \geq 0 .$$

A positive definite kernel k is a *strictly positive definite kernel*, if $x_i = x_j \Leftrightarrow i = j$ implies that

$$\sum_{i,j \in \{1,\ldots,n\}} c_i \, c_j \, k(x_i, x_j) = 0$$

only if $c_1 = \cdots = c_n = 0$.

Note that this definition is equivalent with the matrix K with $K_{ij} = k(x_i, x_j)$ being (strictly) positive definite for all possible choices of $x_1, x_2, \ldots, x_n \in \mathcal{X}$ with $x_i = x_j \Leftrightarrow i = j$ (see also Section 2.1.7).

Every reproducing kernel is a positive definite kernel as

$$\sum_{i,j=1}^{n} c_i \, c_j \, k(x_i, x_j) = \left\langle \sum_{i=1}^{n} c_i \, k(x_i, \cdot), \sum_{i=1}^{n} c_i \, k(x_i, \cdot) \right\rangle \geq 0 \; .$$

For the converse consider the set $\mathcal{F}$ of functions $f : \mathcal{X} \to \mathbb{R}$ of the form $f(\cdot) = \sum_i \alpha_i k(x_i, \cdot); x_1, x_2, \ldots \in \mathcal{X}; \alpha_1, \alpha_2, \ldots \in \mathbb{R}$ with positive definite k. For any two functions $f(\cdot) = \sum_i \alpha_i k(x_i, \cdot)$, $g(\cdot) = \sum_j \beta_j k(x'_j, \cdot)$ in $\mathcal{F}$ we can define an inner product by

$$\langle f(\cdot), g(\cdot) \rangle = \sum_{i,j} \alpha_i \beta_j k(x_i, x'_j) \; . \tag{2.2}$$

This inner product is clearly linear and symmetry follows from k being symmetric. To see that also $f(\cdot) \neq \mathbf{0}(\cdot) \Rightarrow \langle f(\cdot), f(\cdot) \rangle > 0$, assume the contrary. Suppose there was such a function $z(\cdot) = \sum_i c_i k(x_i, \cdot) \neq \mathbf{0}(\cdot)$ with $\langle z(\cdot), z(\cdot) \rangle = 0$ then

$$\|z(\cdot) - \mathbf{0}(\cdot)\|^2 = \langle z(\cdot), z(\cdot) \rangle - 2 \langle z(\cdot), \mathbf{0}(\cdot) \rangle + \langle \mathbf{0}(\cdot), \mathbf{0}(\cdot) \rangle = 0$$

contradicts the assumptions.

Furthermore, as $k(x, \cdot) \in \mathcal{F}$ for all $x \in \mathcal{X}$ we obtain the reproducing property from the inner product (2.2) by

$$\langle f(\cdot), k(x, \cdot) \rangle = \left\langle \sum_i \alpha_i k(x_i, \cdot), k(x, \cdot) \right\rangle = \sum_i \alpha_i k(x_i, x) = f(x) \; .$$

Now, the set $\mathcal{F}$ together with the limits of all Cauchy-sequences of functions from $\mathcal{F}$ forms a Hilbert space.

2.1.7   *Matrix Computations*

Although most statements in this section hold for general matrices we consider for simplicity only real matrices. A real $n \times m$ *matrix* A is a rectangular collection of real numbers. For $i = 1, \ldots, n$ and $j = 1, \ldots, m$ the (i, j)-th element of A is denoted as $A_{ij} \in \mathbb{R}$. Every row (column) of a real matrix forms thus a vector in the Euclidean space $\mathbb{R}^m$ ($\mathbb{R}^n$). Every $n \times m$ matrix denotes a linear transformation $\mathbb{R}^m \to \mathbb{R}^n$.

The *rank* of a matrix is the number of linearly independent rows or columns of the matrix. An $n \times n$ matrix A is *regular* if its rank is equal to n, otherwise *singular*. For regular A there exists a unique matrix (its *inverse*) denoted A^{-1} such that $A^{-1}A = \mathbf{I}$. For singular A there exists no matrix C such that $AC = \mathbf{I}$.

A symmetric matrix A is *positive definite* if $c^\top A c \geq 0$ for all vectors c. A is *strictly positive definite* if $c^\top A c > 0$ for all vectors $c \neq \mathbf{0}$. A is indefinite if there are c_+, c_- such that $c_+^\top A c_+ > 0$ and $c_-^\top A c_- < 0$. For every singular matrix A there is a c such that $Ac = \mathbf{0}$ and thus $c^\top A c = 0$. If A is strictly positive definite, there is no such c and it follows that A is regular.

A vector u is called an *eigenvector* of a matrix A if there is a λ such that $Au = \lambda u$; λ is the *eigenvalue* corresponding to u. A symmetric $n \times n$ matrix A always has real eigenvalues and the eigenvectors can be chosen to form an orthonormal basis of $\mathbb{R}^n$. Denote the eigenvalues (sorted in non-decreasing order) by λ_i and the corresponding normed eigenvectors by u_i. Let D be the diagonal matrix with elements λ_i and let U be the matrix with columns u_i. As the u_i are orthogonal, $U^\top = U^{-1}$. By definition of the eigenvalues and eigenvectors we have $Au_i = u_i \lambda_i$ or in matrix form $AU = UD$. Here $A = UDU^{-1}$ is known as the *diagonal-* or *eigen-decomposition* of A and from

$$\mathbf{I} = U \left(D^{-1} \left(U^{-1} U \right) D \right) U^{-1} = \left(U D^{-1} U^{-1} \right) \left(U D U^{-1} \right)$$

we obtain $A^{-1} = U D^{-1} U^{-1}$ where $\left[D^{-1} \right]_{ii} = 1/\lambda_i$. Equivalently, we can write $A = \sum_i \lambda_i u_i u_i^\top$ and $A^{-1} = \sum_i \lambda_i^{-1} u_i u_i^\top$.

Consider now a symmetric matrix A with only non-negative eigenvalues. Then $\sqrt{D}$ exists and A is positive definite as $c^\top A c = \left(c^\top U \sqrt{D} \right) \left(\sqrt{D} U^\top c \right) \geq 0$. This also shows that for every positive definite matrix A there is a matrix B such that $A = B^\top B$. Now recall that the columns of U form a basis of $\mathbb{R}^n$ and thus at least one component of $U^\top c$ is non-zero. If the eigenvalues of A are all non-negative (positive) it follows that the corresponding component of $\sqrt{D} U^\top c$ is also non-negative (positive) and therefore A is positive definite (strictly positive definite).

The converse also holds, as with a negative (zero) eigenvalue λ_j, and corresponding eigenvector u_j we obtain

$$u_j^\top A u_j = u_j^\top \left(\sum_i \lambda_i u_i u_i^\top \right) u_j = \sum_i (u_j^\top u_i) \lambda_i (u_i^\top u_j) = \lambda_j$$

and A cannot be positive definite (strictly positive definite).

It follows that A is positive definite if and only if A has only non-negative eigenvalues and that A is strictly positive definite if and only if A has only positive eigenvalues.

Now let A, B be two square matrices of dimensionality $n \times n$ and $m \times m$, respectively. Their Kronecker or *tensor product* $H = A \otimes B$ is a $mn \times mn$ matrix with

$$H_{i_{12} j_{12}} = A_{i_1 j_1} B_{i_2 j_2}$$

where $i_{12} = i_1 + n i_2$ and $j_{12} = j_1 + n j_2$.

With u, λ and v, ν eigenpairs of A, B we set $w = u \otimes v$ (i.e., $w_{i_{12}} = u_{i_1} v_{i_2}$) to obtain

$$\sum_{i_{12}} w_{i_{12}} H_{i_{12} j_{12}} = \sum_{i_1 i_2} u_{i_1} v_{i_2} A_{i_1 j_1} B_{i_2, j_2}$$

$$= \left(\sum_{i_1} u_{i_1} A_{i_1 j_1} \right) \left(\sum_{i_2} v_{i_2} B_{i_2, j_2} \right)$$

$$= \lambda u_{j_1} \nu v_{j_2} = \lambda \nu w_{j_{12}}$$

and thus the vector $u \otimes v$ is an eigenvector of the matrix $A \otimes B$ with corresponding eigenvalue $\lambda \nu$. An important conclusion of this is that $A \otimes B$ is (strictly) positive definite, if and only if both A and B are (strictly) positive definite.

2.1.8   *Partitioned Inverse Equations*

Another very useful tool for the following sections are the so called *partitioned inverse equations* [Barnett (1979)]. Let A, B be two regular matrices with

$$A = \begin{pmatrix} A_{11} & A_{12} \\ A_{21} & A_{22} \end{pmatrix} \text{and} B = \begin{pmatrix} B_{11} & B_{12} \\ B_{21} & B_{22} \end{pmatrix} \tag{*}$$

and A_{ij}, B_{ij} of dimensionality $n_i \times n_j$. Now consider the case $AB = \mathbf{I}$, i.e., $B = A^{-1}$. We will show how to obtain the blocks B_{ij} of B only using the blocks A_{ij} of A. Note that as A is regular, so is B and so are the blocks A_{ij}, B_{ij} of A, B. From (*) we obtain

$$A_{11}B_{11} + A_{12}B_{21} = \mathbf{I} \tag{a}$$
$$A_{11}B_{12} + A_{12}B_{22} = \mathbf{0} \tag{b}$$
$$A_{21}B_{11} + A_{22}B_{21} = \mathbf{0} \tag{c}$$
$$A_{21}B_{12} + A_{22}B_{22} = \mathbf{I} . \tag{d}$$

Solving (c) for B_{21} and substituting this in (a) gives

$$\mathbf{I} = A_{11}B_{11} - A_{12}A_{22}^{-1}A_{21}B_{11}$$
$$B_{11}^{-1} = A_{11} - A_{12}A_{22}^{-1}A_{21}$$
$$B_{11} = \left(A_{11} - A_{12}A_{22}^{-1}A_{21}\right)^{-1} .$$

Substituting this back into (c) shows that

$$\mathbf{0} = A_{21}\left(A_{11} - A_{12}A_{22}^{-1}A_{21}\right)^{-1} + A_{22}B_{21}$$
$$B_{21} = -A_{22}^{-1}A_{21}\left(A_{11} - A_{12}A_{22}^{-1}A_{21}\right)^{-1} .$$

Similarly we can of course obtain

$$B_{22} = \left(A_{22} - A_{21}A_{11}^{-1}A_{12}\right)^{-1} .$$

These equations are of particular interest for the case $n_2 = 1$. In that case, for kernel methods whose hypothesis is computed via matrix inversion, the inverse can be updated whenever a new training instance is observed.

2.2 Recognising Patterns with Kernels

In the introduction to this book we already described a machine learning problem. The class of problems similar to the one described there is commonly referred to as supervised learning problems. With the mathematical tools described in the previous section at hand we are now ready to have a closer and more formal look at supervised machine learning.

2.2.1 *Supervised Learning*

The drug design problem described in the introduction was that we wanted to find a function that estimates how effective a chemical compound is in treating a particular illness. The way we wanted to find such a function was by looking at other chemical compounds known to to be effective or not. In more general terms, the chemical compounds for which the effectiveness is known are called training data. The *training data* is a finite set of *instances* (e.g., the chemical compounds) with associated *labels* (e.g., the effectiveness). It is sometimes necessary to distinguish between the instances and their representation in a computer understandable form. This distinction is not necessary in this chapter and we neglect it for simplicity. The task of *supervised* machine learning algorithms is to find a function that estimates the label of instances for which we might not know the label. The instances for which we want to estimate the label are called *test instances*. The set of test instances, the *test data*, is usually only known after an estimating function has been found. This is called *inductive learning*; if it is known beforehand, we speak of *transductive learning*. The set containing all possible instances is called the *instance space*.

We denote the instance space by $\mathcal{X}$ and the set of possible labels by $\mathcal{Y}$. For $\mathcal{Y} = \mathbb{R}$ the learning task is called a *regression* task and for $|\mathcal{Y}| \in \mathbb{N}$ a *classification* task. The special case that $|\mathcal{Y}| = 2$ is called *binary classification*. There, without loss of generality, it is commonly assumed that $\mathcal{Y} = \{-1, +1\}$, $\mathcal{Y} = \{0, +1\}$, or $\mathcal{Y} = \Omega = \{\top, \bot\}$. Often estimating functions for binary classification problems compare a numerical output of one function with some threshold value. If the numerical output is larger that the threshold then the label $+1$ is predicted, otherwise -1. A somewhat different machine learning problem that is gaining importance recently is called *ranking*. There, instead of deciding whether a single instance is more likely to have a positive label rather than a negative label, we want to order (rank) the test data according to every instance's likelihood of having a positive label. A simple approach to ranking, which works with thresholded functions described above, is to use the numerical output directly, rather than compare it to the threshold. The order of the test examples is then the order induced by the order of the reals.

Usually, not all possible functions mapping instances to labels are considered as possible estimating functions. The set of functions that is considered is called the *hypothesis space* $\mathcal{F} \subseteq \{f(\cdot) \mid f : \mathcal{X} \to \mathcal{Y}\}$. A *learning algorithm* can be seen as a function (with some parameters that we neglect here) $a : 2^{\mathcal{X} \times \mathcal{Y}} \to \mathcal{F}$ mapping given training data to a hypothesis.

Given some training data, a function that assigns to every instance in the training data its associated label is called *consistent*. The intersection of the set of consistent functions with the hypothesis space is called the *version space*. A learning algorithm that maps every set of training instances to an element of the corresponding version space is a *consistent learner*.

If the label associated to an instance is independent of the instance, finding a function with good predictive performance is impossible. Thus one needs to assume a functional or conditional dependence between the instance and the associated label. A functional dependence means that there exists a function g such that for all $x \in \mathcal{X}$, the label y of the instance x is determined by g, that is $y = g(x)$. In a binary classification setting this function is called the *concept*. A more general setting only assumes a conditional dependence, meaning that the instance-label pairs are observed according to a fixed but unknown joint probability distribution P with $P(x, y) \neq P(x)P(y)$.

Still, if we make no further assumptions on the kind of dependence between instances and associated labels, for every function $g : \mathcal{X} \to \mathcal{Y}$ that the learning algorithm can approximate well given the training data $Z = \{(x_i, y_i)\}_{i=1}^n \subseteq \mathcal{X} \times \mathcal{Y}$, there is a function $g' : \mathcal{X} \to \mathcal{Y}$ that the learning algorithm can not approximate well given the same training data Z. For example, in a binary classification setting with $\mathcal{Y} = \{-1, +1\}$, a $g'(\cdot)$ can be constructed from $g(\cdot)$ by setting $g'(x) = g(x) = y$ for all $(x, y) \in Z$ and $g'(x) = -g(x)$ for all x not in the training data. In other words, if every possible dependence was equally likely to underly the data, there would be no reason to prefer any consistent function over another. Every consistent function would — on average — estimate the labels equally good (or bad) as randomly guessing the labels of instances not in the training data. This is known as "No Free Lunch" [Wolpert and Macready (1995, 1997)].

The usual way to overcome this problem is by assuming that dependencies occurring in nature are not as illicit as theoretically possible and that "smooth" dependencies are more likely to occur than non-smooth ones. This assumption can directly be incorporated into learning algorithms as we will see later.

2.2.2 *Empirical Risk Minimisation*

The usual learning model of statistical learning theory [Vapnik (1999, 1995)] considers a set $\mathcal{X}$ of instances and a set $\mathcal{Y}$ of labels. The relation between instances and labels is assumed to be a probability measure $P(\cdot, \cdot)$ on the set $\mathcal{X} \times \mathcal{Y}$. In our setting this probability measure is unknown but does not change (e.g., over time). In other words, one assumes conditional dependence of labels on individuals only. The learning task is then — given a set of individuals with associated labels $\{(x_i, y_i)\}_{i=1}^n \subseteq \mathcal{X} \times \mathcal{Y}$ (observed according to $P(\cdot, \cdot)$) — to find a function that estimates the label of instances in $\mathcal{X}$.

Given a hypothesis space $\mathcal{F}$ of functions $\mathcal{F} \subseteq \{f(\cdot) \mid f : \mathcal{X} \rightarrow \mathcal{Y}\}$ considered as possible solutions, the learning task is to find a function in $\mathcal{F}$ that minimises the *true risk*

$$R[f(\cdot)] = \int_{\mathcal{X} \times \mathcal{Y}} V(y, f(x)) dP(x, y) \qquad (2.3)$$

where $V : \mathcal{Y} \times \mathcal{Y} \rightarrow \mathbb{R}$ is a *loss function* that takes on small values whenever $\hat{y} = f(x)$ is a good guess for y and large values whenever it is a bad guess. A typical loss function for regression problems is the *square loss* $V(y, \hat{y}) = (y - \hat{y})^2$. If $P(y|x)$ was known, the ideal prediction function could be computed as: $f(x) = \int y dP(y|x)$.

As neither $P(y|x)$ nor $P(x, y)$ are known, we cannot compute the ideal prediction function nor the true risk of an arbitrary function $f(\cdot) \in \mathcal{F}$. As mentioned in the previous section, just finding any consistent element of the hypothesis space is not sufficient if the hypothesis space contains all possible functions from instances to labels.

One approach to machine learning is to restrict the hypothesis space to smooth functions only and to then look for the element of the hypothesis space that minimises the *empirical risk*, defined as

$$R_{\text{emp}}[f(\cdot)] = \sum_{i=1}^{n} \frac{1}{n} V(y_i, f(x_i)) \ . \qquad (2.4)$$

For binary classification with the so called 0/1-loss ($V_{0/1}(y, y) = 0$ and $V_{0/1}(y, \hat{y}) = 1$ if $y \neq \hat{y}$, the empirical risk equals the training error – the number of misclassified instances.

A different but related approach is to choose a rather large hypothesis space but bias the learning algorithm such that smooth functions are preferred as solutions. In Section 2.3 we will follow this approach to derive the class of learning algorithms known as kernel methods.

2.2.3 *Assessing Predictive Performance*

Learning algorithms compete in different criteria. Two important ones are computation time and predictive performance. The *computation time* can be assessed theoretically in terms of the computational complexity of a learning algorithm or practically by measuring the time needed for a given task. In this section, we describe how the predictive performance of supervised classification algorithms can be assessed. We will not discuss regression problems here.

An important tool in the analysis of the predictive performance is the *contingency table*, a square matrix where each row and column correspond to one class[2] and the i, j-th entry contains the number of examples of class i classified as class j by the learning algorithm. In cases where making a mistake on one class has a different cost than making a mistake on another class, the i, j-th entry of the contingency table is usually multiplied by the associated *misclassification cost*. The diagonal corresponds to correct classifications and has usually cost zero.

Two different ways to compare the performance of supervised classification algorithms are known as error rate and Receiver Operator Characteristic (ROC). We first introduce the error rate criterion which tries to estimate the true risk of a learning algorithm on a given problem. This is usually done by using one or more *validation sets*, consisting of instances for which the label is known but that were not used as training data. The *accuracy* is the number of correctly classified instances in the validation set divided by the total number of examples in the validation set; the *error rate* is the number of incorrectly classified instances divided by the total number of instances in the validation set. If there is more than one validation set, the true risk is estimated by averaging the error rate over these validation sets.

Whenever the amount of labelled data is limited, techniques like *hold-n-out* or *n-fold crossvalidation* are used. In hold-n-out experiments, repeatedly n randomly drawn instances are removed from the training data and used as the validation set. In n-fold crossvalidation, the data set is partitioned into n roughly equally sized sets (the folds) and n experiments are performed, each using $n - 1$ sets for training and one set for validation. The special case where n equals the size of the dataset is known as *leave-one-out* evaluation. Often the folds are stratified, i.e., they are generated such that the class distribution in all folds is roughly the same.

Recently, an alternative way of comparing the predictive performance on binary classification problems has become popular in the machine learning and data mining communities [Provost and Fawcett (2000)]. Instead of using a single criterion like error rate or accuracy, Receiver Operator Characteristic (*ROC*) uses two criteria and is thus able to overcome some shortcomings of merely accuracy based comparisons: Measuring accuracy is only meaningful if the class distribution and misclassification costs in the target environment are known and do never change [Provost *et al.* (1998)].

---

[2]Each class is, for simplicity of notation, here represented by a natural number.

ROC compares the ranking of test examples rather than their binary classification.

In the two-dimensional *ROC space* each classifier is represented by its *true-positive rate* (the fraction of positive examples correctly classified) and its *false-positive rate* (the fraction of negative examples incorrectly classified). The ideal classifier (sometimes called 'ROC heaven') has true-positive rate one and false-positive rate zero; the worst possible classifier (sometimes called 'ROC hell') has true-positive rate zero and false-positive rate one. The default classifiers that classify either all examples as negative or all examples as positive have both rates equal to zero or one, respectively.

Learning algorithms that produce a ranking of examples can be seen as a set of classifiers, each of which corresponds to a cut-point in the ranking. Instances ordered before the cut-point are thought of as positive instance, all others as negative instances. As each classifier corresponds to one point in ROC space, a ranking corresponds to a curve in ROC space. This curve illustrates the possible tradeoffs between true-positive and false-positive rate.

For any set of classifiers in ROC space (including the default classifiers), the tradeoffs corresponding to the convex hull of the classifiers can be achieved by random sampling between the classifiers. The idea behind ROC curves and ROC convex hulls is that instead of committing to a particular misclassification cost setting and class distribution in the test set when learning the classifier, we can instead delay this commitment until a particular test case occurs.

Given a particular misclassification cost setting and class distribution, all classifiers that perform equally well in this setting form a line in ROC space — the *iso-accuracy line*. A more detailed characterisation of common evaluation functions in ROC space can be found in [Flach (2003)]. A set of classifiers dominates another, i.e., is superior to another under all misclassification cost settings and class distributions, if the other set is completely contained in the convex hull of this set. The predictive performance of two sets, none of which dominates the other, can be compared without committing to a particular setting by using the *area under curve* (*AUC*) measure as an aggregate of the predictive performance. This is, however, only beneficial if the misclassification costs are not known. The area under curve for a given set of classifiers is computed as the area of the convex hull of the union of the set of classifiers (including the default classifiers) and ROC hell. In the ranking context, the area under curve estimates the probability that a randomly chosen positive example is ranked before a randomly chosen negative example.

To overcome the dependency of ROC analysis on a single test-set, it is desirable to combine ROC analysis with crossvalidation techniques. How to best average ROC curves, however, is still a matter of scientific dispute. In this work we will consider averages of the area under the curve rather than averages of ROC curves themselves.

2.3 Foundations of Kernel Methods

This section introduces the theoretical background of kernel methods. Parts of this section follow along the lines of [Tan and Fox (2005); Neumaier (1998); Poggio and Smale (2003)]. Before we go into general topics related to kernel methods we begin with a simple example motivating different aspects of kernel methods.

2.3.1 *Model Fitting and Linear Inverse Equations*

Let us first consider the simple case that $\mathcal{X} = \mathcal{Y} = \mathbb{R}$ and assume that the hypothesis space $\mathcal{F}$ is the space of linear functions on $\mathbb{R}$. In this case the general learning problem reduces to the attempt of fitting a linear model to the observed data.

In a more general case, we consider an arbitrary set $\mathcal{X}$ and a hypothesis space $\mathcal{F}$ that consists of all linear combinations of a set of *basis functions* $\mathcal{B}$, i.e., $\mathcal{F} = span(\mathcal{B})$. Often these functions are obtained by "centring" some symmetric function at the elements of $\mathcal{X}$, that is $\mathcal{B} = \{k(x, \cdot) \mid x \in \mathcal{X}\}$ for some symmetric function $k : \mathcal{X} \times \mathcal{X} \to \mathbb{R}$. We now consider the problem of finding a function in $\mathcal{F}$ that best approximates the given training data. In particular we will only consider the case that the hypothesis is a linear combination of basis functions centred at the training instances.

Let K be an $n \times n$ matrix with $K_{ij} = k(x_i, x_j)$, let y be the vector $(y_1, \ldots, y_n)^\top$, and c be an n-dimensional vector with components c_i. Finding c such that Kc best approximates the given training data is known as a model fitting problem. If K is regular, the function minimising the empirical risk with square loss can — in principle — be found by solving $y = Kc$ that is by computing $c = K^{-1}y$. The empirical risk with this choice of c is 0. This kind of linear inverse equations have been studied since Gauss (1880).

However — even if K is regular — this is usually not a good idea. We will now show under which conditions the solution c of $y = Kc$ is very instable under small perturbations of y. This is a crucial point in learning algorithms as usually we can not hope to observe labels y free of noise.

Denote the eigenvalues of K (absolute values sorted in non-decreasing order) by λ_i and the corresponding eigenvectors by u_i. Now recall (from Section 2.1.7) that $K^{-1} = \sum_i \lambda_i^{-1} u_i u_i^{\top}$ and therefore the solution of $y = Kc$ is given by

$$c = \sum_i \frac{u_i u_i^{\top}}{\lambda_i} y = \sum_i u_i \frac{\langle u_i, y \rangle}{\lambda_i} \ .$$

If y is perturbed by random noise, i.e., we observe $y + r$ instead of y, the difference between c and $K^{-1}(y + r)$ is given by

$$\sum_i u_i \frac{\langle u_i, r \rangle}{\lambda_i}$$

where the error term along the direction of u_i arises from the noise along u_i divided by the corresponding eigenvalue. Thus with very small eigenvalues, there is a large random component in c. For linear inverse equations the ratio between the largest and the smallest eigenvalues is known as the *condition number*. Problems with a large condition number are said to be *ill-conditioned*.

To overcome this problem, consider solving $y = (\nu n\mathbf{I} + K)c$ instead of $y = Kc$. In this case the eigenvectors of $\nu n\mathbf{I} + K$ are the same as those of K but the eigenvalues are larger:

$$(K + \nu n\mathbf{I})u_i = Ku_i + \nu n\mathbf{I}u_i = u_i\lambda_i + \nu n u_i = u_i(\lambda_i + \nu n) \ .$$

If all eigenvalues of K are non-negative, it follows that the larger ν becomes, the smaller the condition number of this linear inverse problem becomes and the more stable its solution becomes with respect to noisy training data. The above observations motivate two crucial characteristics of kernel methods: Firstly, as only the condition number of positive definite matrices can be improved in the above way, kernel methods consider only positive definite k. Secondly, kernel methods consider solving regularised problems $(\nu n\mathbf{I} + K)^{-1}y$ rather than the less stable problem $K^{-1}y$, directly. We will return to these characteristics in the next section.

2.3.2 *Common Grounds of Kernel Methods*

In the previous section we already discussed – rather informally – one particular kernel method called regularised least squares. Before we come to describe this and other kernel methods in more detail, we will in this and the next section discuss the common grounds of most kernel methods.

We already described in Section 2.2.2 that minimising the empirical risk is not always sufficient to find a function with good predictive performance. We mentioned there two different methods to overcome this problem. The first was to restrict the hypothesis space, the other was to bias the learning algorithm towards more stable functions. In the example in Section 2.3.1 we then combined these methods. We restricted the hypothesis space to linear combinations of a positive definite function centred at training instances and biased the learning algorithm towards functions that are stable with respect to noisy training data. The restriction to positive definite functions makes the hypothesis space a reproducing kernel Hilbert space.

Techniques to bias learning algorithms to more stable solutions are known as *regularisation* and are build into almost all state of the art learning algorithms. The most common approach to regularisation in Hilbert spaces is *Tikhonov regularisation* [Tikhonov (1963); Tikhonov and Arsenin (1977)], where a regularisation term is added to the empirical risk. This gives rise to the *regularised risk* functional

$$R_{\text{Tikhonov}}[f(\cdot)] = \frac{1}{n} \sum_{i=1}^{n} V(y_i, f(x_i)) + \nu \Omega [f(\cdot)] .$$

Different functionals can be chosen for the regulariser $\Omega : \mathcal{H} \rightarrow \mathbb{R}$. Smoothing splines [Wahba (1990)], for example, use $\Omega[f(\cdot)] = \int_a^b (f^{(m)}(x))^2 dx$ where $f^{(m)}(\cdot)$ denotes the m-th derivative of $f(\cdot)$. Kernel methods like the ones introduced later in this section are characterised by using the square-norm of the function $f(\cdot)$ in the corresponding Hilbert space as the regulariser, that is essentially a smoothing spline with $m = 0$. As we will see later, when choosing square loss, this leads to the approach taken in the previous section to improve the condition number of a linear inverse problem. Another consequence (that we will discuss in the following section) is that the solution of the optimisation problem can be represented in the form $f^*(\cdot) = \sum_{i=1}^{n} c_i k(x_i, \cdot)$. For now we obtain the following optimisation problem

$$\min_{f(\cdot) \in \mathcal{H}} \frac{1}{n} \sum_{i=1}^{n} V(y_i, f(x_i)) + \nu \|f(\cdot)\|_{\mathcal{H}}^2 . \tag{2.5}$$

Different kernel methods arise from using different loss functions. We generally assume that the function $V(y, \cdot)$ is convex in order to ensure uniqueness of the solution and to resolve numerical problems. However, before we turn our attention to the different kernel methods, we will first investigate the form of solutions to the regularised risk minimisation problem.

2.3.3   Representer Theorem

The solutions of (2.5) can always be written in the form

$$f_v(\cdot) = \sum_{i=1}^{n} c_i k(x_i, \cdot) + v(\cdot)$$

where the $\{x_i\}_{i=1}^{n}$ are the training examples for which the labels are known (as above), $k(\cdot, \cdot)$ is the reproducing kernel of the Hilbert space $\mathcal{H}$, and $v(\cdot) \in \mathcal{H}$ is orthogonal to all $k(x_i, \cdot)$ but otherwise arbitrary.

The *representer theorem* [Wahba (1990); Schölkopf *et al.* (2001)] states that the solutions of (2.5) have the form

$$f^*(\cdot) = \sum_{i=1}^{n} c_i k(x_i, \cdot) . \qquad (2.6)$$

This means that we do not have to consider all elements of the reproducing kernel Hilbert space as potential solutions of the regularised risk minimisation problem. Instead it is sufficient — without loss of generality — to only consider linear combinations of kernel functions centred at training instances.

Technically, in this subsection, we first show that the values of $f_v(\cdot)$ are the same on all training points regardless of the choice of $v(\cdot)$. This is known as the *weak representer theorem*. We then show that out of all $f_v(\cdot)$, $f^*(\cdot) = f_0(\cdot)$ is the one with the smallest norm. This is known as the *strong representer theorem*.

For any training example x_j we have

$$f_v(x_j) = \sum_{i=1}^{n} c_i k(x_i, x_j) + v(x_j)$$

$$= \sum_{i=1}^{n} c_i k(x_i, x_j) + \langle k(x_j, \cdot), v(\cdot) \rangle$$

$$= \sum_{i=1}^{n} c_i k(x_i, x_j)$$

$$= f^*(x_j)$$

using the reproducing property of $k(\cdot, \cdot)$ and orthogonality of $k(x_j, \cdot)$ and $v(\cdot)$. This shows that the $f_v(\cdot)$ form an equivalence class of functions that have the same value at all training examples.

Now let us consider the norm of the functions in this equivalence class

$$\|f_v(\cdot)\|_{\mathcal{H}}^2 = \left\| \sum_{i=1}^n c_i k(x_i, \cdot) + v(\cdot) \right\|_{\mathcal{H}}^2$$

$$= \left\| \sum_{i=1}^n c_i k(x_i, \cdot) \right\|_{\mathcal{H}}^2 + \|v(\cdot)\|_{\mathcal{H}}^2$$

$$\geq \left\| \sum_{i=1}^n c_i k(x_i, \cdot) \right\|_{\mathcal{H}}^2$$

$$= \|f^*(\cdot)\|_{\mathcal{H}}^2 .$$

We observe that for every function $v(\cdot)$ that is not equivalent to the function returning always zero, it holds that $\|f_v(\cdot)\|_{\mathcal{H}}^2 > \|f^*(\cdot)\|_{\mathcal{H}}^2$. Thus the optimal solution to (2.5) has the form (2.6) and the regularisation term reads as

$$\|f^*(\cdot)\|_{\mathcal{H}}^2 = \left\langle \sum_{i=1}^n c_i k(x_i, \cdot), \sum_{i=1}^n c_i k(x_i, \cdot) \right\rangle$$

$$= \sum_{i,j=1}^n c_i c_j \langle k(x_i, \cdot), k(x_j, \cdot) \rangle$$

$$= \sum_{i,j=1}^n c_i c_j k(x_i, x_j)$$

$$= c^\top K c$$

where $K_{ij} = k(x_i, x_j)$ and $c = (c_1, \ldots, c_n)^\top$. Note furthermore that $f^*(x) = c^\top \mathbf{k}$ with $\mathbf{k}_i = k(x_i, x)$.

When discussing some kernel methods in more detail in the next section we will use this insight to reduce the problem of minimising the regularised risk functional to a simple problem of linear algebra. Note that in algorithms that enforce sparsity of the solution, the elements of $\{x_i : c_i \neq 0\}$ are called *support vectors*. Sparseness means then $|\{x_i : c_i \neq 0\}| \ll n$.

2.4 Kernel Machines

In this section we describe several learning algorithms that can be applied to an instance space, whenever a kernel function can be defined on the instance space. These algorithms will later be applied to various data structures in the remaining chapters of this book. All but the algorithms described in the last section use the Hilbert space in which the kernel is reproducing as their hypothesis space. The algorithms in the last section exploit that every Hilbert space is a metric space.

2.4.1 *Regularised Least Squares*

The simple algorithm briefly introduced in Section 2.3.1 has become known under several different names: *regularised least squares* [Rifkin (2002)], *proximal support vector machine* [Fung and Mangasarian (2001)], *least squares support vector machines* [Suykens (2000)], *ridge regression* [Saunders *et al.* (1998)]. We will call it the regularised least squares kernel method and describe it in this section in more detail.

We begin our more detailed discussion of this algorithm with the regularised risk functional (2.5)

$$\min_{f(\cdot)\in\mathcal{H}} \frac{1}{n}\sum_{i=1}^{n} V(y_i, f(x_i)) + \nu\|f(\cdot)\|_{\mathcal{H}}^2 \ .$$

While there are variants of this algorithm for classification, we will focus on the regression case here. The regularised least squares problem is obtained by choosing the square loss function, i.e., $V(y, \hat{y}) = (y - \hat{y})^2$. The advantage of choosing square-loss is that in this case — as we shall see below — an analytical solution to the minimisation problem exists. In this case the regularised risk functional reads as follows:

$$\min_{f(\cdot)\in\mathcal{H}} \frac{1}{n}\sum_{i=1}^{n} (y_i - f(x_i))^2 + \nu\|f(\cdot)\|_{\mathcal{H}}^2 \ . \tag{2.7}$$

Now plugging in our knowledge from Section 2.3.3 about the form of solutions (2.6) we can simplify the regularised risk to a linear algebraic form

$$R_{\mathrm{rls}}[f(\cdot)] = \frac{1}{n}\sum_{i=1}^{n}(y_i - f(x_i))^2 + \nu\|f(\cdot)\|_{\mathcal{H}}^2$$

$$= \frac{1}{n}\sum_{i=1}^{n}\left(y_i - \sum_{j=1}^{n}c_j k(x_j, x_i)\right)^2 + \nu c^\top K c$$

$$= \frac{1}{n}\|y - Kc\|^2 + \nu c^\top K c$$

$$= R'_{\mathrm{rls}}[c]$$

and obtain the equivalent optimisation problem

$$\min_{c\in\mathbb{R}^n} \frac{1}{n}\|y - Kc\|^2 + \nu c^\top K c \, . \tag{2.8}$$

We can further rewrite $R'_{\mathrm{rls}}[c]$ to obtain

$$R'_{\mathrm{rls}}[c] = \frac{1}{n}\langle y - Kc, y - Kc\rangle + \nu c^\top K c$$

$$= \frac{1}{n}\langle y, y\rangle - \frac{2}{n}\langle y, Kc\rangle + \frac{1}{n}\langle Kc, Kc\rangle + \nu c^\top K c$$

$$= \frac{1}{n}\langle y, y\rangle - \frac{2}{n}\langle y, Kc\rangle + \frac{1}{n}c^\top K^2 c + \nu c^\top K c \, .$$

Calculating now the gradient with respect to c we obtain

$$\nabla_c R'_{\mathrm{rls}}[c] = -\frac{2}{n}Ky + \frac{2}{n}K^2 c + 2\nu Kc \, .$$

Similarly we obtain the second-order partial derivatives as:

$$\frac{\partial^2}{\partial c_l \partial c_m}R'_{\mathrm{rls}}[c] = +\frac{2}{n}[K^2]_{lm} + 2\nu K_{lm} \, .$$

The matrix H with $H_{lm} = \frac{\partial^2}{\partial c_l \partial c_m}R'_{\mathrm{rls}}[c]$ is called the *Hessian matrix* of $R'_{\mathrm{rls}}[\cdot]$. As K is positive definite, K^2 is also positive definite, and in particular the Hessian is also positive definite. This is sufficient for $R'_{\mathrm{rls}}[\cdot]$ being a *convex function*. That is, for any $c, c' \in \mathbb{R}^n$ and $\lambda \in [0, 1]$ we have $R'_{\mathrm{rls}}[\lambda c + (1-\lambda)c'] \leq \lambda R'_{\mathrm{rls}}[c] + (1-\lambda)R'_{\mathrm{rls}}[c']$.

Therefore any solution to $\frac{d}{dc}R'_{\mathrm{rls}}[c] = \mathbf{0}$ is a globally optimal solution to (2.8) – and therefore to (2.7) by using (2.6). If K is strictly positive definite, $R_{\mathrm{rls}}[f(\cdot)]$ is strictly convex, and there is a unique global optimum that we obtain as:

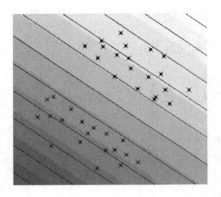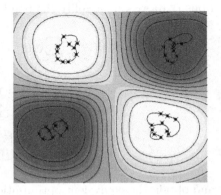

Figure 2.1   Illustration of regularised least squares on two different toy problems.

$$\nabla_c \, R'_{\mathrm{rls}}[c] = \mathbf{0}$$
$$\frac{2}{n}Ky = \frac{2}{n}K^2c + 2\nu Kc$$
$$Ky = K^2c + \nu nKc$$
$$y = Kc + \nu n\mathbf{I}c$$
$$y = (K + \nu\mathbf{I}n)\,c \; .$$

Furthermore, as K is positive definite, the matrix $(K + \nu\mathbf{I}n)$ is strictly positive definite for $\nu > 0$ and thus regular. We can now find the globally optimal solution to (2.8) as:

$$c = (K + \nu\mathbf{I}n)^{-1}\, y$$

This links back to the simple algorithm discussed in Section 2.3.1. A related algorithm will be discussed in Section 2.4.3.

We close this discussion of the regularised least squares algorithm with some illustrations of the type of hypotheses that can be found. In Figure 2.1 the training examples are pairs of real numbers $x \in \mathbb{R}^2$ illustrated by black discs and circles in the figure. The target variable y takes values -1 for the black discs and $+1$ for the black circles. We applied regularised least squares to two different problems and used a different kernel function for both problems. (See Section 3.1.4 for illustrations of other kernel functions.) Test instances consist of all points in the two-dimensional plane and the value of the hypothesis function is illustrated by the colour of the corresponding pixel. Examples with non-zero coefficient in the hypothesis function are marked with a cross.

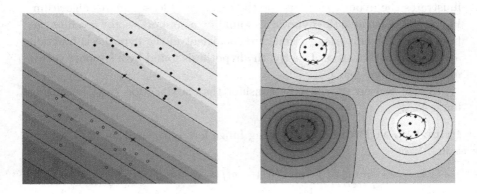

Figure 2.2   Illustration of support vector machines on two different toy problems.

2.4.2   *Support Vector Machines*

Next we introduce the most popular kernel method – the *support vector machine*, first introduced by [Boser *et al.* (1992); Vapnik (1995)].

The motivation for support vector classification often taken in literature is that whenever zero training error can be achieved, the solution can be interpreted as a hyperplane that separates both classes and is maximally distant from the convex hulls of both classes. However, this motivation is lost in the case where zero training error can not be achieved.

Another possible motivation for the support vector machine is that evaluating the function (2.6) as found by the regularised least squares method is expensive. The computational cost could be reduced if the vector c in the solution was sparse. However, this is usually not the case with the square loss function. It turns out that in the pattern recognition case a sparse solution can be found with the so-called *hinge loss* $V(y, \hat{y}) = \max\{0, 1 - y\hat{y}\}$. In the regression case a sparse solution can be found with the so-called ϵ-*insensitive loss* $V(y, \hat{y}) = \max\{0, |y - \hat{y}| - \epsilon\}$. The difference between these loss functions and, say, square loss is that small deviations of the prediction from the true label do not cause a non-zero loss. As can be seen in equation (2.11) below, the smaller the c_i, the smaller the regularisation term. Thus c_i will be set to 0 if this does not cause a too big deviation from the true label.

The impact of this can be seen by comparing Figure 2.1 with Figure 2.2 where we used the same training instances, class labels, and kernel functions in different algorithms. Figure 2.1 is described in Section 2.4.1 and illustrates the hypothesis found be the regularised least squares algorithm. Figure 2.2 illustrates the hypothesis found by a support vector machine. In both figures, examples with non-zero coefficient in the hypothesis function are marked with a cross. Clearly, the hypothesis found by a support vector machine is more sparse.

In this section we will only consider the classification case, i.e., using hinge loss.

Primal SVM Problem   Plugging hinge loss into equation (2.5) we obtain

$$\min_{f(\cdot)\in\mathcal{H}} \frac{1}{n}\sum_{i=1}^{n}\max\{0, 1 - y_i f(x_i)\} + \nu\|f(\cdot)\|_{\mathcal{H}}^2 \ . \tag{2.9}$$

Usually this is written as a constraint quadratic optimisation problem with so called 'slack variables' ξ_i

$$\min_{f(\cdot)\in\mathcal{H},\xi\in\mathbb{R}^n} \frac{1}{n}\sum_{i=1}^{n}\xi_i + \nu\|f(\cdot)\|_{\mathcal{H}}^2$$
$$\text{subject to: } y_i f(x_i) \geq 1 - \xi_i \quad i = 1,\dots,n$$
$$\xi_i \geq 0 \qquad\qquad i = 1,\dots,n \ . \tag{2.10}$$

Using the representer theorem (2.6) we obtain the primal optimisation problem of support vector machines.

$$\min_{c,\xi\in\mathbb{R}^n} \frac{1}{n}\sum_{i=1}^{n}\xi_i + \nu c^\top K c$$
$$\text{subject to: } y_i K_{i\cdot}c \geq 1 - \xi_i \quad i = 1,\dots,n$$
$$\xi_i \geq 0 \qquad\qquad i = 1,\dots,n \ . \tag{2.11}$$

Most literature on support vector machines considers functions of the type $f(\cdot) = \sum_{i=1}^{n} c_i k(x_i, \cdot) + b$ rather than the 'restriction' to $b = 0$ as in (2.6). This restriction can be overcome, however, by using the kernel $k'(x, x') = k(x, x') + 1$ instead [for a discussion of this see, e.g., Rifkin (2002)].

ν-SVM Problem   While we used the parameter ν above, this type of support vector machine is more known as C-SVM. We chose the different parameter for the sake of more consistent notation within this book. The ν-SVM [Smola *et al.* (2000)] has a slightly modified optimisation problem.

$$\min_{c,\xi\in\mathbb{R}^n,\rho\in\mathbb{R}} \frac{1}{n}\sum_{i=1}^{n}\xi_i + \nu\rho + c^\top K c$$
$$\text{subject to: } y_i K_{i\cdot}c \geq \rho - \xi_i \quad i = 1,\dots,n \tag{2.12}$$
$$\xi_i \geq 0 \qquad\qquad i = 1,\dots,n$$
$$\rho \geq 0 \ .$$

The parameter ν in this optimisation problem is an upper bound on the fraction of errors on the training set, i.e., the number of support vectors on the wrong side of the hyperplane. This simplifies choosing the regularisation parameter in domains where one has a good guess of the expected error.

Similar to the discussion of the regularised least squares algorithm we can now see that the objective function of (2.11) and (2.12) is convex because it has a positive definite Hessian matrix. However, this optimisation problem is more difficult, as an analytical solution does not exist. Still, the objective function is a convex quadratic function and the constraints are only linear. There is a lot of literature on general methods for solving this kind of problems. Using tools from mathematical optimisation, the so called 'dual' problem of (2.11) and (2.12) can be derived, which is computationally more tractable than the primal problem derived above.

The Lagrange Dual SVM Problem We now describe how the dual of problem (2.11) can be derived. Consider first the 'Lagrange' function:

$$L = \frac{1}{n}\sum_{i=1}^{n}\xi_i + \nu c^\top K c - \sum_{i=1}^{n}\alpha_i\left(y_i\sum_{j=1}^{n}c_j k(x_i,x_j) - 1 + \xi_i\right) - \sum_{i=1}^{n}\beta_i\xi_i \tag{2.13}$$

or equivalently

$$L = \frac{1}{n}\mathbf{1}^\top\boldsymbol{\xi} + \nu c^\top K c - \boldsymbol{\alpha}^\top Y K c + \mathbf{1}^\top\boldsymbol{\alpha} - \boldsymbol{\alpha}^\top\boldsymbol{\xi} - \boldsymbol{\beta}^\top\boldsymbol{\xi} \tag{2.14}$$

where Y is the diagonal matrix with $Y_{ii} = y_i$ and $\boldsymbol{\alpha},\boldsymbol{\beta},\boldsymbol{\xi}$ are the vectors with compotnents α_i,β_i,ξ_i.

For any $c,\boldsymbol{\xi}$ that satisfy the constraints of (2.11) (these are called 'feasible') and any $\alpha_i,\beta_i \geq 0$ the Lagrange function (2.14) is a lower bound on the solution of (2.11). Indeed, for the case at hand, it can be shown that the saddle point of (2.14) which is a maximum with respect to $\boldsymbol{\alpha},\boldsymbol{\beta}$ and a minimum with respect to $c,\boldsymbol{\xi}$ coincides with the minimum of (2.11). It will turn out that the problem of finding this saddle point is easier to deal with than the original (primal) optimisation problem.

We proceed by differentiating with respect to the parameter ξ of the primal problem and setting the gradient to zero.

$$\nabla_\xi L = \frac{1}{n}\mathbf{1} - \boldsymbol{\alpha} - \boldsymbol{\beta} = 0$$
$$\Leftrightarrow \quad \boldsymbol{\beta} = \frac{1}{n}\mathbf{1} - \boldsymbol{\alpha}$$

As $\beta_i,\alpha_i \geq 0$ we can see that $0 \leq \alpha_i \leq \frac{1}{n}$. If we substitute $\boldsymbol{\beta} = \frac{1}{n}\mathbf{1} - \boldsymbol{\alpha}$ in (2.14) we obtain:

$$L = \nu c^\top K c - \boldsymbol{\alpha}^\top Y K c + \mathbf{1}^\top\boldsymbol{\alpha} \tag{2.15}$$

Differentiating again, now with respect to c, we obtain

$$0 = \nabla_c \, \nu c^\top K c - \alpha^\top Y K c + \mathbf{1}^\top \alpha = 2\nu K c - K Y \alpha$$
$$\Leftrightarrow 0 = 2\nu c - Y \alpha$$
$$\Leftrightarrow c = \tfrac{1}{2\nu} Y \alpha \ .$$

Substituting this into (2.15), we obtain

$$L = \frac{1}{4\nu} \alpha^\top Y K Y \alpha - \frac{1}{2\nu} \alpha^\top Y K Y \alpha + \mathbf{1}^\top \alpha = -\frac{1}{4\nu} \alpha^\top Y K Y \alpha + \mathbf{1}^\top \alpha$$

and with $Q = YKY$ the dual SVM problem

$$\max_{\alpha \in \mathbb{R}^n} \ -\tfrac{1}{4\nu} \alpha^\top Q \alpha + \mathbf{1}^\top \alpha$$

$$\text{subject to: } 0 \leq \alpha_i \leq \tfrac{1}{n} \qquad i = 1, \dots, n \ .$$

If we last but not least substitute α by $2\nu\alpha$ we obtain

$$\max_{\alpha \in \mathbb{R}^n} \ -\tfrac{1}{2} \alpha^\top Q \alpha + \mathbf{1}^\top \alpha$$

$$\text{subject to: } 0 \leq \alpha_i \leq \tfrac{1}{n\nu} \qquad i = 1, \dots, n \ . \tag{2.16}$$

The constraints in (2.16) are known as the *box constraints*. This problem is simpler than (2.11) as it contains simpler constraints. To solve it, standard quadratic programming tools can be used but as the support vector optimisation problem is more specific than the general quadratic programming problem, specialised solutions can be found that are faster than using of-the-shelf optimisation algorithms [Platt (1999); Joachims (1999)].

SVMs with Quadratic Penalties We can alternatively start with squared hinge loss and obtain the optimisation problem:

$$\min_{c, \xi \in \mathbb{R}^n} \ \tfrac{1}{n} \sum_{i=1}^{n} \xi_i^2 + \nu c^\top K c$$

$$\text{subject to: } y_i K_i . c \geq 1 - \xi_i \qquad i = 1, \dots, n \ . \tag{2.17}$$

Following along the lines of the above derivations we arrive at the dual problem

$$\max_{\alpha \in \mathbb{R}^n} \ -\tfrac{1}{2} \alpha^\top Q' \alpha + \mathbf{1}^\top \alpha$$

$$\text{subject to: } 0 \leq \alpha_i \qquad i = 1, \dots, n \ . \tag{2.18}$$

where $Q' = Q + \nu \mathbf{I}$. This regularisation is more similar to the regularisation we used in regularised least squares where we also added a small constant to the diagonal of the kernel matrix.

The reader interested in more details about support vector machines is referred to one of the excellent books on this topic [Cristianini and Shawe-Taylor (2000); Schölkopf and Smola (2002)].

2.4.3 Gaussian Processes

Gaussian processes [MacKay (1997)] are a non-parametric 'Bayesian' regression algorithm. They are based on somewhat different theory than the previously described regularised least squares and the support vector machine algorithms but have some nice properties useful in some application areas.

Bayesian parametric learning techniques assume some prior distribution over the parameters w of the hypothesis functions $\{f_w(\cdot)\}_w$. Given training data, they then compute the posterior distribution over parameter vectors using Bayes' rule. Predictions for unseen test data can then be obtained, for example, by marginalising over the parameters. For that, Bayesian methods assume that the distribution modelling the noise between observed target values and true target values is known.

Gaussian processes are a non-parametric Bayesian method. Instead of parameterising the function class and assuming a prior distribution over the parameter vectors, a prior distribution over the function space itself is assumed, i.e., the prior is $P(f(\cdot))$ rather than $P(w)$. This prior, however, can be defined only implicitly. For that, the distribution of target values and the noise distribution are assumed to be normal. To make learning possible, it has furthermore to be assumed that the target values are correlated and that their correlation depends only on the correlation of the corresponding data points.

To specify a Gaussian process one has to define its mean function $\mu(x) = E[Y(x)]$ and its covariance function $k(x, x') = E[(Y(x) - \mu(x))(Y(x') - \mu(x'))]$, where x, x' are instances, $Y(\cdot)$ is a random function, and $E[\cdot]$ is the expectation over $P(Y(\cdot))$. The choice of covariance functions is thereby only restricted to positive definite kernel functions.

Let $\{x_1, \ldots, x_n\}$ be the training instances, let $\{t_1, \ldots, t_n\}$ be the corresponding observed labels, and let t_{n+1} be a random variable for the label of the unseen example x_{n+1}. We assume that the observed target values t_i are obtained from the true labels y_i by additive Gaussian noise with variance σ. Let K be a matrix with $K_{ij} = k(x_i, x_j)$. The covariance matrix of the resulting Gaussian process is then given by the matrix C with $C = K + \sigma \mathbf{I}$. In the following we will use the convention that bold letters express the restriction of a matrix (vector) to rows and columns (elements) corresponding to training examples only. For example, t is the vector $(t_1, \ldots, t_{n+1})^\top$ and $\mathbf{t}$ is the vector $(t_1, \ldots, t_n)^\top$.

If we assume that the joint distribution of target values is Gaussian then also the conditional distribution $P(t_{n+1}|\mathbf{t})$ is Gaussian:

$$P(t) \propto \exp\left(-\frac{1}{2}t^\top C^{-1}t\right) = \exp\left(-\frac{1}{2}\sum_{i,j=1}^{n+1} t_i t_j [C^{-1}]_{ij}\right)$$

$$P(\mathbf{t}) \propto \exp\left(-\frac{1}{2}\mathbf{t}^\top \mathbf{C}^{-1}\mathbf{t}\right) = \exp\left(-\frac{1}{2}\sum_{i,j=1}^{n} t_i t_j [\mathbf{C}^{-1}]_{ij}\right)$$

$$P(t_{n+1}|\mathbf{t}) = \frac{P(t)}{P(\mathbf{t})} \propto \exp\left(\frac{1}{2}\mathbf{t}^\top \mathbf{C}^{-1}\mathbf{t} - \frac{1}{2}t^\top C^{-1}t\right)$$

$$= \exp\left(\frac{1}{2}\sum_{i,j=1}^{n} t_i t_j [\mathbf{C}^{-1}]_{ij} - \frac{1}{2}\sum_{i,j=1}^{n+1} t_i t_j [C^{-1}]_{ij}\right) \ .$$

For Gaussian distributions, the mean $\hat{t}_{n+1}$ coincides with the most likely value and we need compute the derivative of $P(t_{n+1}|\mathbf{t})$ with respect to t_{n+1}.

$$\frac{d}{dt_{n+1}}P(t_{n+1}|\mathbf{t}) \propto \left(\sum_{i=1}^{n+1} t_i [C^{-1}]_{i(n+1)}\right) \exp(\cdots) \ .$$

Setting $\frac{d}{dt_{n+1}}P(t_{n+1}|\mathbf{t}) = 0$ we obtain the mean and variance of the marginal Gaussian distribution as

$$\hat{t}_{n+1} = -\frac{\sum_{i=1}^{n} t_i [C^{-1}]_{i(n+1)}}{[C^{-1}]_{(n+1)(n+1)}} \quad \text{and} \quad \sigma_{\hat{t}_{n+1}}^2 = \frac{1}{[C^{-1}]_{(n+1)(n+1)}} \ .$$

From a computational point of view it is beneficial – if the label of more than one instance has to be predicted – to make use of the partitioned inverse equations (Section 2.1.8). Now, recall that $\mathbf{C}$ is the $n \times n$ covariance matrix of the training instances only and let $\mathbf{c}$ be the n-dimensional vector of covariances between training examples and one test example. We then obtain $\hat{t}_{n+1} = \mathbf{c}^\top \mathbf{C}^{-1}\mathbf{t}$ and $\sigma_{\hat{t}_{n+1}}^2 = C_{(n+1)(n+1)} - \mathbf{c}^\top \mathbf{C}^{-1}\mathbf{c}$. Here we only have to invert $\mathbf{C}$ once even if the label of different instances have to be predicted.

It can be seen that the mean prediction of a Gaussian process corresponds to the prediction found by a regularised least squares algorithm (Section 2.4.1). Just let $a = \mathbf{C}^{-1}\mathbf{t} = (\mathbf{K} + \sigma\mathbf{I})^{-1}\mathbf{t}$ and note that $f(x_{n+1}) = \sum_{i=1}^{n} a_i k(x_i, x_{n+1}) = a^\top \mathbf{c}$. This links the regularisation parameter ν with the variance of the Gaussian noise distribution assumed above.

2.4.4　Kernel Perceptron

The *kernel perceptron* is a simple binary classification algorithm based on the original perceptron algorithm of Rosenblatt (1957). It finds a hypothesis of the form (2.6) by sequentially updating the hypothesis, whenever a training example is misclassified.

The algorithm begins with all coefficients $c_i = 0$. It then repeatedly cycles through the data and whenever an example, say x_i, is misclassified, the model is updated by changing the corresponding $c_i \leftarrow c_i + y_i$. The algorithm stops as soon as no training example is misclassified by the model any more.

It has been conjectured by Rosenblatt and later been shown by (for example) Novikoff (1963) that, whenever there is a function of the form (2.6) that correctly classifies all training data, the perceptron algorithm will find one such function.

While the original convergence proof has not been for the kernel perceptron but for the original perceptron algorithm, the extension to the kernel case is straightforward.

Let the (unknown) function that correctly classifies the data be given by $f^*(\cdot) = \sum_j d_j k(x_j, \cdot)$. It then exists (as our sample is finite) a margin $\xi \in \mathbb{R}$ such that $y_i \sum_j d_j k(x_j, x_i) > \xi$ and a radius $R \in \mathbb{R}$ such that that $k(x_i, x_i) \le R^2$ for all i.

Let the hypothesis after the l-th update be $f^{(l)}(\cdot) = \sum_j c_j^{(l)} k(x_j, \cdot)$ and let the l-th update be on the i-th example. The inner product between the unknown function and the l-th hypothesis is

$$
\begin{aligned}
\left\langle f^{(l)}(\cdot), f^*(\cdot) \right\rangle &= \sum_{j,j'} d_j c_{j'}^{(l)} k(x_j, x_{j'}) \\
&= \sum_{j,j'} d_j c_{j'}^{(l-1)} k(x_j, x_{j'}) + y_i \sum_j d_j k(x_j, x_i) \\
&> \left\langle f^{(l-1)}(\cdot), f^*(\cdot) \right\rangle + \xi
\end{aligned}
$$

and by recursion then

$$
\left\langle f^{(l)}(\cdot), f^*(\cdot) \right\rangle > l\xi \, .
$$

By geometric reasoning or using the Cauchy-Schwarz inequality we obtain

$$
\| f^{(l)}(\cdot) \|_{\mathcal{H}} \ge \frac{\left\langle f^{(l)}(\cdot), f^*(\cdot) \right\rangle}{\| f^*(\cdot) \|_{\mathcal{H}}}
$$

and thus

$$
\| f^{(l)}(\cdot) \|_{\mathcal{H}} > \frac{l\xi}{\| f^*(\cdot) \|_{\mathcal{H}}} \, . \tag{2.19}
$$

Furthermore, the norm of the hypothesis function is then

$$\left\langle f^{(l)}(\cdot), f^{(l)}(\cdot) \right\rangle$$

$$= \sum_{j,j'} c_j^{(l)} c_{j'}^{(l)} k(x_j, x_{j'})$$

$$= \sum_{j,j'} c_j^{(l-1)} c_{j'}^{(l-1)} k(x_j, x_{j'}) + 2y_i \sum_j c_j^{(l-1)} k(x_i, x_j) + k(x_i, x_i)$$

$$\leq \left\langle f^{(l-1)}(\cdot), f^{(l-1)}(\cdot) \right\rangle + R^2$$

and by recursion

$$\|f^{(l)}(\cdot)\|_{\mathcal{H}}^2 \leq lR^2 . \tag{2.20}$$

Equations (2.19) and (2.20) together yield

$$\frac{l^2 \xi^2}{\|f^*(\cdot)\|_{\mathcal{H}}^2} < \|f^{(l)}(\cdot)\|_{\mathcal{H}}^2 \leq lR^2$$

and thus an upper bound on the number of updates needed to find a consistent hypothesis

$$l < \frac{R^2 \|f^*(\cdot)\|_{\mathcal{H}}^2}{\xi^2} . \tag{2.21}$$

That is, after at most $\frac{R^2 \|f^*(\cdot)\|_{\mathcal{H}}^2}{\xi^2}$ updates the kernel perceptron algorithm converges to a solution that correctly classifies all training data.

2.4.5   *Kernel Principal Component Analysis*

Kernel principal component analysis – *kernel PCA* – [Schoelkopf *et al.* (1997)] is an unsupervised learning technique, i.e., it assumes no knowledge of the value of a target attribute. Kernel PCA extends 'traditional' principal component analysis which tries to find the directions in the data with highest variance or — as we shall see in this section — equivalently, lowest approximation error. Both PCA and kernel PCA are used to project the data (from feature space) to a low dimensional subspace. Projections in two-dimensional space can, for example, be used to visualise sets of instances.

For kernel PCA this corresponds to finding the function for which the function values of the data points have highest variance. As we are only interested in directions, we can without loss of generality restrict our consideration to function with unit norm. If we assume the data has zero mean[3], the corresponding optimisation problem is

$$\max_{f(\cdot)\in\mathcal{H}} \frac{1}{n}\sum_{i=1}^{n} f^2(x_i)$$

subject to $\|f(\cdot)\|_{\mathcal{H}}^2 = 1$

or for the lowest approximation error

$$\min_{f(\cdot)\in\mathcal{H}} \frac{1}{n}\sum_{i=1}^{n} \|\langle k(x_i,\cdot),f(\cdot)\rangle f(\cdot) - k(x_i,\cdot)\|_{\mathcal{H}}^2$$

subject to $\|f(\cdot)\|_{\mathcal{H}}^2 = 1$.

For simplicity of notation we will in the following discussion omit the constraint $\|f(\cdot)\|_{\mathcal{H}}^2 = 1$.

We begin with the latter problem and show next that it is equivalent to the former problem. Using the reproducing property of $k(\cdot,\cdot)$ we obtain

$$\min_{f(\cdot)\in\mathcal{H}} \frac{1}{n}\sum_{i=1}^{n} \|f(x_i)f(\cdot) - k(x_i,\cdot)\|_{\mathcal{H}}^2$$

and by explicit multiplication

$$\min_{f(\cdot)\in\mathcal{H}} \frac{1}{n}\sum_{i=1}^{n} [\langle f(x_i)f(\cdot),f(x_i)f(\cdot)\rangle - 2\langle f(x_i)f(\cdot),k(x_i,\cdot)\rangle + \langle k(x_i,\cdot),k(x_i,\cdot)\rangle]$$

which we can simplify using the reproducing property to

$$\min_{f(\cdot)\in\mathcal{H}} \frac{1}{n}\sum_{i=1}^{n} [f^2(x_i)\langle f(\cdot),f(\cdot)\rangle - 2f^2(x_i) + k(x_i,x_i)] .$$

As $\langle f(\cdot),f(\cdot)\rangle = \|f(\cdot)\|_{\mathcal{H}}^2 = 1$ and $k(x_i,x_i)$ is independent of $f(\cdot)$, we obtain

$$\min_{f(\cdot)\in\mathcal{H}} \frac{1}{n}\sum_{i=1}^{n} [-f^2(x_i)]$$

and thus the problem of maximising the variance along $f(\cdot)$. We proceed with an analytic solution of this optimisation problem.

The weak representer theorem can be applied to this problem and we can make use of (2.6) to write $f(x_i) = \tilde{K}_{i\cdot}c$ where $\tilde{K}$ is a centred version of K with $K_{ij} = k(x_i,x_j)$. As then $f^2(x_i) = \left(c^\top\tilde{K}_{\cdot i}\right)\left(\tilde{K}_{i\cdot}c\right)$ we obtain the optimisation problem

$$\max_{c\in\mathbb{R}^n} \frac{1}{n}c^\top\tilde{K}^2 c .$$

---

[3]We will later in this subsection discuss how this can be achieved in the general case.

Now, let $\{(u_i, \lambda_i)\}$ be the Eigenpairs of $\tilde{K}$ sorted such that $\lambda_i \geq \lambda_j$ if $i < j$. As then $\tilde{K}^2 = \sum_i u_i \lambda_i^2 u_i^\top$ we obtain

$$\max_{c \in \mathbb{R}^n} \frac{1}{n} \sum_i \langle c, u_i \rangle \lambda_i^2 \langle u_i, c \rangle$$

as furthermore the eigenvectors form a basis, we can view c as a linear combination of eigenvectors, say $c = \sum_j \alpha_j u_j$, and the optimisation problem simplifies to

$$\max_{\alpha \in \mathbb{R}^n} \frac{1}{n} \sum_i \alpha_i^2 \lambda_i^2 .$$

The norm of $f(\cdot)$ can be computed as $c^\top K c = \sum_i \alpha_i^2 \lambda_i$ and the restriction to functions with unit norm means we have to solve

$$\max_{\beta \in \mathbb{R}^n} \frac{1}{n} \sum_i \beta_i \lambda_i$$

subject to $\sum_i \beta_i = 1$

by the order assumed on λ_i a maximum is at $\beta_1 = 1; \beta_i = 0 (i > 1)$.

This means that the function with unit norm for which the data has maximal variance is a linear combination of the kernels 'centred' at the training data and with the coefficients c_i, where $c = \lambda_1^{\frac{-1}{2}} u_1$.

Kernel PCA proceeds further by finding the function for which the data has maximal variance but which is orthogonal to the above function. This function is given by $c = \lambda_2^{\frac{-1}{2}} u_2$. The third function, orthogonal to the first two, is given by $c = \lambda_3^{\frac{-1}{2}} u_3$; the fourth by $c = \lambda_4^{\frac{-1}{2}} u_4$ and so forth.

It remains to show how we can deal with data that does not have a zero mean. That is, we know the function $k(x_i, x_j) = \langle k(x_i, \cdot), k(x_j, \cdot) \rangle$ and want to compute $\tilde{k}(x_i, x_j) = \langle k(x_i, \cdot) - \mu(\cdot), k(x_j, \cdot) - \mu(\cdot) \rangle$, where $\mu(\cdot) = \frac{1}{n} \sum_i k(x_i, \cdot)$ is the mean function. We obtain

$$\tilde{k}(x_i, x_j) = \langle k(x_i, \cdot) - \mu(\cdot), k(x_j, \cdot) - \mu(\cdot) \rangle$$
$$= \langle k(x_i, \cdot), k(x_j, \cdot) \rangle - \langle k(x_i, \cdot), \mu(\cdot) \rangle - \langle \mu(\cdot), k(x_j, \cdot) \rangle + \langle \mu(\cdot), \mu(\cdot) \rangle$$
$$= k(x_i, x_j) - \frac{1}{n} \sum_l k(x_i, x_l) - \frac{1}{n} \sum_l k(x_l, x_j) + \frac{1}{n^2} \sum_{l,l'} k(x_l, x_{l'}) .$$

In matrix notation, the second summand in the last line of the above equation is the average of a row, the third the average of a column, and the last one the average of the whole matrix. Thus the centred kernel matrix can be computed as

$$\tilde{K} = K - \frac{1}{n} K \mathbf{1} - \frac{1}{n} \mathbf{1} K + \frac{1}{n^2} \mathbf{1} K \mathbf{1} . \tag{2.22}$$

2.4.6 *Distance-Based Algorithms*

Distance-based learning algorithms [see for example Mitchell (1996)] are a set of learning algorithms that can be applied to a learning task whenever the instance space is a (pseudo-)metric space (Section 2.1.3). As every inner product space is a metric space (see Section 2.1.5), distance based algorithms can be applied to data on which a positive definite kernel function has been defined. The metric is then given by $d(x, x') = \sqrt{k(x,x) - 2k(x,x') + k(x',x')}$. This subsection describes briefly two simple distance-based learning-algorithms: the k-nearest neighbour algorithm and the k-means algorithm.

The *nearest neighbour* algorithm is a supervised learning algorithm that can be applied to regression and classification problems. In the regression case it predicts the target value of an unseen instance as the average target value of its nearest training instances. In the classification case it predicts the class that is most common among the nearest training instances. The number of neighbours that is taken into account in both cases is a parameter of the learning algorithm. Increasing this parameter leads to a kind of smoothing of the predicted values and makes the algorithm more stable with respect to label-noise. Implementations of nearest neighbour differ in the way conflicts are resolved, i.e., how equally distant instances are treated and how equally frequent class labels are handled.

The *k-means* algorithm is an unsupervised learning algorithm that tries to find sets (clusters) of instances such that the instances in the same set are more similar to each other than to the instances in other sets. k-means starts with a random assignment of instances to clusters. If the instance space is an inner product space (Section 2.1.5), it then repeats the following two steps: (1) compute the mean of each cluster, and (2) assign each instance to the cluster whose mean is nearest. For our purposes it is important that step (1) is not necessary — though it is computationally attractive — as we can implicitly represent the cluster mean by the set of instances in a cluster. Then, the distance between the mean of a cluster C

and an instance x can be computed as follows

$$
d \left(x, \frac{1}{|C|} \sum_{x' \in C} x' \right)
$$

$$
= \sqrt{ \langle x, x \rangle - 2 \left\langle x, \frac{1}{|C|} \sum_{x' \in C} x' \right\rangle + \left\langle \frac{1}{|C|} \sum_{x' \in C} x', \frac{1}{|C|} \sum_{x' \in C} x' \right\rangle }
$$

$$
= \sqrt{ \langle x, x \rangle - 2 \frac{1}{|C|} \sum_{x' \in C} \langle x, x' \rangle + \frac{1}{|C|^2} \sum_{x', x'' \in C} \langle x', x'' \rangle } \, .
$$

The last line of this equation only contains inner products between examples which can be replaced by an arbitrary kernel function defined on the instances. This is necessary if the instance space is not an inner product space. The number of clusters initially created is a parameter of the learning algorithm.

2.5   Summary

In this section we described the most important basics needed for the further developments in this book. Starting with measurable sets we introduced metric spaces, linear spaces, normed linear spaces, and inner product spaces; as well as Banach and Hilbert spaces. After that we reviewed the relation between reproducing kernels of Hilbert spaces and positive definite functions, and the isomorphism of different realisations of Hilbert spaces. In the following sections the basics of supervised learning and the foundations of kernel methods have been summarised. Last but not least we gave an overview over a number of different kernel methods.

The most important topic of the first section was probably the characterisation of the class of positive definite functions which coincides with the class reproducing kernels of Hilbert spaces. Though less important to the further developments, it is important for the illustration of such functions to note that for every positive definite function $k(\cdot, \cdot) : \mathcal{X} \times \mathcal{X} \to \mathbb{R}$ on a finite or countable set $\mathcal{X}$, there is a map $\phi : \mathcal{X} \to l_2$ for which $k(x, x') = \langle \phi(x), \phi(x') \rangle$ for all $x, x' \in \mathcal{X}$. The subspace of l_2, spanned by the images of elements of $\mathcal{X}$ under ϕ, is often called the *feature space*. The feature space has clearly dimension at most $|\mathcal{X}|$ and the existence of ϕ is guaranteed by isomorphism of different realisations of the Hilbert space. How to find one such ϕ for finite $\mathcal{X}$ is described in the section on matrix computations.

Very important topics in the third section were the foundation of kernel methods in basic model fitting methods and the discussion of the need for regularisation; leading to the regularised risk optimisation problem (2.5). However, the most important and fundamental result is the representer theorem that is at the heart of all kernel methods described in the third section of this chapter. Equation (2.6) gives the form of solutions of the regularised risk optimisation problem under rather general assumptions.

With this background we are now ready to have a closer look at kernel functions.

Chapter 3

Kernel Design

*When I examine myself and my methods of thought, I come
close to the conclusion that the gift of fantasy has meant more
to me than my talent for absorbing positive knowledge.*

(Albert Einstein, On Science)

In Chapter we illustrated the general supervised learning task and motivated the need to consider learning from structured data. The class of learning algorithms we are most interested in is the class of kernel methods. In Chapter 1.6 we then introduced the necessary formal background of kernel methods. This included a brief review of relevant topics from model fitting and regularisation theory, as well as the characterisation of hypothesis spaces that form a reproducing kernel Hilbert space. For that we discussed different properties of positive definite and reproducing kernel functions.

In this chapter we will investigate, which positive definite functions can successfully be applied in kernel methods. This is a necessary foundation needed in the following chapters that will concentrate on the definition of kernel functions for particular knowledge representation languages. Thus, in the following sections we will try to characterise kernel functions that lead to good learning performance and we will motivate the need for choosing the 'right' kernel for a particular learning problem. After that we will investigate different possibilities of defining kernel functions for simple data structures like sets. Last but not least we will review a number of kernel functions for structured data that have been defined prior to or at the same time as this book.

3.1   General Remarks on Kernels and Examples

We will begin this section with an attempt to classify kernel functions according to the 'driving force' behind their definition. This driving force may, for example, be the syntax of a representation language or based on a generative model of a given set of training instances. We will then describe different properties of kernel functions that are of importance for good predictive performance. The first of these properties is, for example, that for any two instances with different class, there needs to be a function in the hypothesis space that is able to distinguish between them. After that we describe different kernel functions that can be (and have been) used for instances that are readily described as elements of an inner product space like $\mathbb{R}^n$. After that we will illustrate the impact of choosing one particular kernel function and motivate the importance of picking the 'right one'.

3.1.1   *Classes of Kernels*

A useful conceptual distinction between different kernels is based on the 'driving-force' of their definition. We distinguish between semantics, syntax, model, and data as the driving-force of the kernel definition. This distinction will help later in Section 3.4 to review kernel functions defined in the literature in a systematic way. The most popular of these driving forces is the syntax, usually combined with some semantic understanding of the representation language. The kernels presented in Chapters 3.5 and 4.6 are examples of this combination.

Semantics is in some sense the ideal driving-force for the definition of kernels. It is related to so-called 'knowledge-driven' approaches of incorporating expert knowledge into the domain representation. Semantics-driven kernel definitions, however, often lead to proprietary special case kernels that can be used in one application only. This motivates the definition of syntax-driven kernel functions on knowledge representations that are able to represent some semantics explicitly.

Syntax is often used in typed systems to formally describe the semantics of the data. It is the most common driving force. In its simplest case, i.e., untyped attribute-value representations, it treats every attribute in the same way. More complex syntactic representations are graphs, restricted subsets of graphs such as lists and trees, or terms in some (possibly typed) logic. Whenever kernels are syntax-driven, they are either special case kernels, assuming some underlying semantics of the application, or they are parameterised and offer the possibility to adapt the kernel function to certain semantics.

Models contain some kind of knowledge about the instance space, i.e., about the relationships among instances. These models can either be generative models of instances or they can be given by some sort of transformation relations. Hidden Markov models are a frequently used generative model. Edit operations on a lists are one example for operations that transform one list into another. The graph defined on the set of lists by these operations can be seen as a model of the instance space. While each edge of a graph only contains local information about neighbouring vertices, the set of all edges, i.e., the graph itself, also contains information about the global structure of the instance space.

Data-driven approaches use results obtained by analysing the training data. Data-driven approaches are hardly ever used for kernel definition but they are frequently used to choose a kernel from a class of kernel functions.

Often more than one of the above described driving-forces of kernel definitions are applied together. Models of instance spaces contain either semantic background knowledge or are learnt from the training data itself. In both cases the model-driven kernel definition is combined with another driving force. Whenever a set of kernels is defined on some syntactic representation, either semantic background knowledge or training data will be used to choose one particular kernel from this set. Either way, the syntax-driven kernel definition is combined with another driving force.

3.1.2 *Good Kernels*

For a kernel method to perform well on some domain, positive definiteness of the kernel is not the only issue. To discuss the characteristics of good kernels, we need the notion of a concept class. In a binary classification problem (Section 2.2.1), with a functional dependence between object representations and labels, the function underlying this dependence is called a *concept* $c : \mathcal{X} \to \Omega$. A *concept class* $\mathcal{C}$ is a set of concepts.

While there is always a valid kernel that performs poorly $(k_0(x, x') = 0)$, there is also always a valid kernel $(k_c(x, x') = +1 \Leftrightarrow c(x) = c(x')$ and $k_c(x, x') = -1 \Leftrightarrow c(x) \neq c(x'))$ that performs ideally. However, the learning problem is that $c(\cdot)$ is unknown. We distinguish the following three issues crucial to 'good' kernels: completeness, correctness, and appropriateness.

Completeness refers to the extent to which the knowledge incorporated in the kernel is sufficient for solving the problem at hand. A kernel is said to be complete if it takes into account all the information necessary to represent the concept that underlies the problem domain. Formally, we call a kernel complete if $k(x, \cdot) = k(x', \cdot)$ implies $x = x'$ [1]. With respect to some concept class, however, it is not important to distinguish between instances that are equally classified by all concepts in that particular concept class. We call a kernel complete with respect to a concept class $\mathcal{C}$ if $k(x, \cdot) = k(x', \cdot)$ implies $c(x) = c(x')$ for all $c \in \mathcal{C}$.

Correctness refers to the extent to which the underlying semantics of the problem are obeyed in the kernel. Correctness can formally only be expressed with respect to a certain concept class and a certain hypothesis space. In particular, we call a kernel correct with respect to a concept class $\mathcal{C}$ and linear combinations of kernels (as in Equation (2.6)) if for all concepts $c \in \mathcal{C}$ there exist $\alpha_i \in \mathbb{R}, x_i \in \mathcal{X}, \theta \in \mathbb{R}$ such that $\forall x \in \mathcal{X} : \sum_i \alpha_i k(x_i, x) \geq \theta \Leftrightarrow c(x)$. A kernel that is not complete with respect to a concept class can not be correct with respect to that concept class and any hypothesis space. For the remainder of the paper we will use 'correct' only with respect to linear combinations of kernels as the hypothesis space.

Appropriateness refers to the extent to which examples that are close to each other in class membership are also 'close' to each other in feature space. Appropriateness can formally only be defined with respect to a concept class and a learning algorithm. For example, a kernel is appropriate for learning concepts in a concept class with the kernel perceptron, if the maximal number of mistakes can be bound by a polynomial. This problem is most apparent in the *matching kernel* $k_\delta(x, x') = 1 \Leftrightarrow x = x'$ and $k_\delta(x, x') = 0 \Leftrightarrow x \neq x'$ which is always complete and correct but not appropriate.

Empirically, a complete, correct and appropriate kernel exhibits two properties. A complete and correct kernel separates the concept well, i.e., a learning algorithm achieves high accuracy when learning and validating on the same part of the data. An appropriate kernel generalises well, i.e., a learning algorithm achieves high accuracy when learning and validating on different parts of the data. In other words an appropriate kernel avoids overfitting (Section 2.2.2).

3.1.3 *Kernels on Inner Product Spaces*

In this section we review the traditionally used kernels on inner product spaces and give some intuitions.

---

[1]This corresponds to the map ϕ, with $\langle \phi(x), \phi(x') \rangle = k(x, x')$ for all x, x', being injective.

For some inner product space $\mathcal{R}$, let $x, x' \in \mathcal{R}$ and let $\langle \cdot, \cdot \rangle$ denote the scalar product in $\mathcal{R}$. In real world applications, often $\mathcal{R} = \mathbb{R}^n$ and $\langle x, x' \rangle = \sum_{i=1}^{n} x_i x_i'$.

Apart from the linear kernel

$$k(x, x') = \langle x, x' \rangle$$

and the normalised linear kernel

$$k(x, x') = \frac{\langle x, x' \rangle}{\sqrt{\langle x, x \rangle \langle x', x' \rangle}}$$

which corresponds to the cosine of the angle enclosed by the vectors, the two most frequently used kernels on inner product spaces are the polynomial kernel and the Gaussian kernel. Given two parameters $l \in \mathbb{R}, p \in \mathbb{N}$ the polynomial kernel is defined as:

$$k(x, x') = (\langle x, x' \rangle + l)^p \ .$$

The intuition behind this kernel definition is that it is often useful to construct new features as products of original features. This way for example the XOR problem can be turned into a linearly separable problem. The parameter p is the maximal order of monomials making up the new feature space, the parameter l is the bias towards lower order monomials. If $l = 0$ the feature space consists only of monomials of order p of the original features.

Example 3.1 (xor). *Consider the positive examples* $(+1, +1), (-1, -1)$ *and the negative examples* $(+1, -1), (-1, +1)$. *Clearly, there is no straight line separating positive from negative examples. However, if we use the transformation* $\phi : (x_1, x_2) \mapsto (x_1^2, \sqrt{2} x_1 x_2, x_2^2)$ *separation is possible with the plane orthonormal to* $(0, 1, 0)$ *as the the sign of* $x_1 x_2$ *already corresponds to the class. To see that this transformation can be performed implicitly by a polynomial kernel, let* $x = (x_1, x_2), z = (z_1, z_2)$ *and* $k(x, z) = \langle x, z \rangle^2$. *Then*

$$k(x, z) = \langle (x_1, x_2), (z_1, z_2) \rangle^2 = (x_1 z_1 + x_2 z_2)^2$$
$$= (x_1 z_1)^2 + 2 x_1 x_2 z_1 z_2 + (x_2 z_2)^2$$
$$= \left\langle \left(x_1^2, \sqrt{2} x_1 x_2, x_2^2 \right), \left(z_1^2, \sqrt{2} z_1 z_2, z_2^2 \right) \right\rangle$$

The last line is the inner product under the map ϕ. *Now, let* $x_+(x_-)$ *be either of the positive (negative) examples given above. An unseen example* x *can be classified without explicitly transforming instances, as* $k(x, x_+) - k(x, x_-)$ *corresponds to implicitly projecting the new examples onto the vector* $\phi(x_+) - \phi(x_-)$

Given the bandwidth parameter σ the Gaussian kernel is defined as:

$$k(x, x') = e^{-||x-x'||^2/\sigma^2} \ .$$

Using this kernel function in a support vector machine results in a classifier that can be seen as a radial basis function network with Gaussian kernels centred at the support vectors. The images of the points from the vector space $\mathbb{R}^n$ under the map $\phi : \mathbb{R}^n \to \mathcal{H}$ with $k(x, x') = \langle \phi(x), \phi(x') \rangle$ lie all on the surface of a hyperball in the Hilbert space $\mathcal{H}$. No two images are orthogonal and any set of images is linearly independent. The parameter σ can be used to tune how much generalisation is done. For very large σ, all vectors $\phi(x)$ are almost parallel and thus almost identical. For very small σ, the vectors $\phi(x)$ are almost orthogonal to each other and the Gaussian kernel behaves almost like the matching kernel. In applications this often causes a problem known as the *ridge problem*, which means that the learning algorithm functions more or less just as a lookup table. In Section 3.1.2 we called such kernels inappropriate.

3.1.4 *Some Illustrations*

To illustrate the importance of choosing the 'right' kernel function, we next illustrate the hypothesis found by a Gaussian process with different kernel functions.

In Figure 3.1 the training examples are pairs of real numbers $x \in \mathbb{R}^2$ illustrated by black discs and circles in the figure. The (unknown) target function is an XOR-type function, the target variable y takes values -1 for the black discs and $+1$ for the black circles. The probability of a test example being of class $+1$ is illustrated by the colour of the corresponding pixel in the figure. The different kernels used are the linear kernel $k(x, x') = \langle x, x' \rangle$, the polynomial kernel $k(x, x') = (\langle x, x' \rangle + l)^p$, the sigmoid kernel $k(x, x') = \tanh(\gamma \langle x, x' \rangle)$, and the Gaussian kernel function $k(x, x') = \exp\left[-||x - x'||^2/\sigma^2\right]$.

Figure 3.2 illustrates the impact of choosing the parameter of a Gaussian kernel function on the regularisation of the solution found by a Gaussian process. Training examples are single real numbers and the target value is also a real number. The unknown target function is a sinusoid function shown by a thin line in the figure. Training examples perturbed by random noise are depicted by black circles. The colour of each pixel illustrates the distribution of target values given the example, the most likely value is always coloured in white.

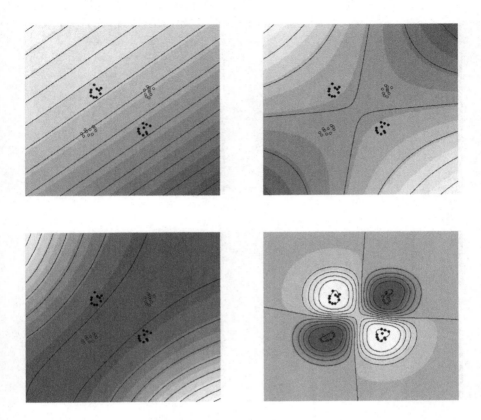

Figure 3.1 Impact of different kernel functions on the solution found by Gaussian processes. Kernel functions from left to right, top to bottom are: linear kernel, polynomial kernel of degree 2, sigmoid kernel, and Gaussian kernel.

3.2 Kernel Functions

When defining kernels for structured data, it is often useful to build them up from kernel functions defined on simpler data structures. In this section we will first review which combinations of positive definite matrices and functions are again positive definite. We will thereby first focus on certain sums and products of kernels. These considerations will prove useful when looking at kernels defined in the literature in Section 3.4 and when defining kernels for other representation languages in Chapters 3.5 and 4.6.

After that we investigate whether minima or maxima of kernels are positive definite. This investigation is motivated by observing that many

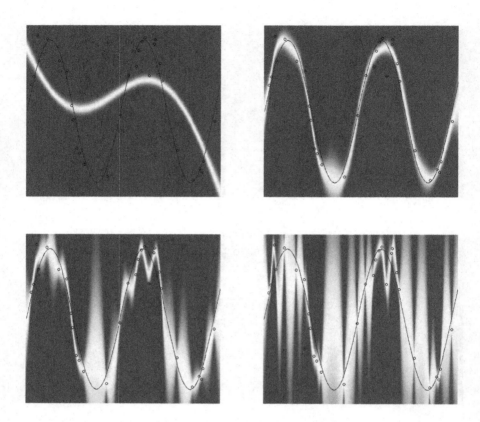

Figure 3.2   Impact of the bandwidth of a Gaussian kernel function on the regularisation of the solution found by Gaussian processes. The bandwidth is decreasing from left to right, top to bottom.

distances on structured data defined in the literature are based on minima or maxima over more simple distance functions. We will show there, that minima and maxima over kernels are, in general, not positive definite. This motivates the definition of kernel functions on particular representation languages in Chapters 3.5 and 4.6.

3.2.1   *Closure Properties*

Before we describe, which combinations of positive definite functions are positive definite, we will first review and extend some results from Section 2.1.7 on which combinations of matrices are positive definite.

Proposition 3.1. *The following matrices are positive definite:*

(1) For any matrix B, the matrix $B^{\top}B$ is positive definite.

(2) For any two positive definite matrices G, H, the tensor product $G \otimes H$ is positive definite.

(3) For any strictly positive definite matrix G and integer n, G^n is strictly positive definite. For any positive definite matrix G and integer $n > 0$, G^n is positive definite.

(4) For any positive definite matrix G and real number $\gamma \geq 0$, the limit of the power series $\sum_n^{\infty} \gamma^n G^n$ exists if γ is smaller than the inverse of the largest eigenvalue of G. Then also the limit is positive definite.

(5) For any symmetric matrix G and real number β, the limit of the power series $\sum_n^{\infty} \frac{\beta^n}{n!} G^n$ exists and is positive definite.

Proof.

(1) This holds as $c^{\top} B^{\top} B c = \|Bc\|^2 = \sum_i [Bc]_i^2 \geq 0$.

(2) This is shown in Section 2.1.7.

(3) Let D be a diagonal matrix with the eigenvalues of G as its elements and T be the matrix with the eigenvectors of G as columns. Then $GT = TD$ and $G = TDT^{-1} = TDT^{\top}$. For $n > 0$ we have

$$G^n = \left(TDT^{-1}\right)^n = T \left(DT^{-1}T\right)^{n-1} DT^{-1} = TD^n T^{-1}$$

and it follows that G^n is positive definite. The result also holds for negative n as the eigenvalues of the inverse of G are equal to the inverse of the eigenvalues of G.

Before continuing the discussion we need a result concerning both 4. and 5.: For any symmetric matrix G with eigendecomposition $G = TDT^{-1}$ as above, we can compute the limit of the power series $\sum_n^{\infty} \lambda_n G^n$ as

$$\sum_n^{\infty} \lambda_n G^n = T \left(\sum_n^{\infty} \lambda_n D^n \right) T^{-1}$$

where $\sum_n^{\infty} \lambda_n D^n$ can be computed componentwise. Now:

4. For any positive real number $d < \gamma^{-1}$, we have $\sum_n^{\infty} \gamma^n d^n = \frac{1}{1-\gamma d} > 0$.

5. For any real number d, we have $\sum_n^{\infty} \frac{\beta^n}{n!} d^n = e^{\beta n} > 0$. $\qquad \square$

Next we have a look at the closure properties of kernel functions.

Proposition 3.2. *Let the functions $g, h, k_1, k_2, \ldots$ be positive definite functions such that the sequence of functions $k_1, k_2, \ldots$ converges and let $\alpha, \beta \geq 0$. Then the following functions are also positive definite:*

(1) $k\left((x,z),(x',z')\right) = g(x,x') * h(z,z')$
(2) $k(x,x') = g(x,x') * h(x,x')$
(3) $k(x,x') = \alpha g(x,x') + \beta h(x,x')$
(4) $k(x,x') = \lim_{m\to\infty} k_m(x,x')$

Proof.

(1) The matrix K with $K_{(i_{12})(j_{12})} = k\left((x_{i_1}, z_{i_2}), (x_{j_1}, z_{j_2})\right)$ is the tensor product of the matrices G, H with $G_{i_1 j_1} = g(x_{i_1}, x_{j_1})$ and $H_{i_2 j_2} = h(z_{i_2}, z_{j_2})$. It follows that K is positive definite if and only if both G and H are positive definite (Section 2.1.7).

(2) Assume that there is a choice of $c_1, \ldots, c_n$ such that

$$\sum_{i,j} c_i c_j g(x_i, x_j) * h(x_i, x_j) < 0 \ .$$

With $a_{i_1 i_2} = c_{i_1}$ if $i_1 = i_2$ and $a_{i_1 i_2} = 0$ otherwise, we have a choice of $a_{i_1 i_2}$ such that

$$\sum_{i_1, i_2, j_1, j_2} a_{i_1 i_2} a_{j_1 j_2} g(x_{i_1}, x_{j_1}) * h(x_{i_2}, x_{j_2}) < 0$$

which contradicts the proof of the previous item.

(3) Compute

$$\sum_{i,j} c_i c_j \left[\alpha g(x_i, x_j) + \beta h(x_i, x_j)\right]$$

$$= \alpha \left[\sum_{i,j} c_i c_j g(x_i, x_j)\right] + \beta \left[\sum_{i,j} c_i c_j h(x_i, x_j)\right] \ .$$

(4) This   holds   as
    $\sum_{i,j} c_i c_j \lim_{m\to\infty} k_m(x_i, x_j) = \lim_{m\to\infty} \sum_{i,j} c_i c_j k_m(x_i, x_j).$ $\square$

Last but not least we have the following proposition for constant bounded kernel functions:

Proposition 3.3. *Let* $h : \mathcal{X} \times \mathcal{X} \to \mathbb{R}$ *be a positive definite function and* $c \in \mathbb{R}$ *such that* $\forall x \in \mathcal{X} : h(x,x) < c$. *Then the function* $k : \mathcal{X} \times \mathcal{X} \to \mathbb{R}$ *defined by*

$$k(x,x') = \frac{1}{c - h(x,x')}$$

is positive definite.

The proof follows long the lines of Gower (1971).

Proof. First notice that $c > h(x, x) \geq 0$ and

$$2|h(x, x')| \leq h(x, x) + h(x', x') \leq 2c \ .$$

Therefore, $\left|\frac{h(x,x')}{c}\right| < 1$ and

$$\lim_{m \to \infty} \sum_{i=0}^{m} \left(\frac{h(x, x')}{c}\right)^i = \frac{c}{c - h(x, x')} \ .$$

As $h(\cdot, \cdot)$ is positive definite, it follows from the above proposition that the left hand side of the equation is positive definte. Then, also $k(x, x') = \frac{1}{c - h(x,x')}$ is positive definite. □

3.2.2 *Kernel Modifiers*

The commonly used kernel functions for vectors (Subsection 3.1.3) can be seen as kernel functions built up by applying a function $\kappa : \mathcal{P} \to (\mathcal{X} \times \mathcal{X} \to \mathbb{R}) \to (\mathcal{X} \times \mathcal{X} \to \mathbb{R})$ to the usual inner product, that given some parameters (an element of the parameter space $\mathcal{P}$) – maps a kernel to a modified kernel.

While this point of view does not add much when considering kernels on vectors only, it is very helpful when defining kernels for arbitrary data. There it is sufficient to define a 'default kernel' (corresponding to the inner product between vectors), implicitly giving rise to a family of kernels (corresponding to polynomial, Gaussian, or normal kernels)

- A *polynomial modifier* is defined as
$$\kappa_{\text{polynomial}}(p, l)(k)(x, x') = (k(x, x') + l)^p \ (l \geq 0, \ p \in \mathbb{Z}^+)$$
- A *Gaussian modifier* is defined as:
$$\kappa_{\text{gaussian}}(\gamma)(k)(x, x') = e^{-[k(x,x) - 2k(x,x') + k(x',x')]/\sigma^2} (\gamma > 0)$$
- A *normalisation modifier* is defined as
$$\kappa_{\text{normalised}}(k)(x, x') = \frac{k(x, x')}{\sqrt{k(x, x)k(x', x')}}$$

where $\sqrt{k(x, x)}$ is the norm of x in the feature space, and thus the normalisation kernel is equal to the cosine of the angle between x and x' in the feature space corresponding to k.

It follows from the closure properties discussed in the previous section that modified kernels are positive definite if the underlying kernel is positive definite. The traditionally used kernels on inner product spaces are from this point of view modified versions of the canonical inner product.

3.2.3   *Minimal and Maximal Functions*

In the literature distances are often defined using the minima and/or maxima over a set of distances, e.g., the distances described in [Eiter and Mannila (1997)] between point sets, the string edit distance [Fischer and Fischer (1974)] between sequences, or the subgraph distance [Messmer (1995); Bunke and Allerman (1983)] between graphs. It is thus interesting to investigate whether in general kernel functions can be defined as the minimum and/or maximum of a set of kernels. In this section we investigate whether certain uses of minima and/or maxima give rise to positive definite kernels. Kernels on instances represented by sets will be discussed in Section 3.3.1 and 3.3.2.

We begin our discussion with two very simple uses of minima and maxima:

- The function $\min\{x, x'\}$ defined on non-negative real numbers is positive definite: Let $\theta_x(\cdot)$ be the function such that $\theta_x(z) = 1$ if $z \in [0; x]$ and $\theta_x(z) = 0$ otherwise. Then,

$$\min\{x, x'\} = \int_{\mathbb{R}} \theta_x(\cdot)\theta_{x'}(\cdot)d\mu$$

  coincides with the usual (L_2, see Subsection 2.1.5) inner product between the functions $\theta_x(\cdot)$ and $\theta_{x'}(\cdot)$. Thus it is positive definite.
- The function $\max\{x, x'\}$ defined on non-negative real numbers is not positive definite. Setting $x = 0, x' = 1$ we obtain the indefinite matrix

$$\begin{pmatrix} 0 & 1 \\ 1 & 1 \end{pmatrix}.$$

We show next, that – in general – functions built from positive definite kernels using the min or max function are not positive definite.

- The function $\min_i k_i(x, x')$, where each k_i is a positive definite kernel, is not necessarily positive definite: Setting $x = 1; x' = 2; k_1(x, x') = xx'; k_2(x, x') = (3 - x)(3 - x')$ gives rise to the indefinite matrix

$$\begin{pmatrix} 1 & 2 \\ 2 & 1 \end{pmatrix}.$$

- The function $\max_i k_i(x, x')$ where again each k_i is a positive definite kernel, is not necessarily positive definite: If this function was positive definite then the component-wise maximum of two positive definite matrices would also be positive definite. Consider the matrices

$$A = \begin{pmatrix} 1 & 1 & 0 \\ 1 & 1 & 0 \\ 0 & 0 & 1 \end{pmatrix} \qquad \text{and} \qquad B = \begin{pmatrix} 1 & 0 & 0 \\ 0 & 1 & 1 \\ 0 & 1 & 1 \end{pmatrix} .$$

Here, A has the eigenvectors $(1,1,0)^\top; (0,0,1)^\top; (1,-1,0)^\top$ with corresponding eigenvalues $2,1,0 \geq 0$, showing that both matrices are positive definite. However, the component-wise maximum of A and B,

$$D = \begin{pmatrix} 1 & 1 & 0 \\ 1 & 1 & 1 \\ 0 & 1 & 1 \end{pmatrix}$$

is indefinite: $(1,0,0)D(1,0,0)^\top = 1 > 0$ and $(1,-1,1)D(1,-1,1)^\top = -1 < 0$.

We will return to min and max functions in Section 3.3.2 where we turn our attention to kernels on sets. In the next section we discuss how kernel functions can be combined such that the combination is dominated by the maximal kernel value.

3.2.4 *Soft-Maximal Kernels*

A 'soft-max' function is a sequence of functions that in the limit converges to the function $\max_i k_i(x, x')$. Two simple examples of soft-max functions are

$$\sqrt[m]{\sum_i k_i^m(x, x')}$$

and

$$\frac{1}{\gamma} \ln \sum_i \exp\left[\gamma k_i(x, x')\right] .$$

The former converges to the maximum for $m \in \mathbb{N}, m \to \infty$, and the latter for $\gamma \in \mathbb{R}, \gamma \to \infty$. As the corresponding max function is not positive definite (Section 3.2.3) and kernels are closed under the limit (Section 3.2.1), it is clear that there is an infinite number of soft-max functions in each sequence that is not positive definite.

However, we can define simple positive definite functions whose value is dominated by the maximal kernel value. We call such a function a *soft-maximal kernel*. The soft-maximal kernels related to the above soft-max functions are

$$\sum_i k_i^m(x, x')$$

and

$$\sum_i \exp\left[\gamma k_i(x, x')\right]$$

which are both positive definite if the k_i are positive definite (Section 3.2.1).

Thus albeit the max function itself is not positive definite, we can hope that it is possible to mimic its behaviour by using one of these alternative functions. We later discuss soft-maximal kernels in the context of instances that can be represented by sets in Section 3.3.2 and use them instead of a maximal set kernel in Section 4.3.

3.3 Introduction to Kernels for Structured Data

Before investigating kernels on complex structured data in detail in the remainder of this book, we now concentrate on kernels for sets. These considerations will be the basis for kernel definitions in the remaining sections and chapters.

3.3.1 *Intersection and Crossproduct Kernels on Sets*

As we will see later, an integral part of many kernels for structured data is the *decomposition* of an object into a set of its parts and the *intersection* of two sets of parts. The kernel on two objects is then defined as a measure of the intersection of the two corresponding sets of parts.

The general case of interest for set kernels is when the instances X_i are elements of a semiring of sets $\mathfrak{S}$ and there is a measure μ with $\mathfrak{S}$ as its domain of definition (Section 2.1.2). A natural choice of a kernel on such data is the following kernel function:

Definition 3.1. Let $\mu(\cdot)$ be a measure defined on the semiring of sets $\mathfrak{S}$. The *intersection kernel* $k_\cap : \mathfrak{S} \times \mathfrak{S} \to \mathbb{R}$ is defined as

$$k_\cap(X_i, X_j) = \mu(X_i \cap X_j); \qquad X_i, X_j \in \mathfrak{S} . \tag{3.1}$$

Proposition 3.4. *The intersection kernel is a positive definite kernel function.*

Proof.   Let $\mu(\cdot)$, $\mathfrak{S}$, and $k_\cap(\cdot, \cdot)$ be as in Definition 3.1.

It is known [see for example Kolmogorov and Fomin (1960a)] that for any $X_1, \ldots, X_n$ belonging to the semiring $\mathfrak{S}$ there is a finite system of pairwise disjoint sets $\mathcal{A} = \{A_1, \ldots, A_m\} \subseteq \mathfrak{S}$ such that every X_i is a union of some A_l. Let $\mathcal{B}_i \subseteq \mathcal{A}$ be such that $X_i = \bigcup_{B \in \mathcal{B}_i} B$. Furthermore let the characteristic function $\Gamma_X : \mathcal{A} \to \{0; 1\}$ be defined as $\Gamma_X(A) = 1 \Leftrightarrow A \subseteq X$ and $\Gamma_X(A) = 0$ otherwise. With these definitions we can write

$$\mu(X_i \cap X_j) = \sum_{B \in \mathcal{B}_i \cap \mathcal{B}_j} \mu(B) = \sum_{A \in \mathcal{A}} \Gamma_{X_i}(A)\Gamma_{X_j}(A)\mu(A) .$$

The intersection kernel is then positive definite on $X_1, \ldots, X_n$ as

$$\sum_{ij} c_i c_j \mu(X_i \cap X_j) = \sum_{ij} c_i c_j \sum_{A \in \mathcal{A}} \Gamma_{X_i}(A)\Gamma_{X_j}(A)\mu(A)$$

$$= \sum_{A \in \mathcal{A}} \left(\sum_i c_i \Gamma_{X_i}(A) \right)^2 \mu(A)$$

$$\geq 0 . \qquad \qquad \square$$

Note that in the simplest case (finite sets with $\mu(\cdot)$ being the set cardinality) the intersection kernel coincides with the inner product of the bitvector representations of the sets.

For nonempty sets we furthermore define the following kernels.

Definition 3.2. Let $\mu(\cdot)$ be a measure defined on the ring of sets $\mathfrak{S}$ with unit $\mathcal{X}$ such that $\mu(\mathcal{X}) < \infty$. We define functions $(\mathfrak{S} \setminus \{\emptyset\}) \times (\mathfrak{S} \setminus \{\emptyset\}) \to \mathbb{R}$:

$$k_\cup(X_i, X_j) = \tfrac{1}{\mu(X_i \cup X_j)}; \qquad (3.2)$$

$$k_{\underset{\cup}{\cap}}(X_i, X_j) = \tfrac{\mu(X_i \cap X_j)}{\mu(X_i \cup X_j)}; \qquad (3.3)$$

Proposition 3.5. *The functions (3.2) and (3.3) are positive definite.*

Proof. With all sets and functions as in Definition 3.2, it holds that

$$\mu(X_i \cup X_j) = \mu(\mathcal{X}) - \mu((\mathcal{X} \setminus X_i) \cap (\mathcal{X} \setminus X_i)) .$$

As $\mu((\mathcal{X} \setminus X_i) \cap (\mathcal{X} \setminus X_j))$ is an intersection kernel and

$$\mu(\mathcal{X}) > \mu((\mathcal{X} \setminus X_i) \cap (\mathcal{X} \setminus X_j)) \qquad X_i, X_j \neq \emptyset ,$$

by Proposition 3.3 $k_\cup(\cdot, \cdot)$ is positive definite. That $k_{\underset{\cup}{\cap}}(\cdot, \cdot)$ is positive definite follows then directly from Proposition 3.2. $\qquad \square$

The kernel function (3.3) is known as the *Tanimoto coefficient* or *Jaccard coefficient*. Its positive definiteness is shown in [Gower (1971)] and it has been used in kernel methods by Baldi and Ralaivola (2004).

In the case that the sets X_i are finite or countable sets of elements on which a kernel has been defined, it is often beneficial to use set kernels other than the intersection kernel. For example the following kernel function:

Definition 3.3. Let $X_1, \ldots, X_n$ be arbitrary finite sets and let $k : \mathcal{X} \times \mathcal{X} \to$ $\mathbb{R}$ be a positive definite kernel function on $\mathcal{X} = \bigcup_{i=1}^{n} X_i$. The *crossproduct kernel* is defined as

$$k_\times(X, X') = \sum_{x \in X, x' \in X'} k(x, x') \qquad X, X' \in \{X_1, \ldots, X_n\} . \qquad (3.4)$$

Proposition 3.6. *The crossproduct kernel is positive definite.*

Proof. Let all functions and variables be as defined in Definition 3.3. The crossproduct kernel is a positive definite kernel function as

$$k_\times(X, X') = \sum_{x \in X, x' \in X'} k(x, x') = \left\langle \sum_{x \in X} k(x, \cdot), \sum_{x' \in X'} k(x', \cdot) \right\rangle$$

using the reproducing property of $k(\cdot, \cdot)$. □

In the case that the right hand side kernel is the matching kernel, the crossproduct kernel coincides with the intersection kernel.

In the remainder of this section we are more interested in the case that $\mathfrak{S}$ is a Borel algebra (Section 2.1.2) with unit $\mathcal{X}$ and measure μ which is countably additive and satisfies $\mu(\mathcal{X}) < \infty$. We can then extend the definition of the characteristic functions to $\mathcal{X}$ by $\Gamma_X(x) = 1 \Leftrightarrow x \in X$ and $\Gamma_X(x) = 0$ otherwise. We can then write the intersection kernel as

$$k_\cap(X_i, X_j) = \mu(X \cap X') = \int_{\mathcal{X}} \Gamma_{X_i}(x) \Gamma_{X_j}(x) d\mu \qquad (3.5)$$

this shows the relation of the intersection kernel to the usual (L_2 – see Subsection 2.1.5) inner product between the characteristic functions $\Gamma_X(\cdot), \Gamma_{X'}(\cdot)$ of the sets.

Similarly, for the crossproduct kernel (3.4) we obtain in this setting the integral equation

$$\int_X \int_{X'} k(x, x') d\mu d\mu = \int_{\mathcal{X}} \int_{\mathcal{X}} \Gamma_X(x) k(x, x') \Gamma_{X'}(x') d\mu d\mu$$

with any positive definite kernel k defined on the elements. Positive definiteness of this integral can be seen directly as it is equal to

$$\left\langle \int_{\mathcal{X}} \Gamma_X(x) k(x, \cdot) d\mu, \int_{\mathcal{X}} \Gamma_{X'}(x') k(x', \cdot) d\mu \right\rangle .$$

Note, that with the matching kernel k_δ we recover the intersection kernel from equation (3.5) albeit with different measure (μ^2 rather than μ).

3.3.2 *Minimal and Maximal Functions on Sets*

As many distance functions defined on structured data use minima or maxima over a set of distances (Section 3.2.3), we proceed with two simple cases in which positive definiteness holds for kernels on sets that use minima or maxima functions.

- The function $\min_{x \in X, x' \in X'} x x'$ defined on sets of non-negative real numbers $X, X' \subset \mathbb{R}^+$ is positive definite as

$$\min_{x \in X, x' \in X'} x x' = \left(\min_{x \in X} x \right) \left(\min_{x' \in X'} x' \right) .$$

- The function $\max_{x \in X, x' \in X'} x x'$ defined on sets of non-negative real numbers $X, X' \subset \mathbb{R}^+$ is positive definite as

$$\max_{x \in X, x' \in X'} x x' = \left(\max_{x \in X} x \right) \left(\max_{x' \in X'} x' \right) .$$

Now we turn to the more general functions

$$\min_{x \in X, x' \in X'} k(x, x') \text{and} \max_{x \in X, x' \in X'} k(x, x') .$$

These are related to the functions $\min_i k_i(x, x')$ and $\max_i k_i(x, x')$ considered in Section 3.2.3. To see this let $X = \{x_i\}_i; X' = \{x'_j\}_j$ and $k_{ij}(X, X') = k(x_i, x'_j)$. Then

$$\min_{x \in X, x' \in X'} k(x, x') = \min_{ij} k_{ij}(X, X')$$

and

$$\max_{x \in X, x' \in X'} k(x, x') = \max_{ij} k_{ij}(X, X') .$$

Though this indicates that $\min_{x \in X, x' \in X'} k(x, x')$ and $\max_{x \in X, x' \in X'} k(x, x')$ might not be positive definite, it is not a proof yet. Thus we continue with two counter-examples.

For $\min_{x \in X, x' \in X'} k(x, x')$ with $X = \{(1, 2)^\top, (2, 1)^\top, (2, 0)^\top\}$, $X' = \{(2, 1)^\top\}$, and using $k(x, x') = \langle x, x' \rangle$ we obtain the indefinite matrix

$$\begin{pmatrix} 2 & 4 \\ 4 & 5 \end{pmatrix} .$$

Similarly, for $\max_{x \in X, x' \in X'} k(x, x')$ with $x_1 = \{(1, 0)^\top\}$, $x_2 = \{(1, 0)^\top, (0, 1)^\top\}$, $x_3 = \{(0, 1)^\top\}$, and again $k(x, x') = \langle x, x' \rangle$ we obtain the matrix

$$D = \begin{pmatrix} 1 & 1 & 0 \\ 1 & 1 & 1 \\ 0 & 1 & 1 \end{pmatrix} ,$$

which is again indefinite (compare Section 3.2.3).

One approach to overcome these problems with using the min and/or max functions in the definition of positive definite kernel functions is to use a soft-maximal kernel introduced in Section 3.2.4. We then obtain a *soft-maximal set kernel*

$$\sum_{x \in X; x' \in X'} k^n(x, x')$$

and

$$\sum_{x \in X; x' \in X'} \exp\left[\gamma k(x, x')\right]$$

which are both positive definite if k is positive definite and which are both dominated by the maximal kernel on a pair of instances. It is interesting to note here that soft-max kernels for sets can be seen as a crossproduct kernel with a modified kernel on the elements. In Section 4.3 we discuss these kernels in more detail in the context of multi-instance learning.

3.3.3 Kernels on Multisets

For knowledge representation often multisets are used instead of sets. The difference is that every element of a multiset is not required to be different from all other elements of that multiset. We restrict our attention here to finite multisets, as this is the most interesting practical case and will be pursued further in Chapter 3.5.

For such multisets, we can define a characteristic function $\Gamma_X : \mathcal{X} \to \mathbb{N}$ such that $\Gamma_X(x)$ is equal to the number of times x occurs in the multiset X. For every finite multiset trivially $\sum_{x \in \mathcal{X}} \Gamma_X^2(x) < \infty$. Similar to Subsection 3.3.1 we then obtain the crossproduct kernel for multisets as

$$\sum_{x, x' \in \mathcal{X}} \Gamma_X(x) k(x, x') \Gamma_{X'}(x') .$$

Using the matching kernel k_δ on the elements we obtain

$$\sum_{x \in \mathcal{X}} \Gamma_X(x) \Gamma_{X'}(x) .$$

To also generalise the intersection kernel to multisets we can use the function

$$\sum_{x \in \mathcal{X}} \min\left\{\Gamma_X(x); \Gamma_{X'}(x)\right\} .$$

As a generalisation of both intersection and crossproduct kernels, we will later (in Chapter 3.5) consider functions of the form

$$\sum_{x, x' \in \mathcal{X}} k\left(\Gamma_X(x), \Gamma_{X'}(x')\right) k(x, x') .$$

3.3.4 *Convolution Kernels*

The best known kernel for representation spaces that are not mere attribute-value tuples is the *convolution kernel* proposed by Haussler (1999). The basic idea of convolution kernels is that the semantics of composite objects can often be captured by a relation R between the object and its parts. The kernel on the object is then made up from kernels defined on different parts.

Let $x, x' \in \mathcal{X}$ be the objects and $\vec{x}, \vec{x}' \in \mathcal{X}_1 \times \cdots \times \mathcal{X}_D$ be tuples of parts of these objects. Given the relation $R \subseteq (\mathcal{X}_1 \times \cdots \times \mathcal{X}_D) \times \mathcal{X}$ we can define the decomposition R^{-1} as $R^{-1}(x) = \{\vec{x} : (\vec{x}, x) \in R\}$. Then the convolution kernel is defined as

$$k_{conv}(x, x') = \sum_{\substack{\vec{x} \in R^{-1}(x) \\ \vec{x}' \in R^{-1}(x')}} \prod_{d=1}^{D} k_d(x_d, x_d') \ .$$

The term 'convolution kernel' refers to a class of kernels that can be formulated in the above way. The advantage of convolution kernels is that they are very general and can be applied in many different problems. However, because of that generality, they require a significant amount of work to adapt them to a specific problem. In particular, choosing R in 'real-world' applications is a non-trivial task.

3.4 Prior Work

In this section we describe related and prior work on defining kernel functions for structured data. As described in Section 3.1.1, we distinguish between model-driven and syntax-driven kernel functions.

Subsection 3.4.1 deals with kernel functions defined on probabilistic, generative models of the instance space. Subsection 3.4.2 describes kernel functions defined using some kind of similarity relation or transformation operation between instances. Subsection 3.4.3 describes several kernel functions defined on sequences of discrete symbols. The idea is always to extract all possible subsequences (of some kind) and to define the kernel function based on the occurrence and similarity of these subsequences. Subsection 3.4.4 shows how this idea can be generalised to extracting subtrees of trees and defining a kernel function based on occurrence and similarity of subtrees in two trees.

3.4.1 *Kernels from Generative Models*

Generative models in general and hidden Markov models [Rabiner (1989)] in particular are widely used in computer science. One of their application areas is protein fold recognition where one tries to understand how proteins fold up in nature. Another application area is speech recognition. One motivation behind the development of kernels on generative models is to be able to apply kernel methods to sequence data. Sequences occur frequently in nature, for example, proteins are sequences of amino acids, genes are sequences of nucleic acids, and spoken words are sequences of phonemes. Another motivation is to improve the classification accuracy of generative models.

The first and most prominent kernel function based on a generative model is the *Fisher kernel* [Jaakkola and Haussler (1999a,b)]. The key idea is to use the gradient of the log-likelihood with respect to the parameters of a generative model as the features in a discriminative classifier. The motivation to use this feature space is that the gradient of the log-likelihood with respect to the parameters of a generative model captures the generative process of a sequence rather that just the posterior probabilities.

Let U_x be the Fisher-score, that is, the gradient of the log-likelihood with respect to the parameters of the generative model $P(x \mid \theta)$ at x:

$$U_x = \nabla_\theta \log P(x \mid \theta) \ .$$

Furthermore, let I be the *Fisher information matrix*, i.e., the expected value of the outer product $U_x U_x^\top$ over $P(x \mid \theta)$. The Fisher kernel is then defined as $k(x, x') = U_x^\top I^{-1} U_{x'}$. The Fisher kernel can be calculated whenever the probability model $P(x \mid \theta)$ of the instances given the parameters of the model has a twice differentiable likelihood and the Fisher information matrix is positive definite at the chosen θ. Learning algorithms using the Fisher kernel can be shown to perform well if the class variable is contained as a latent variable in the probability model. In [Jaakkola and Haussler (1999a)] it has been shown that under this condition kernel machines using the Fisher kernel are asymptotically at least as good as choosing the maximum a posteriori class for each instance based on the model. In practise often the role of the Fisher information matrix is ignored, yielding the kernel $k(x, x') = U_x^\top U_{x'}$.

Usually, as a generative model a hidden Markov model is used and as a discriminative classifier a support vector machine is used. The Fisher kernel has successfully been applied in many learning problems where the instances are sequences of symbols, such as protein classification [Jaakkola *et al.* (2000); Karchin *et al.* (2002)] and promoter region detection [Pavlidis *et al.* (2001)].

The key ingredient of the Fisher kernel is the Fisher score mapping U_x that extracts a feature vector from a generative model. In [Tsuda *et al.* (2002a)] performance measures for comparing such feature extractors are discussed. Based on this discussion, a kernel is defined on models where the class is an explicit variable in the generative model rather than only a latent variable as it is required in the case of Fisher kernels. Empirically, this kernel performs favourably to the Fisher kernel on a protein fold recognition task. A similar approach has been applied to speech recognition [Smith and Gales (2002)].

Recently, a general framework for defining kernel functions on generative models has been described [Tsuda *et al.* (2002b)]. The so-called *marginalised kernels* contain the above described Fisher kernel as a special case. The paper compares other marginalised kernels with the Fisher kernel and argues that these have some advantages over the Fisher kernel. While, for example, Fisher kernels only allow for the incorporation of second order information by using a second order hidden Markov model [Durbin *et al.* (1998)], other marginalised kernels allow for the use of second-order information with a first order hidden Markov model. In [Tsuda *et al.* (2002b)] it is shown that incorporating this second-order information in a kernel function is useful in the prediction of bacterial genera from their DNA.

In general, marginalised kernels are defined on any generative model with some visible and some hidden information. Let the visible information be an element of the finite set $\mathcal{X}$ and the hidden information be an element of the finite set $\mathcal{S}$. If the hidden information was known, a joint kernel $k_z : (\mathcal{X} \times \mathcal{S}) \times (\mathcal{X} \times \mathcal{S}) \to \mathbb{R}$ could be used. Usually, the hidden information is unknown but the expectation of a joint kernel with respect to the hidden information can be used. Let $x, x' \in \mathcal{X}$ and $s, s' \in \mathcal{S}$. Given a joint kernel k_z and the posterior distribution $p(s|x)$ (usually estimated from a generative model), the marginalised kernel in $\mathcal{X}$ is defined as:

$$k(x, x') \sum_{s, s' \in \mathcal{S}} p(s|x) p(s'|x') k_z((x, s), (x', s')) .$$

To complete this section on kernels from generative models, the idea of defining kernel functions between sequences based on a pair hidden Markov model [Durbin *et al.* (1998)] has to be mentioned. Such kernels have independently been developed by Haussler (1999) and Watkins (1999a). Strictly speaking pair hidden Markov models are not models of the instance space, they are generative models of an aligned pair of sequences [Durbin *et al.* (1998)].

Recently, Saunders *et al.* (2003) have shown that syntactic string kernels (presented in Section 3.4.3) can be seen as a special case of Fisher kernels of a k-stage Markov process with uniform distributions over the transitions.

3.4.2 *Kernels from Instance Space Graphs*

This section describes kernels that are based on knowledge about common properties of instances or relations between instances. The best known kernel in this class is the *diffusion kernel* [Kondor and Lafferty (2002)]. The motivation behind this and similar kernel functions is that it is often more easy to describe the local neighbourhood of an instance than to describe the structure of the whole instance space or to compute a similarity between two arbitrary instances. The neighbourhood of an instance might be all instances that differ with this one only by the presence or absence of one particular property. When working with molecules, for example, such properties might be functional groups or bonds. The neighbourhood relation obviously induces global information about the make up of the instance space. The approach taken in the kernels described in this section is to try to capture this global information in a kernel function merely based on the neighbourhood description.

To model the structure of instance spaces, often undirected graphs or hypergraphs are used. While the use of hypergraphs is less common in literature, it appears more systematic and intuitive.

A hypergraph is described by a set of vertices $\mathcal{V}$ – the instances – and a set of edges $\mathcal{E}$, where each edge corresponds to a set of vertices. Each edge of the hypergraph can be interpreted as some property that all vertices of the edge have in common. For documents, for example, the edges could correspond to words or citations that they have in common; in a metric space the hyperedge could include all vertices with distance less than a given threshold from some point.

For a hypergraph with n vertices and m edges, we define the $n \times m$ matrix B by $B_{ij} = 1$ if and only if $v_i \in e_j$ and $B_{ij} = 0$, otherwise. Let then the $n \times n$ matrix D by defined by $D_{ii} = \sum_j \left[B^\top B \right]_{ij} = \sum_j \left[B^\top B \right]_{ji}$. The matrices $B^\top B$ and $L = D - B^\top B$ are positive definite by construction. The matrix L is known as the graph Laplacian. Often also the normalised Laplacian is used.

Conceptually, kernel matrices are then defined as the limits of matrix power series of the form

$$K = \sum_{i=0}^{\infty} \lambda_i \left(B^\top B\right)^i \qquad \text{or} \qquad K = \sum_{i=0}^{\infty} \lambda_i \left(-L\right)^i$$

with parameters λ_i. These power series can be interpreted as measuring the number of walks of different lengths between given vertices.

As outlined in Section 3.2.1, limits of such power series can be computed by means of an eigenvalue decomposition of $-L$ or $B^\top B$, and a 'recomposition' with modified eigenvalues. The modification of the eigenvalues is usually such that the order of eigenvalues is kept, while all eigenvalues are forced to become positive.

Examples for such kernel functions are the *diffusion kernel* [Kondor and Lafferty (2002)]

$$K = \sum_{i=0}^{\infty} \frac{\beta^n}{n!} (-L)^i \; ,$$

the *von Neumann kernel* [Kandola *et al.* (2003)]

$$K = \sum_{i=1}^{\infty} \gamma^{i-1} \left(B^\top B\right)^i \; ,$$

and the *regularised Laplacian kernel* [Smola and Kondor (2003)]

$$K = \sum_{i=1}^{\infty} \gamma^i (-L)^i \; .$$

For exponential power series like the diffusion kernel, the limit can be computed by exponentiating the eigenvalues, while for geometrical power series, the limit can be computed by the formula $1/(1 - \gamma e)$, where e is an eigenvalue of $B^\top B$ or $-L$, respectively. A general framework and analysis of these kernels can be found in [Smola and Kondor (2003)].

If the instance space is big, the computation of these limits might be too expensive. For some special instance space structures, such as regular trees, complete graphs, and closed chains Kondor and Lafferty (2002) give closed forms for directly computing the the kernel matrix. An application of the diffusion kernel to gene function prediction has been described in [Vert and Kanehisa (2003)]. An application of the von Neumann kernel to document classification has been presented in [Kandola *et al.* (2003)].

A similar idea of defining a kernel function on the structure of the instance space is described in [Vert (2002)]. In that paper it is described how global patterns of inheritance can be incorporated into a kernel function and how missing information can be dealt with using a probabilistic model of inheritance. The main difference to the diffusion kernel is that the structures considered are directed trees and that instances correspond to sets of vertices in these trees rather than single instances. Trees are connected acyclic graphs where one vertex has no incoming edge and all other nodes have exactly one incoming edge. The application considered in that paper is that of classifying phylogenetic profiles. A phylogenetic profile contains information about the organisms in which a particular gene occurs. The phylogenetic information considered in [Vert (2002)] is represented as a tree such that each leaf (a vertex with no outgoing edge) corresponds to one living organism and every other vertex corresponds to some ancestor of the living organisms. To represent genes, every vertex of the tree is assigned a random variable. The value of this random variable indicates whether the corresponding organism has a homologue of the particular gene or not.

If the genomes of all ancestor organisms were available, this information could be used to define a kernel function reflecting the similarity between evolutions. A subtree of the above described tree along with an assignment of indicator values to this tree is called an evolution pattern. Ideally the kernel function on two genes would be defined as the number of evolution patterns that agree with the phylogenetic histories of both genes. An evolution pattern agrees with a phylogenetic history if the assignment of indicator variables is the same for all vertices in the evolution pattern. As the genomes are only known for some ancestor organisms, a probabilistic model that can be used to estimate missing indicator variables is suggested in [Vert (2002)].

For two given phylogenetic profiles x_L, y_L the kernel is defined as follows. Let T be a tree, L be the leaf nodes and $C(T)$ the set of all possible subtrees of T. One particular evolution pattern can be expressed as a subtree $S \in C(T)$ and the corresponding assignment z_S of indicator values. $p(z_s)$ denotes the probability of such an evolution pattern having occurred in nature and $p(x_L|z_S)$ is the probability of observing a particular phylogenetic profile x_L given the evolution pattern z_S (obtained from the probabilistic model mentioned above). Then the tree kernel for phylogenetic profiles is defined as:

$$k(x_L, y_L) = \sum_{S \in C(T)} \sum_{z_s} p(z_S) p(x_L|z_S) p(y_L|z_S) \ .$$

In [Vert (2002)] it is shown that this kernel function can be computed in time linear in the size of the tree.

3.4.3 *String Kernels*

The traditional kernel function used for text classification is simply the scalar product of two texts in their 'bag-of-words' representation [Joachims (2002)]. A bag-of-words represents each text by a vector in a Euclidean space, where each component counts how often a particular word occurs in a text. This kernel function does not take the structure of the text or words into account but simply the number of times each word occurs. More sophisticated approaches try to define a kernel function on the sequence of characters. Similar approaches define kernel functions on other sequences of symbols, e.g., on the sequence of symbols each corresponding to one amino acid and together describing a protein.

The first kernel function defined on strings can be found in [Watkins (1999b); Lodhi *et al.* (2001)] and is also described in [Cristianini and Shawe-Taylor (2000); Schölkopf and Smola (2002)]. The idea behind this kernel is to base the similarity of two strings on the number of common subsequences. These substrings need not be contiguous in the strings but the more gaps in the occurrence of the subsequence, the less weight is given to it in the kernel function. This can be best illustrated by an example.

Consider the two strings 'cat' and 'cart'. The common subsequences are 'c', 'a', 't', 'ca', 'at', 'ct', 'cat'. As mentioned above, it is useful to penalise gaps in the occurrence of the subsequence. This can be done using the total length of a subsequence in the two strings. We now list the common subsequences again and give the total length of their occurrence in 'cat' and 'cart' as well: 'c':1/1, 'a':1/1, 't':1/1, 'ca':2/2, 'at':2/3, 'ct':3/4, 'cat':3/4. Usually, an exponential decay is used. With a decay factor λ the penalty associated with each substring is 'c':$(\lambda^1\lambda^1)$, 'a':$(\lambda^1\lambda^1)$, 't':$(\lambda^1\lambda^1)$, 'ca':$(\lambda^2\lambda^2)$, 'at':$(\lambda^2\lambda^3)$, 'ct':$(\lambda^3\lambda^4)$, 'cat':$(\lambda^3\lambda^4)$. The kernel function is then simply the sum over these penalties, i.e., $k(\text{'cat'}, \text{'cart'}) = 2\lambda^7 + \lambda^5 + \lambda^4 + 3\lambda^2$.

Let Σ be a finite alphabet, Σ^n the set of strings of length n from that alphabet and Σ^* the set of all strings from that alphabet. Let $|s|$ denote the length of the string $s \in \Sigma^*$ and let the symbols in s be indexed such that $s = s_1 s_2 \ldots s_{|s|}$. For a set of indices i let $s[i]$ be the subsequence of s induced by this set of indices and let $l(i)$ denote the total length of $s[i]$ in s, i.e., the biggest index in i minus the smallest index in i plus one. We are now able to define the feature transformation ϕ underlying the string kernel. For some string $u \in \Sigma^n$ the value of the feature $\phi_u(s)$ is defined as:

$$\phi_u(s) = \sum_{i:u=s[i]} \lambda^{l(i)} .$$

The kernel between two strings $s, t \in \Sigma^*$ is then simply the scalar product of $\phi(s)$ and $\phi(t)$ and can be written as:

$$k_n(s, t) = \sum_{u \in \Sigma^n} \phi_u(s)\phi_u(t) = \sum_{u \in \Sigma^n} \sum_{i:u=s[i]} \sum_{j:u=t[j]} \lambda^{l(i)+l(j)} .$$

While this computation appears very expensive, using recursive computation, it can be performed in $O(n|s||t|)$ [Lodhi *et al.* (2001)].

An alternative to the above kernel has been used in [Paass *et al.* (2002)] and [Leslie *et al.* (2002)] where only contiguous substrings of a given string are considered. A string is then represented by the number of times each unique substring of n symbols occurs in the sequence. This representation of strings by their contiguous substrings is known as the spectrum of a string or as its n-gram representation. The kernel function is simply the scalar product in this representation. It is shown in [Leslie *et al.* (2002)] that this kernel can be computed in time linear in the length of the strings and the length of the considered substrings. In [Paass *et al.* (2002)] not all possible n-grams are used but a simple statistical test is employed as a feature subset selection heuristic. This kernel has been applied to protein [Leslie *et al.* (2002)] and spoken text [Paass *et al.* (2002)] classification. Spoken text is represented by a sequence of phonemes, syllables, or words.

Many empirical results comparing the above kernel functions can be found in [Lodhi *et al.* (2002)]. As shown in [Saunders *et al.* (2003)] these kernels can be seen as Fisher kernels (presented in section 3.4.1) of a k-stage Markov process with uniform distribution over the transitions. This perspective leads to a generalisation of the above kernel that is able to deal with variable length substrings. In [Vishwanathan and Smola (2003)] and [Leslie *et al.* (2003)] string kernels similar to the n-gram kernel are considered and it is shown how these can be computed efficiently by using suffix and mismatch trees, respectively. The main conceptual difference to the n-gram kernel is that a given number of mismatches is allowed when comparing the n-grams to the substrings.

A quite different kernel on strings can be found in [Zien *et al.* (2000)]. The focus of that paper is on the recognition of translation initiation sites in DNA or mRNA sequences. This problem is quite different from the above considered applications. The main difference is that rather than classifying whole sequences, in this task one codon (three consecutive symbols) from a sequence has to be identified as the translation initiation site. Each sequence can have arbitrarily many candidate solutions of which one has to be chosen. However, in [Zien *et al.* (2000)] and earlier work this problem is converted into a traditional classification problem on sequences of equal length.

Fixed length windows of symbols centred at each candidate solution are extracted from each sequence. The class of one such window corresponds to the candidate solution being a true translation initiation site or not. One valid kernel on these sequences is simply the number of symbols that coincide in the two sequences. Other kernels can, for example, be defined as a polynomial function of this kernel.

Better classification accuracy is, however, reported in [Zien *et al.* (2000)] for a kernel that puts more emphasis on local correlations. Let n be the length of each window and $\mathcal{X}$ be the set of possible symbols, then each window is an element of $\mathcal{X}^n$. For $x, x' \in \mathcal{X}^n$ let x_i, x'_i denote the i-th element of each sequence. Using the matching kernel k_δ on $\mathcal{X}$ first a polynomial kernel on a small sub-window of length $2l + 1$ with weights $w_j \in \mathbb{R}$ and power d_1 is defined:

$$k_i(x, x') = \left(\sum_{j=-l}^{l} w_j k_\delta(x_{i+j}, x'_{i+j}) \right)^{d_1} .$$

Then the kernel on the full window is simply the polynomial of power d_2 of the kernels on the sub-windows:

$$k(x, x') = \left(\sum_{i=l}^{n-l} k_i(x, x') \right)^{d_2} .$$

This kernel is called the *locality-improved kernel*. An empirical comparison to other general purpose machine learning algorithms shows competitive results for $l = 0$ and better results for larger l. These results were obtained on the above mentioned translation initiation site recognition task.

Even better results can be achieved by replacing the symbol at some position in the above definition with the conditional probability of that symbol given the previous symbol. Let $p_{i,\text{TIS}}(x_i|x_{i-1})$ be the probability of symbol x_i at position i given symbol x_{i-1} at position $i - 1$, estimated over all true translation initiation sites. Furthermore, let $p_{i,\text{ALL}}(x_i|x_{i-1})$ be the probability of symbol x_i at position i given symbol x_{i-1} at position $i - 1$, estimated over all candidate sites. Then we define

$$s_i(x) = \log p_{i,\text{TIS}}(x_i|x_{i-1}) - \log p_{i,\text{ALL}}(x_i|x_{i-1})$$

and replace x_{i+j} in the locality-improved kernel by $s_{i+j}(x)$ and the matching kernel by the product. A support vector machine using this kernel function outperforms all other approaches applied in [Zien *et al.* (2000)].

3.4.4 *Tree Kernels*

A kernel function that can be applied in many natural language processing tasks has been proposed by Collins and Duffy (2002). The instances of the learning task are considered to be labelled ordered directed trees. The key idea to capture structural information about the trees in the kernel function is to consider all subtrees occurring in a parse tree. Here, a subtree is defined as a connected subgraph of a tree such that either all children or no child of a vertex is in the subgraph. The children of a vertex are the vertices that can be reached from the vertex by traversing one directed edge. The kernel function is the inner product in the space which describes the number of occurrences of all possible subtrees.

Consider some enumeration of all possible subtrees and let $h_i(T)$ be the number of times the i-th subtree occurs in tree T. For two trees T_1, T_2 the kernel is then defined as

$$k(T_1, T_2) = \sum_i h_i(T_1) h_i(T_2) \ .$$

Furthermore, for the sets of vertices $\mathcal{V}_1$ and $\mathcal{V}_2$ of the trees T_1 and T_2, let $S(v_1, v_2)$ with $v_1 \in \mathcal{V}_1, v_2 \in \mathcal{V}_2$ be the number of subtrees rooted at vertex v_1 and v_2 that are isomorphic. Then the tree kernel can be computed as

$$k(T_1, T_2) = \sum_i h_i(T_1) h_i(T_2) = \sum_{v_1 \in \mathcal{V}_1, v_2 \in \mathcal{V}_2} S(v_1, v_2) \ .$$

Let *label*(v) be a function that returns the label of vertex v, let $|\delta^+(v)|$ denote the number of children of vertex v, and let $\delta^+(v, j)$ be the j-th child of vertex v (only ordered trees are considered). $S(v_1, v_2)$ can efficiently be calculated as follows: $S(v_1, v_2) = 0$ if *label*$(v_1) \neq$ *label*(v_2). $S(v_1, v_2) = 1$ if *label*$(v_1) =$ *label*(v_2) and $|\delta^+(v_1)| = |\delta^+(v_2)| = 0$. Otherwise[2],

$$S(v_1, v_2) = \prod_{k=1}^{|\delta^+(v_1)|} \left(1 + S(\delta^+(v_1, j), \delta^+(v_2, j))\right) \ .$$

This recursive computation has time complexity $\mathcal{O}(|\mathcal{V}_1||\mathcal{V}_2|)$.

Experiments investigated how much the application of a kernelised perceptron algorithm to trees generated by a probabilistic context free grammar outperforms the use of the probabilistic context free grammar alone. The empirical results achieved in [Collins and Duffy (2002)] are promising.

---

[2] Note that in this case $|\delta^+(v_1)| = |\delta^+(v_2)|$, as actually the number of children of a vertex is determined by its label. This is due to the nature of the natural language processing applications that are considered.

The kernel function used in these experiments is actually a weighted variant of the kernel function presented above.

A generalisation of this kernel to also take into account other substructures of the trees is described in [Kashima and Koyanagi (2002)]. A substructure of a tree is defined as a tree such that there is a descendants preserving mapping from vertices in the substructure to vertices in the tree[3]. Another generalisation considered in that paper is that of allowing labels to partially match. Promising results have been achieved with this kernel function in HTML document classification tasks.

Recently, Vishwanathan and Smola (2003) proposed the application of string kernels to trees by representing each tree by the sequence of labels generated by a depth-first traversal of the trees, written in preorder notation. To ensure that trees only differing in the order of their children are represented in the same way, the children of each vertex are ordered according to the lexical order of their string representation.

3.5 Summary

In the previous part of this book we have described the foundations of kernel methods and the design of kernel functions. In this chapter we have first described the importance of choosing the 'right' kernel function, and how that kernel function can be characterised. Afterwards we have summarised some more or less well known results on kernel combinations, and we have given a general overview of kernels for sets. Last but not least we gave an overview of prior work.

In the following two chapters we will now define kernel functions for two particular knowledge representation formalisms: terms in a higher-order logic and graphs.

---

[3]A descendant of a vertex v is any vertex that occurs in the subtree rooted at v.

Chapter 4

Basic Term Kernels

Logic takes care of itself; all we have to do is to look and see how it does it.

(Ludwig Wittgenstein, Tractatus Logico-Philosophicus)

The topic of this book is the application of kernel methods to structured data. While this clearly involves background from (at least) two research directions, the previous chapters have mainly focused on different aspects of kernel methods only. This was necessary as understanding kernel functions and how they can be applied in learning algorithms is essential to the definition of good kernel functions for structured data.

Having provided this understanding, we are now ready to look at kernel functions for particular instance spaces of structured data. In the introduction to this book we have already — rather informally — described sets of molecules as one structured instance space. An important aspect is the presence of identifiers (for the atoms/vertices) and links (for the bonds/edges).

In this chapter we focus on data structures without identifiers and links. To represent these, we chose to use terms in a typed higher-order logic. While this logic is powerful enough to also represent identifiers and links, we will here choose to ignore them. The logic we are using is the variant of the λ-calculus with polymorphic types introduced by Lloyd (2003). We will consider data structures with identifiers and links in Chapter 4.6, separately.

The outline of this chapter is as follows. Section 4.1 gives an account of the different logics typically used as representation languages for structured data and introduces the higher-order logic with polymorphic types that we use in the remainder of this chapter. Section 4.2 defines a kernel on the terms of this logic, investigates some theoretical properties, and describes how these kernels can be adapted to particular domains. Section 4.3 discusses in more depth the implications of using this kernel function for one particular concept class, so-called multi-instance concepts. Section 4.5 provides a variety of experimental results showing that kernel methods with kernel functions defined in the framework of this chapter, perform competitive or better than other algorithms applied in the literature. Section 4.6 concludes this chapter.

4.1 Logics for Learning

The uses of logic as a representation language in learning algorithms are manifold. The simplest type of logic that can be — and has been — used to represent instances is propositional logic. The research field inductive logic programming has been using various variants of first-order logic. Lloyd (2003) recently suggested the use of a typed and polymorphic higher-order logic for learning; we will adopt this logic. Now, we give a brief introduction to the different types of logic, focusing on those aspects that are most important for knowledge representation. The logic we will use is then described in Section 4.1.5. To give a coherent view on this logic, we will there repeat some of the topics of the other sections.

First of all, we need to distinguish between the syntax and semantics of the logic. The syntax defines a set of symbols and how they can be combined to form valid statements of the logic. The semantics of the logic describes the intended meaning of the symbols and their combination. Whether a valid logical statement is true or false depends only on the semantics – on how we interpret the symbols and their combination. In the following we will neglect those aspects of the different logics that are usually not used for knowledge representation.

4.1.1 *Propositional Logic for Learning*

Formally, an alphabet of *propositional logic* consists of a set of atoms, the five connectives $\neg, \vee, \wedge, \leftarrow, \leftrightarrow$, and the punctuation symbols '(' and ')'. The formulae of propositional logic can be defined inductively. Every atom is a formula. Given a formula ϕ, the negation of this formula $\neg\phi$ is a formula. Given two formulae ϕ, ϕ' the connections $(\phi\vee\phi'), (\phi\wedge\phi'), (\phi \leftarrow \phi'), (\phi \leftrightarrow \phi')$ are formulae. In propositional learning, usually, each instance is represented by (possibly negated) symbols connected by conjunctions (with $\wedge$) such that the interpretation of the resulting formula is true for the instance we want to represent. The interpretation of $(\phi \wedge \phi')$ is true if and only if both ϕ and ϕ' are true. For example, if the instances reflect particular weather conditions, different symbols that could be available are: sunny, rainy, and windy. The representation of a rainy day with no sun and no wind would then be $\neg$sunny $\wedge$ rainy $\wedge$ $\neg$windy. A shorter but otherwise equivalent representation of each instance is to use the set of all symbols whose interpretation is true for the instance we want to represent. Thus, the above weather conditions could be represented by {rainy}, having exactly the same interpretation as above.

A strongly related representation language is the so called *attribute-value representation*. There, every instance is essentially represented in one row of a table. Every column of the table corresponds to one attribute. For every instance, each attribute can take different values. In propositional logic, the attributes were called atoms and the different possible values were Booleans such that the resulting conjunction is true for the given instance. In attribute-value learning, the set of possible values an attribute can take is called the range or domain of the attribute. For learning problems with a finite set of possible values of each attribute, propositional representation and attribute-value representation are essentially equivalent as there is a straight-forward mapping in either direction.

4.1.2 *First-Order Logic for Learning*

The knowledge representation usually used in first-order learning extends this definition most importantly by allowing for a set of so-called background predicates. First-order logic allows for the following symbols: constants, variables, function symbols, predicate symbols, connectives, punctuation symbols, and quantifiers. Apart from the connectives and punctuation symbols introduced above, ',' is used as a punctuation symbol. For each function and predicate symbol, there is a number called its *arity*. The quantifiers are $\exists$ and $\forall$. As in propositional logic, the smallest valid formula is called an atom. Before we can define atoms, we need the notion of a *term*. All constants are terms, all variables are terms, and given a n-ary function symbol f and n terms $t_1, t_2 \ldots, t_n$, the expression $f(t_1, t_2, \ldots, t_n)$ is a term. An *atom* can then be constructed from an n-ary predicate symbol P and n terms $t_1, t_2 \ldots, t_n$ as $P(t_1, t_2, \ldots, t_n)$. A *literal* is an atom or a negated atom.

The *formulae* of first-order logic can be defined inductively. Every atom is a formula. Given a formula ϕ, the negation of this formula $\neg\phi$ is a formula. Given two formulae ϕ, ϕ' the connections $(\phi \vee \phi'), (\phi \wedge \phi'), (\phi \leftarrow \phi'), (\phi \leftrightarrow \phi')$ are formulae. Last but not least, given a formula ϕ and a variable x, the expressions $\exists x\ \phi$ and $\forall x\ \phi$ are formulae. A formula or term is *ground* if it does not contain any variables. The occurrence of a variable in a formula is *bound* if it follows directly after a quantifier or if it occurs within the scope of a quantifier that is directly followed by the same variable. A formula is *closed* if every occurrence of every variable is bound.

A *clause* is a finite (possibly empty) disjunction of literals. An alternative representation of the clause $H_1 \vee \ldots \vee H_m \vee \neg B_1 \vee \ldots \vee \neg B_n$ with atoms $H_1, H_2, \ldots H_m, B_1, B_2, \ldots B_n$ is the expression $H_1 \vee \ldots \vee H_m \leftarrow B_1 \wedge \ldots \wedge B_n$. The lefthand-side of $\leftarrow$ is here called the head of the clause and the righthand-side is called the body. A *program clause* is a clause of the form $H \leftarrow L_1 \wedge \ldots \wedge L_l$ where H is an atom and $L_1, \ldots, L_l$ are literals. A *predicate definition* is a finite and non-empty set of program clauses whose head has the same predicate with the same arity.

The subfield of machine learning concerned with learning in first-order logic is called *inductive logic programming*. The usual learning task considerd in inductive logic programming is essentially binary classification of instances. The class is thereby given by a particular predicate called *target predicate*. The instances are literals of this target predicate and the class of an instance is positive if the literal is an atom and negative if it is a negated atom. Additionally, inductive logic programming considers frequently the presence of a set of predicate definitions called the *background predicates*. One frequently considered task in inductive logic programming is that of *relational rule learning*. There one tries to find a predicate definition of the target predicate such that this predicate definition together with the background predicates logically implies all positive instances and none of the negative instances. The details of logical implication in first-order logic are beyond the scope of this book and are thus omitted.

4.1.3   *Lambda Calculus*

We now begin the discussion of the logic we will use to represent instances. This logic is based on the usual type-free *lambda calculus*. In lambda calculus, every formula represents a function with one argument. Functions with many arguments can be obtained by *currying* the function, that is by transforming it into two functions with one argument each.

Formally, we are again given a set of variables, the punctuation symbols '(', ')', and '.', as well as the symbol 'λ'. The role of λ is thereby related to the role of $\exists$ and $\forall$ in first-order logic as it also 'binds variables'. The set of λ-*terms* is defined inductively: Every variable is a term. Given a term M and a variable x, the expression $(\lambda x.M)$ is a term called an *abstraction*. Given two terms M, N the expression $(M\ N)$ is a term, called an *application*. Furthermore we use the following notational conventions: $F\ M_1 \ldots M_n$ represents $(\ldots (F\ M_1)\ldots)M_n)$ and $\lambda x_1 x_2 \ldots x_n.M$ represents $(\lambda x_1.(\lambda x_2.\ \ldots (\lambda x_n.M)\ldots)))$. The occurrence of a variable in a term is *bound*, if it follows directly after λ or if it occurs within the scope of a λ that is directly followed by the same variable. A formula is *closed* if every occurrence of every variable is bound. A substitution $M[x := N]$ denotes the operation of replacing every free occurrence of x in M by N.

Numbers and Boolean values are usually not defined as constants in lambda calculus, rather are they used as shorthand for some λ-term. For example, Boolean truth values can be defined by $true = \lambda xy.x$ and $false = \lambda xy.y$. Using this definition, the conditional *if B then P else Q* is simply represented by $B\ P\ Q$ whenever B is a term that is either *true* or *false*. This can be seen as

$$true\ P\ Q = \lambda xy.x\ P\ Q = (((\lambda x.(\lambda y.x))\ P)\ Q) = ((\lambda y.P)\ Q) = P$$

and

$$false\ P\ Q = \lambda xy.y\ P\ Q = (((\lambda x.(\lambda y.y))\ P)\ Q) = ((\lambda y.y)\ Q) = Q\ .$$

The usual arithmetic operators on numbers can similarly be recovered as shorthands for some λ-terms. Without proof we will also use this convenient abbreviation.

The difference between the function symbols used in first-order logic and the functions of the lambda calculus is that the function symbols are never evaluated, there is not even a definition of how to compute them. The functions of lambda calculus, however, are evaluated whenever given an argument. As we will see later the availability of (real) functions allows us to model sets and similar data structured within a term rather than using the background predicates. Still some uses of functions and function symbols are similar. One example is the representation of lists in either language. We begin with the representation of an ordered pair in lambda calculus and define $pair = \lambda x.\lambda y.\lambda c.cxy$. Applying this function to A and B we obtain $pair\ A\ B = (\lambda x.(\lambda y.(\lambda c.(cxy)))) A\ B = \lambda c.cAB$. To extract the first element we apply the result to *true*:

$$pair\ A\ B\ true = \lambda c.(cAB)(\lambda x.(\lambda y.x)) = (\lambda x.(\lambda y.x))AB = A\ .$$

To extract the second element we apply the result to *false*:

$$pair \; A \; B \; false = \lambda c.(cAB)(\lambda x.(\lambda y.y)) = (\lambda x.(\lambda y.y))AB = B \;\;.$$

To represent lists we need to define the empty list $[] = \lambda x.true$ and can then, for example represent the list $[A, B, C, D]$ by the term

$$(pair \; A \; (pair \; B \; (pair \; C \; (pair \; D \; [])))) \;\;.$$

To access elements of the list, we use combinations of the functions $head = \lambda x.(x \; true)$ and $tail = \lambda x.(x \; false)$. To test whether a list is empty, we use the function $null = \lambda d.(d \; \lambda x.(\lambda y.false))$.

It can be shown that all recursive functions can be represented in the lambda calculus and that exactly the functions that can be computed by a Turing machine can be represented in the lambda calculus. Although we omitted important topics of the lambda calculus like conversion and normalisations, the discussion above should be sufficient to provide a basic understanding of those aspects of the lambda calculus needed in the further development of this chapter. We now turn to variants of the lambda calculus with types. Typed versions of lambda calculus are sometimes called *combinatory logic*.

4.1.4 *Lambda Calculus with Polymorphic Types*

So far we have only described untyped logics for knowledge representation. So why do we need a type system at all? The first reason is the same as for all programming languages. A type system helps detecting errors in the representation that would otherwise result in errors at run time or — even worse — never be detected. The other reason is that whenever we assume that a complex data structure is composed from different simpler data structures, we need to account for the possibility that the different parts have different semantics. Whenever the different parts have different semantics we need to provide means to associate different kernel functions with them. Our approach to make this possible is by using types and associating kernels to particular types.

The types of the logic are built up from a set of type constructors using the symbol $\rightarrow$ (for function types) and $\times$ (for product types). With every type constructor there is a number called the arity of the type constructor. For example the type constructor for the Booleans Ω and the type constructor for the integers *Int* have both arity zero. The type constructor for lists *List* has arity 1 and we can write the type of a list of integers simply as *List Int*. Suppose now, we have declared a function *head* that maps a list of type *List Int* to its first element which has type *Int*. This type declaration is called the *signature* of the function *head* and denoted by *head* : *List Int* → *Int*. If we need a function that maps a list of Booleans to its first element, with types in place, we would need to declare a new function. This creates a lot of overhead which can be avoided in two ways. Firstly, we could omit the type system or, secondly, we could use a polymorphic type system. For the above reasons we do not want to omit the type system. We thus need to introduce polymorphic types.

The *types* of the logic are then expressions built up from the set of type constructors and a set of parameters (that is, type variables), using the symbol → and ×. For example, consider again the type constructor *List* of arity one, used to provide the list types. We can now declare the function *head* using a type variable a as *head* : *List a* → a. A closed type is a type not containing any parameters, the set of all closed types is denoted by $\mathfrak{S}^c$.

We have now introduced separately all ingredients of the logic we will use for representing structured instances. In the next section we will clarify how these ingredients interact, revise the definition of terms of the logic with the type system in place, and outline which terms are used for knowledge representation in learning systems – the so-called basic terms.

4.1.5 *Basic Terms for Learning*

In the logic for learning algorithms proposed by Lloyd (2003), instances are represented by basic terms in a typed higher-order logic. The alphabet of the logic consists of a set of type constructors with a given arity, a set of parameters, a set of constants with given signature, and a set of variables. The types of the logic are built up from a set of type constructors and the set of parameters using the symbol → (for function types) and × (for product types). They are defined inductively. Every parameter is a type. Given a type constructor T of arity n and types $\alpha_1, \ldots, \alpha_n$, the expression $T\,\alpha_1 \ldots \alpha_n$ is a type. Given types α, β, the expression $\alpha \to \beta$ is a type. Given types $\alpha_1, \ldots, \alpha_n$, the expression $\alpha_1 \times \cdots \times \alpha_n$ is a type.

An example of the constants of the logic are the symbols $\top$ (true) and $\bot$ (false). Furthermore, two different kinds of constants, *data constructors* and *functions*, are distinguished. Data constructors are the function symbols of first-order logic, functions are the 'true' functions of the typed lambda calculus. A *signature* is the declared type of a constant. For example, the empty list constructor [] has signature *List* α, where α is a parameter and

List is a type constructor. The list constructor # (usually written infix) has signature $\alpha \to List\ \alpha \to List\ \alpha$. Thus # expects two arguments, an element of type α and a list of type $List\ \alpha$, and produces a new list of type $List\ a$. If a constant C has signature α, we denote this by $C : \alpha$.

The *terms* of the logic are the terms of the typed λ-calculus, which are formed in the usual way by abstraction, tupling, and application from constants in $\mathfrak{C}$ and a set of variables. $\mathfrak{L}$ denotes the set of all terms (obtained from a particular alphabet). A term of type Ω is called a *formula*. A function whose codomain type is Ω is called a *predicate*. In the logic, one can introduce the usual connectives and quantifiers as functions of appropriate types. Thus the connectives conjunction, $\wedge$, and disjunction, $\vee$, are functions of type $\Omega \to \Omega \to \Omega$. In addition, if t is of type Ω, the abstraction $\lambda x.t$ is written $\{x \mid t\}$ to emphasise its intended meaning as a set. There is also a tuple-forming notation $(\ldots)$. Thus, if $t_1, \ldots, t_n$ are terms of type $\tau_1, \ldots, \tau_n$, respectively, then $(t_1, \ldots, t_n)$ is a term of type $\tau_1 \times \cdots \times \tau_n$.

Now we come to the key definition of basic terms. Intuitively, basic terms represent the instances that are the subject of learning. Basic terms fall into one of three kinds: those that represent individuals that are lists, trees, and so on; those that represent sets, multisets, and so on; and those that represent tuples. The second kind are abstractions. For example, the basic term representing the set $\{1, 2\}$ is

$$\lambda x.\textit{if } x = 1 \textit{ then } \top \textit{ else if } x = 2 \textit{ then } \top \textit{ else } \bot,$$

and

$$\lambda x.\textit{if } x = A \textit{ then } 42 \textit{ else if } x = B \textit{ then } 21 \textit{ else } 0$$

is the representation of the multiset with 42 occurrences of A and 21 occurrences of B (and nothing else). Thus we adopt abstractions of the form

$$\lambda x.\textit{if } x = t_1 \textit{ then } s_1 \textit{ else } \ldots \textit{ if } x = t_n \textit{ then } s_n \textit{ else } s_0$$

to represent (extensional) sets, multisets, and so on. The term s_0 here is called a default term and for the case of sets is $\bot$ and for multisets is 0. Generally, one can define default terms for each (closed) type. The set of default terms is denoted by $\mathfrak{D}$ [for full details on default terms see Lloyd (2003)].

Definition 4.1 (Basic terms). *The set of* basic terms, $\mathfrak{B}$, *is defined inductively as follows.*

(1) If C is a data constructor having signature $\sigma_1 \to \cdots \to \sigma_n \to (T\ a_1 \ldots a_k)$, $t_1, \ldots, t_n \in \mathfrak{B}$ $(n \geq 0)$, and t is $C\ t_1 \ldots t_n \in \mathfrak{L}$, then $t \in \mathfrak{B}$.

(2) If $t_1, \ldots, t_n \in \mathfrak{B}$, $s_1, \ldots, s_n \in \mathfrak{B}$ $(n \geq 0)$, $s_0 \in \mathfrak{D}$ and t is

$$\lambda x. \text{if } x = t_1 \text{ then } s_1 \text{ else } \ldots \text{ if } x = t_n \text{ then } s_n \text{ else } s_0 \in \mathfrak{L},$$

then $t \in \mathfrak{B}$.

(3) If $t_1, \ldots, t_n \in \mathfrak{B}$ $(n \geq 0)$ and t is $(t_1, \ldots, t_n) \in \mathfrak{L}$, then $t \in \mathfrak{B}$.

Part 1 of the definition of the set of basic terms states, in particular, that individual natural numbers, integers, and so on, are basic terms. Also a term formed by applying a data constructor to (all of) its arguments, each of which is a basic term, is a basic term. Consider again lists formed using the data constructors [] having signature *List* α, and # having signature $\alpha \to List\ a \to List\ \alpha$. Then $A\#B\#C\#[]$ is the basic term of type *List* α representing the list $[A, B, C]$, where A, B, and C are constants having signature α. Basic terms coming from Part 1 of the definition are called *basic structures* and always have a type of the form $T\alpha_1 \ldots \alpha_n$.

The abstractions formed in Part 2 of the definition are "almost constant" abstractions since they take the default term s_0 as value for all except a finite number of points in the domain. They are called *basic abstractions* and always have a type of the form $\beta \to \gamma$. This class of abstractions includes useful data types such as (finite) sets and multisets (assuming $\bot$ and 0 are default terms). More generally, basic abstractions can be regarded as lookup tables, with s_0 as the value for items not in the table. In fact, the precise definition of basic terms in [Lloyd (2003)] is a little more complicated in that, in the definition of basic abstractions, $t_1, \ldots, t_n$ are ordered and $s_1, \ldots, s_n$ cannot be default terms. These conditions avoid redundant representations of abstractions.

Part 3 of the definition of basic terms just states that one can form a tuple from basic terms and obtain a basic term. These terms are called *basic tuples* and always have a type of the form $\alpha_1 \times \cdots \times \alpha_n$.

Compared with Prolog, our knowledge representation offers a type system which can be used to express the structure of the hypothesis space and thus acts as a declarative bias which simplifies the definition of kernel functions. The other important extension are the abstractions, which allow us to use genuine sets and multisets. In fact, Prolog only has data constructors (functors), which are also used to emulate tuples.

It will be convenient to gather together all basic terms that have a type more general than some specific closed type. In this definition, if α and β

are types, then α is *more general than* β if there exists a type substitution ξ such that $\beta = \alpha\xi$.

Definition 4.2 (Basic terms of a given type). *For each $\alpha \in \mathfrak{S}^c$, define $\mathfrak{B}_\alpha = \{t \in \mathfrak{B} \mid t$ has type more general than $\alpha\}$.*

The intuitive meaning of $\mathfrak{B}_\alpha$ is that it is the set of terms representing individuals of type α.

For use in the definition of a kernel, we introduce some notation. If $s \in \mathfrak{B}_{\beta\to\gamma}$ and $t \in \mathfrak{B}_\beta$, then $V(s\ t)$ denotes the "value" returned when s is applied to t [the precise definition is in Lloyd (2003)]. For example, if s is $\lambda x.if\ x = A\ then\ 42\ else\ if\ x = B\ then\ 21\ else\ 0$ and t is A, then $V(s\ t) = 42$. Also, if $u \in \mathfrak{B}_{\beta\to\gamma}$, the *support* of u, denoted $supp(u)$, is the set $\{v \in \mathfrak{B}_\beta \mid V(u\ v) \notin \mathfrak{D}\}$. Thus, for the s above, $supp(s) = \{A, B\}$.

We now show how to represent directed graphs in this logic: There is a type constructor *Graph* such that the type of a graph is *Graph ν ε*, where ν is the type of information in the vertices and ε is the type of information in the edges. *Graph* is defined by

$$Graph\ \nu\ \varepsilon = \{ID \times \nu\} \times \{(ID \times ID) \times \varepsilon\},$$

where *ID* is the type of identifiers. Note that this definition corresponds closely to the mathematical definition of a graph: each vertex has a unique ID and each edge is uniquely identified by the ordered pair of labels of the vertices it connects.

The edges of graphs can be seen as links connecting different parts of one term with each other. In this chapter we will not exploit this sort of identifier and link structures. The main reason for this is that a recursive kernel definition exploiting identifiers and links need not necessarily converge. A related problem is how to actually compute these kernels. Chapter 4.6 will investigate these topics for directed and undirected graphs in detail. In the remainder of this chapter we will ignore the special nature of identifiers and links.

4.2   Kernels for Basic Terms

Having introduced our knowledge representation formalism in Section 4.1, we are now ready to define kernels for basic terms. In Section 4.2.1 we define a default kernel on basic terms. In Section 4.2.2 we show that the kernel is positive definite. In Section 4.2.3 we show how to adapt the default kernel to match more closely the domain under investigation.

4.2.1 *Default Kernels for Basic Terms*

Our definition of a kernel on basic terms assumes the existence of kernels on the various sets of data constructors. More precisely, for each type constructor $T \in \mathfrak{T}$, κ_T is assumed to be a positive definite kernel on the set of data constructors associated with T. For example, for the type constructor *Nat*, κ_{Nat} could be the *product kernel* defined by $\kappa_{Nat}(n, m) = nm$. For other type constructors, say M, the matching kernel could be used, i.e., $\kappa_M(x, x') = k_\delta(x, x')$.

Definition 4.3 (Default kernel for basic terms). *The function* k : $\mathfrak{B} \times \mathfrak{B} \to \mathbb{R}$ *is defined inductively on the structure of terms in* $\mathfrak{B}$ *as follows.*

(1) If $s, t \in \mathfrak{B}_\alpha$, where $\alpha = T \ \alpha_1 \ldots \alpha_k$ for some $T, \alpha_1, \ldots, \alpha_k$, s is $C \ s_1 \ldots s_n$, and t is $D \ t_1 \ldots t_m$ then

$$k(s, t) = \begin{cases} \kappa_T(C, D) & \text{if } C \neq D \\ \kappa_T(C, C) + \sum_{i=1}^{n} k(s_i, t_i) & \text{otherwise} \end{cases} .$$

(2) If $s, t \in \mathfrak{B}_\alpha$, where $\alpha = \beta \to \gamma$, for some β, γ, then

$$k(s, t) = \sum_{\substack{u \in supp(s) \\ v \in supp(t)}} k(V(s \ u), V(t \ v)) \cdot k(u, v).$$

(3) If $s, t \in \mathfrak{B}_\alpha$, where $\alpha = \alpha_1 \times \cdots \times \alpha_n$ for some $\alpha_1, \ldots, \alpha_n$, s is $(s_1, \ldots, s_n)$ and t is $(t_1, \ldots, t_n)$ then

$$k(s, t) = \sum_{i=1}^{n} k(s_i, t_i) .$$

(4) If there does not exist $\alpha \in \mathfrak{S}^c$ such that $s, t \in \mathfrak{B}_\alpha$, then $k(s, t) = 0$.

Definition 4.3 originates from work first presented in [Gärtner *et al.* (2002b)]. Lloyd (2003, Definition 3.7.4) gives a less general definition for which some nicer theoretical properties can be shown but which is not flexible enough for practical applications. In particular, Lloyd (2003) restricts Part 2 of the definition to the case where k is the matching kernel on $\mathfrak{B}_\beta$ so that

$$k(s, t) = \sum_{u \in supp(s) \cap supp(t)} k(V(s \ u), V(t \ u)),$$

for $s, t \in \mathfrak{B}_{\beta \to \gamma}$. The generalisation above is important in practise and each of the applications described in Section 4.5 will use it.

We proceed by giving examples and some intuition of the default kernel defined above. In the following examples we will be somewhat sloppy with our notation and identify basic terms with the lists, sets, and multisets they represent.

Example 4.1 (Default kernel on lists). *Let M be a nullary type constructor and $A, B, C, D : M$. Let $\#$ and $[]$ be the usual data constructors for lists. Choose κ_M and κ_{List} to be the matching kernel. Let s be the list $[A, B, C] \in \mathfrak{B}_{List\ M}$, $t = [A, D]$, and $u = [B, C]$. Then*

$$
\begin{aligned}
k(s, t) &= \kappa_{List}((\#), (\#)) + k(A, A) + k([B, C], [D]) \\
&= 1 + \kappa_M(A, A) + \kappa_{List}((\#), (\#)) + k(B, D) + k([C], []) \\
&= 1 + 1 + 1 + \kappa_M(B, D) + \kappa_{List}((\#), []) \\
&= 3 + 0 + 0 \\
&= 3.
\end{aligned}
$$

Similarly, $k(s, u) = 2$ and $k(t, u) = 3$.

The intuition here is that if we use the matching kernel on the list constructors and on the elements of the lists, then we can decompose the kernel as $k(s, t) = l + m + n$ where l is the length of the shorter list, m is the number of consecutive matching elements at the start of both lists, and $n = 1$ if the lists are of the same length and 0 otherwise.

The kernel used in the above example is related to string kernels [Lodhi *et al.* (2002)] in so far as they apply to the same kind of data. However, the underlying intuition of list/string similarity is very different. String kernels measure similarity of two strings by the number of common (not necessarily consecutive) substrings. The list kernel defined above only takes the longest common consecutive sublist at the start of the two lists into account. This is more in line with the interpretation of lists as head-tail trees (used also in inductive logic programming), and the kind of matching performed by anti-unification.

Example 4.2 (Default kernel on sets). *Let M be a nullary type constructor and $A, B, C, D : M$. Choose κ_M and κ_Ω to be the matching kernel.*

Let s be the set $\{A, B, C\} \in \mathfrak{B}_{M \to \Omega}$, $t = \{A, D\}$, *and* $u = \{B, C\}$. *Then*

$$
\begin{aligned}
k(s,t) &= k(A,A)k(\top,\top) + k(A,D)k(\top,\top) + k(B,A)k(\top,\top) \\
&\quad + k(B,D)k(\top,\top) + k(C,A)k(\top,\top) + k(C,D)k(\top,\top) \\
&= \kappa_M(A,A) + \kappa_M(A,D) + \kappa_M(B,A) + \kappa_M(B,D) \\
&\quad + \kappa_M(C,A) + \kappa_M(C,D) \\
&= 1 + 0 + 0 + 0 + 0 + 0 \\
&= 1.
\end{aligned}
$$

Similarly, $k(s,u) = 2$ *and* $k(t,u) = 0$.

The intuition here is that using the matching kernel for the elements of the set corresponds to computing the cardinality of the intersection of the two sets. Alternatively, this computation can be seen as the inner product of the bit-vectors representing the two sets. Set kernels have been described in more detail in Section 3.3.1.

Example 4.3 (Default kernel on multisets). *Let M be a nullary type constructor and $A, B, C, D : M$. Choose κ_M to be the matching kernel, and κ_{Nat} to be the product kernel. Let s be $\langle A, A, B, C, C, C \rangle \in \mathfrak{B}_{M \to Nat}$ (i.e., s is the multiset containing two occurrences of A, one of B, and three of C), $t = \langle A, D, D \rangle$, and $u = \langle B, B, C, C \rangle$. Then*

$$
\begin{aligned}
k(s,t) &= k(2,1)k(A,A) + k(2,2)k(A,D) \\
&\quad + k(1,1)k(B,A) + k(1,2)k(B,D) \\
&\quad + k(3,1)k(C,A) + k(3,2)k(C,D) \\
&= 2 \times 1 + 4 \times 0 + 1 \times 0 + 2 \times 0 + 3 \times 0 + 6 \times 0 \\
&= 2.
\end{aligned}
$$

Similarly, $k(s,u) = 8$ *and* $k(t,u) = 0$.

The intuition here is that using the product kernel for the elements of the multiset corresponds to computing the inner product of the multiplicity vectors representing the two multisets. Multiset kernels have been described in more detail in Section 3.3.3.

These examples were kept deliberately simple in order to illustrate the main points. The kernel defined in Definition 4.3 provides much more flexibility in three important respects: (i) it allows nesting of types, such that e.g. sets can range over objects that are themselves structured; (ii) it allows flexibility in the choice of the kernels on data constructors, such that e.g. elements of lists can partially match as in DNA sequences; and (iii) it allows flexibility in the way in which examples are modelled in the framework, such that e.g. a list does not have to be represented by a head-tail tree if that does not match its semantics.

4.2.2 Positive Definiteness of the Default Kernel

Now we can formulate the main theoretical result of this chapter.

Proposition 4.1 (Positive definiteness). *Let $k : \mathfrak{B} \times \mathfrak{B} \to \mathbb{R}$ be the function defined in Definition 4.3. For each $\alpha \in \mathfrak{S}^c$, it holds that k is a positive definite kernel on $\mathfrak{B}_\alpha$ if the kernels κ_T on the data constructors associated with the same type constructor T are positive definite.*

As mentioned above, the kernel of Definition 4.3 originates from work first presented in [Gärtner *et al.* (2002b)]. The kernel presented in (Lloyd, 2003, Definition 3.7.4) is less general which allows for a stronger proposition to hold but which is not flexible enough for practical applications. Before giving the full inductive proof of this Proposition, we give the relevant definitions and an intuitive outline of the proof. The key idea of the proof is to base the induction on a 'bottom-up' definition of $\mathfrak{B}$.

Definition 4.4. Define $\{\mathfrak{B}_m\}_{m\in\mathbb{N}\cup\{0\}}$ inductively as follows.

$$\mathfrak{B}_0 = \{C \mid C \text{ is a data constructor of arity } 0\}$$

$$\mathfrak{B}_{m+1} = \{C\, t_1 \dots t_n \in \mathfrak{L} \mid C \text{ is a data constructor of arity } n \text{ and}$$

$$t_1, \dots, t_n \in \mathfrak{B}_m (n \geq 0)\}$$

$$\cup \{\lambda x. \text{if } x = t_1 \text{ then } s_1 \text{ else} \dots \text{if } x = t_n \text{ then } s_n \text{ else } s_0 \in \mathfrak{L} \mid$$

$$t_1, \dots, t_n \in \mathfrak{B}_m, s_1, \dots, s_n \in \mathfrak{B}_m, \text{ and } s_0 \in \mathfrak{D}\}$$

$$\cup \{(t_1, \dots, t_n) \in \mathfrak{L} \mid t_1, \dots, t_n \in \mathfrak{B}_m\}.$$

One can prove that $\mathfrak{B}_m \subseteq \mathfrak{B}_{m+1}$, for $m \in \mathbb{N}$, and that $\mathfrak{B} = \bigcup_{m\in\mathbb{N}} \mathfrak{B}_m$.

The intuitive outline of the proof of Proposition 4.1 is as follows: First, assume that those kernels occurring on the right-hand side in Definition 4.3 are positive definite. Then the positive definiteness of the (left-hand side) kernel follows from the closure properties of the class of positive definite kernels. The kernel on basic structures is positive definite because of closure under sum, zero extension, and direct sum, and because the kernels defined on the data constructors are assumed to be positive definite. The kernel on basic abstractions is positive definite as the function *supp* returns a finite set, and kernels are closed under zero extension, sum, and tensor product. The kernel on basic tuples is positive definite because of closure under direct sum.

Proof. First the symmetry of k on each $\mathfrak{B}_\alpha$ is established. For each $m \in \mathbb{N} \cup \{0\}$, let $SYM(m)$ be the property:

For all $\alpha \in \mathfrak{S}^c$ and $s, t \in \mathfrak{B}_\alpha \cap \mathfrak{B}_m$, it follows that $k(s,t) = k(t,s)$.

It is shown by induction that $SYM(m)$ holds, for all $m \in \mathbb{N}$. The symmetry of k on each $\mathfrak{B}_\alpha$ follows immediately from this since, given $s, t \in \mathfrak{B}_\alpha$, there exists an m such that $s, t \in \mathfrak{B}_m$ (because $\mathfrak{B} = \bigcup_{m \in \mathbb{N}} \mathfrak{B}_m$ and $\mathfrak{B}_m \subseteq \mathfrak{B}_{m+1}$, for all $m \in \mathbb{N}$).

First it is shown that $SYM(0)$ holds. In this case, s and t are data constructors of arity 0 associated with the same type constructor T, say. By definition, $k(s,t) = \kappa_T(s,t)$ and the result follows because κ_T is symmetric.

Now assume that $SYM(m)$ holds. It is proved that $SYM(m+1)$ also holds. Thus suppose that $\alpha \in \mathfrak{S}^c$ and $s, t \in \mathfrak{B}_\alpha \cap \mathfrak{B}_{m+1}$. It has to be shown that $k(s,t) = k(t,s)$. There are three cases to consider corresponding to α having the form $T \, \alpha_1 \ldots \alpha_k$, $\beta \to \gamma$, or $\alpha_1 \times \cdots \times \alpha_m$. In each case, it is easy to see from the definition of k and the induction hypothesis that $k(s,t) = k(t,s)$. This completes the proof that k is symmetric on each $\mathfrak{B}_\alpha$.

For the remaining part of the proof, for each $m \in \mathbb{N} \cup \{0\}$, let $PD(m)$ be the property:

For all $n \in \mathbb{N}, \alpha \in \mathfrak{S}^c, t_1, \ldots, t_n \in \mathfrak{B}_\alpha \cap \mathfrak{B}_m$, and $c_1, \ldots, c_n \in \mathbb{R}$, it holds that $\sum_{i,j \in \{1,\ldots,n\}} c_i \, c_j \, k(t_i, t_j) \geq 0$.

It is shown by induction that $PD(m)$ holds, for all $m \in \mathbb{N}$. The remaining condition for positive definiteness follows immediately from this since, given $t_1, \ldots, t_n \in \mathfrak{B}_\alpha$, there exists an m such that $t_1, \ldots, t_n \in \mathfrak{B}_m$.

First it is shown that $PD(0)$ holds. In this case, each t_i is a data constructor of arity 0 associated with the same type constructor T, say. By definition, $k(t_i, t_j) = \kappa_T(t_i, t_j)$, for each i and j, and the result follows since κ_T is assumed to be positive definite.

Now assume that $PD(m)$ holds. It is proved that $PD(m+1)$ also holds. Thus suppose that $n \in \mathbb{Z}^+, \alpha \in \mathfrak{S}^c, t_1, \ldots, t_n \in \mathfrak{B}_\alpha \cap \mathfrak{B}_{m+1}$, and $c_1, \ldots, c_n \in \mathbb{R}$. It has to be shown that $\sum_{i,j \in \{1,\ldots,n\}} c_i \, c_j \, k(t_i, t_j) \geq 0$. There are three cases to consider.

(1) Let $\alpha = T \, \alpha_1 \ldots \alpha_k$. Suppose that $t_i = C_i \, t_i^{(1)} \ldots t_i^{(m_i)}$, where $m_i \geq 0$,

for $i = 1, \ldots, n$. Let $\mathcal{C} = \{C_i \mid i = 1, \ldots, n\}$. Then

$$\sum_{i,j \in \{1,\ldots,n\}} c_i\, c_j\, k(t_i, t_j)$$

$$= \sum_{i,j \in \{1,\ldots,n\}} c_i\, c_j\, \kappa_T(C_i, C_j)$$

$$+ \sum_{\substack{i,j \in \{1,\ldots,n\} \\ C_i = C_j}} c_i\, c_j \sum_{l \in \{1,\ldots,arity(C_i)\}} k(t_i^{(l)}, t_j^{(l)}).$$

Now

$$\sum_{i,j \in \{1,\ldots,n\}} c_i\, c_j\, \kappa_T(C_i, C_j) \geq 0$$

using the fact that κ_T is a positive definite kernel on the set of data constructors associated with T. Also

$$\sum_{\substack{i,j \in \{1,\ldots,n\} \\ C_i = C_j}} c_i\, c_j \sum_{l \in \{1,\ldots,arity(C_i)\}} k(t_i^{(l)}, t_j^{(l)})$$

$$= \sum_{C \in \mathcal{C}} \sum_{\substack{i,j \in \{1,\ldots,n\} \\ C_i = C_j = C}} \sum_{l \in \{1,\ldots,arity(C)\}} c_i\, c_j\, k(t_i^{(l)}, t_j^{(l)})$$

$$= \sum_{C \in \mathcal{C}} \sum_{l \in \{1,\ldots,arity(C)\}} \sum_{\substack{i,j \in \{1,\ldots,n\} \\ C_i = C_j = C}} c_i\, c_j\, k(t_i^{(l)}, t_j^{(l)})$$

$$\geq 0,$$

by the induction hypothesis.

(2) Let $\alpha = \beta \to \gamma$. Then

$$\sum_{i,j \in \{1,\ldots,n\}} c_i\, c_j\, k(t_i, t_j)$$

$$= \sum_{i,j \in \{1,\ldots,n\}} c_i\, c_j \sum_{\substack{u \in supp(t_i) \\ v \in supp(t_j)}} k\left(V(t_i\, u), V(t_j\, v)\right) \cdot k(u, v)$$

$$= \sum_{i,j \in \{1,\ldots,n\}} \sum_{\substack{u \in supp(t_i) \\ v \in supp(t_j)}} c_i\, c_j\, k\left(V(t_i\, u), V(t_j\, v)\right) \cdot k(u, v)$$

$$= \sum_{\substack{(i,u),(j,v) \in \\ \{(k,w)\ \mid\ k=1,\ldots,n\ \text{and}\ w \in supp(t_k)\}}} c_i\, c_j\, k\left(V(t_i\, u), V(t_j\, v)\right) \cdot k(u, v)$$

$$\geq 0.$$

For the last step, we proceed as follows. By the induction hypothesis, k is positive definite on both $\mathfrak{B}_\beta \cap \mathfrak{B}_m$ and $\mathfrak{B}_\gamma \cap \mathfrak{B}_m$. Hence the function

$$h : ((\mathfrak{B}_\beta \cap \mathfrak{B}_m) \times (\mathfrak{B}_\gamma \cap \mathfrak{B}_m)) \times ((\mathfrak{B}_\beta \cap \mathfrak{B}_m) \times (\mathfrak{B}_\gamma \cap \mathfrak{B}_m)) \to \mathbb{R}$$

defined by

$$h\left((u, y), (v, z)\right) = k(u, v) \cdot k(y, z)$$

is positive definite, since h is a tensor product of positive definite kernels (Section 3.2.1). Now consider the set

$$\{(u, V(t_i\ u)) \mid i = 1, \ldots, n \text{ and } u \in supp(t_i)\}$$

of points in $(\mathfrak{B}_\beta \cap \mathfrak{B}_m) \times (\mathfrak{B}_\gamma \cap \mathfrak{B}_m)$ and the corresponding set of constants

$$\{c_{i,u} \mid i = 1, \ldots, n \text{ and } u \in supp(t_i)\},$$

where $c_{i,u} = c_i$, for all $i = 1, \ldots, n$ and $u \in supp(t_i)$.

(3) Let $\alpha = \alpha_1 \times \cdots \times \alpha_m$. Suppose that $t_i = (t_i^{(1)}, \ldots, t_i^{(m)})$, for $i = 1, \ldots, n$. Then

$$\sum_{i,j \in \{1, \ldots, n\}} c_i\, c_j\, k(t_i, t_j)$$

$$= \sum_{i,j \in \{1, \ldots, n\}} c_i\, c_j \left(\sum_{l=1}^{m} k(t_i^{(l)}, t_j^{(l)}) \right)$$

$$= \sum_{l=1}^{m} \sum_{i,j \in \{1, \ldots, n\}} c_i\, c_j\, k(t_i^{(l)}, t_j^{(l)})$$

$$\geq 0,$$

by the induction hypothesis. ☐

4.2.3 *Specifying Kernels*

The kernel defined in the previous section closely follows the type structure of the individuals that are used for learning. As indicated, the kernel assumes the existence of atomic kernels for all data constructors used. These kernels can be the product kernel for numbers, the matching kernel which just checks whether the two constructors are the same, or a user-defined kernel. In addition, kernel modifiers (see Section 3.2.2) can be used to customise the kernel definition to the domain at hand. In this section, we suggest how atomic kernels and kernel modifiers could be specified by an extension of the Haskell language [Jones and Hughes (1998)].

To incorporate domain knowledge into the kernel definition, it will frequently be necessary to modify the default kernels for a type. For these modifiers, the choices discussed in Section 3.2.2 are offered. Other modifiers can be defined by the user, using the syntax below.

We suggest that kernels be defined directly on the type structure (specifying the structure of the domain and the declarative bias). We introduce our suggested kernel definition syntax by means of an example: the East/West challenge [Michie *et al.* (1994)] that describes an instance space of trains with different cars, each of which is described by a number of attributes. The learning task is to classify trains as eastbound or westbound.

```
eastbound :: Train -> Bool
type Train = Car -> Bool with modifier gaussian 0.1
type Car = (Shape,Length,Roof,Wheels,Load)
data Shape = Rectangle | Oval
data Length = Long | Short
data Roof = Flat | Peaked | None with kernel roofK
type Wheels = Int with kernel discreteKernel
type Load = (LShape,LNumber)
data LShape = Rectangle | Circle | Triangle
type LNumber = Int
```

The first line declares the learning target **eastbound** as a mapping from trains to the booleans. A train is a set of cars, and a car is a 5-tuple describing its shape, its length, its roof, its number of wheels, and its load. All of these are specified by data constructors except the load, which itself is a pair of data constructors describing the shape and number of loads.

The **with** keyword describes a property of a type, in this case kernels and kernel modifiers. The above declarations state that on trains we use a Gaussian kernel modifier with bandwidth $\gamma = 0.1$. By default, for **Shape**, **Length** and **LShape** the matching kernel is used, while for **LNumber** the product kernel is used. The default kernel is overridden for **Wheels**, which is defined as an integer but uses the matching kernel instead. Finally, **Roof** has been endowed with a user-defined atomic kernel which could be defined as follows:

```
roofK :: Roof -> Roof -> Real
roofK x x = 1
```

```
roofK Flat Peaked = 0.5
roofK Peaked Flat = 0.5
roofK x y = 0
```

This kernel counts 1 for identical roofs, 0.5 for matching flat against peaked roofs, and 0 in all other cases (i.e., whenever one car is open and the other is closed).

Finally, the normalisation modifier could be implemented as the following higher-order function:

```
normalised :: (t->t->Real) -> t -> t -> Real
normalised k x y = (k x y) / sqrt((k x x)*(k y y))
```

In this section we have presented a kernel for structured data that closely follows the syntactic structure of individuals as expressed by their higher-order type signature. The default setting assumes the product kernel for numbers and the matching kernel for symbols, but this can be overridden to match the semantics of the data more closely. The simplicity with which different kernels (kernel modifiers) can be defined on the different parts of the instances clearly advocates the use of a typed knowledge representation language like the one we use.

4.3 Multi-Instance Learning

To investigate in more depth the implications of using the basic term kernel, we now consider one particular problem class, so called *multi-instance learning* problems. This class of problems has recently received a significant amount of interest from the machine learning community. One popular application of multi-instance learning is drug activity prediction problems in which chemical compounds are described by the surface shape of several low-energy conformations.

Multi-instance (MI) learning problems [Dieterich *et al.* (1997)] occur whenever example objects, individuals, can not be described by a single characteristic feature vector, but by a set of vectors. Any of these vectors could be responsible for the classification of the set. The inherent difficulty of MI problems is to identify the characteristic element of each bag.

To apply basic term kernels to MI problems, we view every set of vectors as an abstraction. The corresponding kernel is then the default kernel for basic abstractions. To incorporate our knowledge about multi-instance concepts, we use a polynomial modifier on the elements of the sets, that is, on basic tuples. In particular, the kernel we consider coincides with the soft-maximal set kernel of Section 3.3.2.

The main result of this section is that these basic term kernels can be shown to separate positive and negative MI sets under natural assumptions. We furthermore give a Novikoff type bound for the kernel perceptron (Section 2.4.4) with this kernels. Most importantly, this bound is polynomial in the number of instances per bag and does not depend on the dimensionality of the feature space. This is important in kernel methods as the dimensionality of the feature space is often infinite.

Subsection 4.3.1 introduces the MI setting under various aspects. Subsection 4.3.2 gives an account of the separability of MI problems in kernel feature space and devises a suitable kernel. Subsection 4.3.3 gives a Novikoff (1963) type bound for the kernel perceptron on the same kind of problems. Subsection 4.3.5 discusses an alternative way to apply attribute-value learning algorithms to MI problems.

Later, in Section 4.5.2, empirical studies compare this kernel to other MI learning algorithms. On one hand, an SVM using this kernel is compared to state of the art MI algorithms. On the other hand, it is compared to other methods that can be used to apply SVMs to MI data. In both studies the kernel proposed in this section compares favourably.

4.3.1   *The Multi-Instance Setting*

MI problems have been introduced under this name in [Dietterich *et al.* (1997)]. However, similar problems and algorithms have been considered earlier, for example in pattern recognition [Keeler *et al.* (1991)]. Within the last couple of years, several approaches have been made to upgrade attribute-value learning algorithms to tackle MI problems. Other approaches focused on new algorithms specifically designed for MI learning.

Recall that concepts are functions $\nu_{\mathrm{I}} : \mathcal{X} \to \{+1, -1\}$, where $\mathcal{X}$ is often referred to as the instance space and $\{+1, -1\}$ are the labels. There are $2^{|\mathcal{X}|}$ concepts on the instance space $\mathcal{X}$. A function $f : \mathcal{X} \to \mathbb{R}$ is said to separate the concept if $f(x) > 0 \Leftrightarrow \nu_{\mathrm{I}}(x) = +1$.

If examples are represented by subsets of some domain $\mathcal{X}$ concepts are functions $\nu_{\mathrm{set}} : 2^{\mathcal{X}} \to \{+1, -1\}$. There are $2^{2^{|\mathcal{X}|}}$ different concepts on sets. Such concepts are sometimes referred to as multi-part concepts. MI concepts are a specific kind of these concepts.

Definition 4.5. A *multi-instance concept* is a function $\nu_{\mathrm{MI}} : 2^{\mathcal{X}} \to \{+1, -1\}$. It is defined as:

$$\nu_{\mathrm{MI}}(X) = +1 \Leftrightarrow \exists\, x \in X : \nu_{\mathrm{I}}(x) = +1$$

where ν_{I} is a concept over an instance space (referred to as the 'underlying concept'), and $X \subseteq \mathcal{X}$ is a set.

There are $2^{|\mathcal{X}|}$ different MI concepts. The difficulty in this task is not just to generalise beyond examples, but also to identify the characteristic element of each bag. Any learning algorithm that sees a positive bag (a bag with label $+1$) cannot infer much about the elements of the bag, except that one of its elements is positive in the underlying concept. With large bag sizes this information is of limited use.

A popular real-world example of a multi-instance problem is the prediction of drug activity, introduced in the musk domain [Dietterich *et al.* (1997)]. A drug is active if it binds well to enzymes or cell-surface receptors. The binding strength is determined by the shape of the drug molecule. However, most molecules can change their shape by rotating some of their internal bonds. The possible shapes of a molecule, i.e., a combination of the angles of the rotatable bonds of the molecule, are known as conformations. A drug binds well to enzymes or cell-surface receptors if one of its conformations binds well. Thus the drug activity prediction problem is a multi-instance problem. A molecule is represented by a set of descriptions of its different conformations. The shape of each conformation is described by a feature vector where each component corresponds to the length of one ray from the origin to the molecule surface. More details on the musk domain are given in Section 4.5.2.

4.3.2   *Separating MI Problems*

In this subsection we define a kernel function on sets of instances that separates MI problems under natural assumptions. Using this kernel function, SVMs and other kernel methods can easily be applied to MI problems. We begin by introducing the notion of separability.

Separability   A concept $\nu_{\mathrm{I}} : \mathcal{X} \to \{-1, +1\}$ is called *linearly separable* in input space if

$$\forall\, x \in \mathcal{X} : \langle x, c \rangle \geq \theta \Leftrightarrow \nu_{\mathrm{I}}(x) = +1$$

holds for some constant c and threshold θ. Likewise, a concept is called linearly separable with respect to a feature map ϕ if

$$\forall\, x \in \mathcal{X} : \langle \phi(x), c_\phi \rangle \geq \theta \Leftrightarrow \nu_{\mathrm{I}}(x) = +1$$

holds for some $c_\phi \in \mathrm{span}\{\phi(x) : x \in \mathcal{X}\}$. In what follows we often use the term *separable* to refer to concepts that are linearly separable with respect to a feature transformation given implicitly by a kernel.

In particular, we will later assume that for some c_ϕ, b the following holds for every $x \in \mathcal{X}$:

$$\begin{aligned}
\nu_{\mathrm{I}}(x) = +1 &\Rightarrow \quad \langle \phi(x), c_\phi \rangle + b \geq 1 \\
\nu_{\mathrm{I}}(x) = -1 &\Rightarrow 0 \leq \langle \phi(x), c_\phi \rangle + b \leq 1 - \epsilon.
\end{aligned} \tag{4.1}$$

Note that we can, without loss of generality, assume that $b = 0$, since for given ϕ, c_ϕ, b the map $x \mapsto (\phi(x), 1)$ together with (c_ϕ, b) will satisfy the above condition without a constant offset.

We will now discuss the soft-maximal set kernel from Section 3.3.2 in more detail:

Multi-Instance Kernel Given a kernel $k_{\mathrm{I}}(\cdot, \cdot)$ and a constant $p > 0$, we define:

$$k_{\mathrm{MI}}(X, X') = \sum_{x \in X, x' \in X'} k_{\mathrm{I}}^p(x, x') . \tag{4.2}$$

If $k_{\mathrm{I}}(\cdot, \cdot)$ is, for example, a Gaussian RBF kernel, then it is not necessary to require $p \in \mathbb{N}$, since in this case $k_{\mathrm{I}}^p(\cdot, \cdot)$ is a Gaussian RBF kernel itself, albeit with width σ^2/p instead of σ^2. In general, however, we need to require that $p \in \mathbb{N}$. Then, since products of kernels are kernels, also $k_{\mathrm{I}}^p(\cdot, \cdot)$ is a kernel, and consequently also $k_{\mathrm{MI}}(\cdot, \cdot)$ is a kernel.

The specification of a multi-instance kernel in the context of the basic term kernel framework can be found in Section 4.5.2 where we also present empirical results.

We are now able to give the main result of this section.

Lemma 4.1. *A MI concept ν_{MI} is separable with the kernel k_{MI}, as defined in (4.2), for sufficiently large p, if the underlying concept ν_{I} is separable with the kernel k_{I} and some ϵ, according to (4.1).*

Proof. Let $p > 0$ if $\epsilon = 1$, and $p > -\frac{\ln m}{\ln(1-\epsilon)}$ otherwise. Here m is a bound on the cardinality of the bags X.

Since the concept is separable, there exists a c_ϕ satisfying (4.1). Now consider the function

$$f(X) = \sum_{x \in X} \langle \phi(x), c_\phi \rangle^p .$$

One can see that if $\nu_{\mathrm{MI}}(X) = +1$, i.e., there is a $x \in X$ satisfying $\nu_{\mathrm{I}}(x) = +1$, then

$$f(X) \geq 1^p = 1 \ .$$

Furthermore, if $\nu_{\mathrm{MI}}(X) = -1$, i.e., there is no $x \in X$ satisfying $\nu_{\mathrm{I}}(x) = +1$, then

$$f(X) \leq m(1 - \epsilon)^p < m(1 - \epsilon)^{-\frac{\ln m}{\ln(1-\epsilon)}} = 1 \ ,$$

$\square$

Discussion Before we proceed with the next section, it is useful to discuss — in general terms — the relationship between functions like $k_{\mathrm{MI}}(\cdot, \cdot)$ and $f(\cdot)$ above.

Let $k : \mathcal{X} \times \mathcal{X} \to \mathbb{R}$ be a positive definite kernel with $k(x, x') = \langle \phi(x), \phi(x') \rangle$ and let $h(\cdot)$ be a function that takes a positive definite kernel as an argument and returns another positive definite kernel. When applied to the inner product $\langle \cdot, \cdot \rangle$, it performs the following map $h : \langle \cdot, \cdot \rangle \mapsto \langle \psi(\cdot), \psi(\cdot) \rangle$.

We are now interested in the function $K(X, X') = \sum_{x \in X, x' \in X'} h(k(x, x'))$. Obviously $h(k(x, x')) = \langle \psi(\phi(x)), \psi(\phi(x')) \rangle$ and $K(X, X') = \langle \Phi(X), \Phi(X') \rangle$ with $\Phi(X) = \sum_{x \in X} \psi(\phi(x))$.

Now we can rewrite functions like $f(X)$ in these terms:

$$f(X) = \sum_{x \in X} h(\langle \phi(x), c_\phi \rangle) = \left\langle \sum_{x \in X} \psi(\phi(X)), \psi(c_\phi) \right\rangle = \langle \Phi(X), c_\Phi \rangle \ .$$

The above lemma then says that if $\nu_{\mathrm{I}}(\cdot)$ is linearly separable with respect to ϕ then $\nu_{\mathrm{MI}}(\cdot)$ is linearly separable with respect to Φ. In the next section we will provide a bound on the number of steps needed by the kernel perceptron with the MI kernel to converge to a consistent solution.

Example 4.4. Let $\mathcal{X} = \Omega^4 = \{\top, \bot\}^4$, $x \in \mathcal{X}$, $x = (x_1, x_2, x_3, x_4)$, $\nu_{\mathrm{I}}(x) \Leftrightarrow x_2 \wedge x_4$, and

$$k_{\mathrm{I}}(x, y) = \sum_{x_i = y_i = \top} 1 \ .$$

Then $m = 16$, as $\max_i |X_i| \leq |\mathcal{X}| = 2^4 = 16$, and $\epsilon = 1/2$. Here we have $p = 5 > \log 16 / \log 2$.

The following example illustrates that the intersection kernel (and thus also the crossproduct kernel) separates MI concepts on discrete sets.

Example 4.5. Let $\mathcal{X} = \{a, b, c, d\}$, $\mathcal{C} = \{a, c\}$, $\nu_{\mathrm{I}}(x) \Leftrightarrow x \in \mathcal{C}$, and $k_{\mathrm{I}}(x, y) = k_\delta(x, y)$. Then $\epsilon = 1$, $m = 4$ as $\max_i |X_i| \leq |\mathcal{X}| = 4$), and $p = 1 > 0$. It follows that:

$$k_{\mathrm{MI}}(X, Y) = \sum_{x \in X, y \in Y} k_\delta(x, y) = |X \cap Y| = k_{\mathrm{set}}(X, Y) \ .$$

It follows directly from the lemma above and from the definition of convolution kernels [Haussler (1999)] that (for finite example sets) MI concepts can be separated with convolutions of Gaussian RBF kernels if the underlying concept can be separated with Gaussian RBF kernels, since in this case k_{I}^p is a Gaussian RBF kernel itself, albeit with width σ^2/p instead of σ^2. In this case the MI kernel does not require an additional parameter to be chosen. Also note that for RBF kernels, Equation (4.1) always holds with $b = 0$.

We need one further lemma:

Lemma 4.2. *If an MI concept* ν_{MI} *is separable then the underlying concept* ν_{I} *is separable.*

Proof. Say $f_{\mathrm{MI}}(Z)$ is a function that separates positive and negative bags $(f_{\mathrm{MI}}(Z) > \theta \Leftrightarrow \nu_{\mathrm{MI}}(Z) = +1)$. Then $f_{\mathrm{I}}(z) = f_{\mathrm{MI}}(\{z\})$ is a function that separates the underlying concept (with $f_{\mathrm{I}}(z) > \theta \Leftrightarrow \nu_{\mathrm{I}}(z) = +1$). $\quad \square$

It is now easy to show:

Theorem 4.1. *An MI concept* $\nu_{\mathrm{MI}}(\cdot)$ *is separable by* $k_{\mathrm{MI}}(\cdot, \cdot)$ *with a non-zero margin if and only if the underlying concept* $\nu_{\mathrm{I}}(\cdot)$ *is separable by the kernel* $k_{\mathrm{I}}(\cdot, \cdot)$ *with a non-zero margin.*

Proof. In Lemma 4.1 the margin of the MI problem is

$$\epsilon_{\mathrm{MI}} = 1 - m(1 - \epsilon)^p > 0 \ .$$

Furthermore, assuming a margin ϵ on $f_{\mathrm{MI}}(\cdot)$ in Lemma 4.2, a margin of ϵ can be found on $f_{\mathrm{I}}(\cdot)$. The lower bounds are maintained similarly. $\quad \square$

4.3.3   *Convergence of the MI Kernel Perceptron*

In this section we show a Novikoff type bound (Section 2.4.4) for the kernel perceptron using the MI kernel function (4.2). Most importantly, if all parameters of the underlying classification problem are considered constant then this bound is polynomial in the number of instances per bag.

The Novikoff (1963) theorem for perceptrons (see Section 2.4.4) states: If there are $R, \xi > 0, c_\phi \in \mathbb{R}^N$ such that $\|x_i\| \leq R$ and $y_i \langle c_\phi, x_i \rangle \geq \xi$ then the perceptron makes at most $\left(\frac{R \|c_\phi\|}{\xi} \right)^2$ mistakes.

The importance of the Novikoff theorem is that the number of errors does not depend on the dimensionality of the feature space. Therefore it is possible to replace the inner product in $\mathbb{R}^N$ by any kernel function k without losing the convergence property. In Section 2.4.4 we derived this bound for the kernel perceptron. The only difference is that here we use $\|c_\phi\|^2$ in the enumerator instead of $\|f^*(\cdot)\|_{\mathcal{H}}^2$. Their relationship can be seen by computing

$$\|f^*(\cdot)\|_{\mathcal{H}}^2 = \left\langle \sum_i \alpha_i k(x_i, \cdot), \sum_i \alpha_i k(x_i, \cdot) \right\rangle$$

and replacing $k(x_i, \cdot)$ by $\phi : \mathcal{X} \to l_2$ with $k(x_i, x_j) = \langle \phi(x_i), \phi(x_j) \rangle$ which is possible as all realisations of Hilbert spaces are isomorphic. Then

$$\|f^*(\cdot)\|_{\mathcal{H}}^2 = \left\langle \sum_i \alpha_i \phi(x_i), \sum_i \alpha_i \phi(x_i) \right\rangle = \langle c_\phi, c_\phi \rangle .$$

To show that the kernel perceptron can learn MI data, it remains to be shown that the above bound is not exponential. Most interesting is thereby the dependence on the number of instances per bag.

Theorem 4.2. *The number of mistakes made by the kernel perceptron with the MI kernel as defined in (4.2) can be bounded by a quasi-polynomial in the size m of the bags and in the parameters $R_{\mathrm{I}}, \epsilon, \|c_\phi\|$ of the underlying concept.*

Proof. Let all variables and functions be defined as in the proof of Lemma 4.1. Let $p = -\frac{\ln m}{\ln(1-\epsilon)} + 1$. Let Φ be such that $k_{\mathrm{MI}}(X, X') = \langle \Phi(X), \Phi(X') \rangle$ and let c_Φ be such that

$$\sum_{x \in X} \langle \phi(x), c_\phi \rangle^p = \langle \Phi(X), c_\Phi \rangle .$$

Let R_{I} be such that $k_{\mathrm{I}}(x, x) \leq R_{\mathrm{I}}^2$ and let $(X_1, Y_1), \ldots (X_n, Y_n); X_i \subseteq \mathcal{X}; Y_i \in \{-1, +1\}$ be a sequence of labelled bags.
If $\nu_{\mathrm{MI}}(X) = +1$ then

$$f(X) = \sum_{x \in X} \langle \phi(x), c_\phi \rangle^p \geq 1^p = 1 .$$

If $\nu_{\text{MI}}(X) = -1$ then

$$f(X) = \sum_{x \in X} \langle \phi(x), c_\phi \rangle^p \leq \sum_{x \in X} (1 - \epsilon)^p \leq m(1 - \epsilon)^p = 1 - \epsilon .$$

To ap-
ply Novikoff's theorem, we consider $Y_i \langle (\Phi(X_i), -1), (c_\Phi, \xi_{\text{MI}} + 1) \rangle \geq \xi_{\text{MI}}$
with $\xi_{\text{MI}} = \frac{\epsilon}{2}$. Now, we need to find $\|(c_\Phi, \xi_{\text{MI}} + 1)\|^2$ and R_{MI} such that for
all X_i it holds that $\|(\Phi(X_i), -1)\|^2 \leq R_{\text{MI}}^2$.

From positive definiteness of k_{I} it follows directly that $k_{\text{I}}(x, x) \pm 2k_{\text{I}}(x, x') + k_{\text{I}}(x', x') \geq 0$ and thus $2|k_{\text{I}}(x, x')| \leq k_{\text{I}}(x, x) + k_{\text{I}}(x', x') \leq 2R_{\text{I}}^2$.
Then we obtain $R_{\text{MI}}^2 = m^2 R_{\text{I}}^{2p} + 1$ as

$$\|(\Phi(X), -1)\|^2 = 1 + k_{\text{MI}}(X, X) = 1 + \sum_{x, x' \in X} k_{\text{I}}^p(x, x') \leq 1 + m^2 R_{\text{I}}^{2p} .$$

By construction of c_Φ we know that $\|c_\Phi\| = \|c_\phi\|^p$. Then

$$\|(c_\Phi, \xi_{\text{MI}} + 1)\|^2 = \|c_\phi\|^{2p} + (1 + \xi_{\text{MI}})^2 .$$

It follows that:

$$\frac{R_{\text{MI}}^2 \|(c_\Phi, \xi_{\text{MI}} + 1)\|^2}{\xi_{\text{MI}}^2} = \frac{(m^2 R_{\text{I}}^{2p} + 1)(4\|c_\phi\|^{2p} + (2 + \epsilon)^2)}{\epsilon^2} .$$

Then as $p = -\frac{\ln m}{\ln(1 - \epsilon)} + 1$ and setting

$$s = -\frac{2 \ln \|c_\phi\|}{\ln(1 - \epsilon)} \text{ and } q = -\frac{2 \ln R_{\text{I}}}{\ln(1 - \epsilon)}$$

the number of errors made by the MI kernel perceptron is bound by:

$$\frac{4R_{\text{I}}^2 \|c_\phi\|^2 m^2 m^{s+q}}{\epsilon^2} + \frac{(2 + \epsilon)^2 m^2 m^q}{\epsilon^2} + \frac{4\|c_\phi\|^2 m^s}{\epsilon^2} + \frac{(2 + \epsilon)^2}{\epsilon^2} . \qquad (4.3)$$

□

Note that sometimes, for k_{MI} to be positive definite, it is necessary that
$p \in \mathbb{N}$. In this case we use $\lceil p \rceil$ instead of p. The proof is then different from
the above one only in some constants.

To simplify the bound given in equation (4.3), we proceed as follows:
Using $\epsilon < 1$ we obtain

$$\frac{4R_{\text{I}}^2 \|c_\phi\|^2 m^2 m^{s+q}}{\epsilon^2} + \frac{9m^2 m^q}{\epsilon^2} + \frac{4\|c_\phi\|^2 m^s}{\epsilon^2} + \frac{9}{\epsilon^2} .$$

Furthermore assuming that $\|c_\phi\|, R_{\text{I}} \geq 1$ and thus $s, q \geq 0$; $m^s, m^q \geq 1$ we
obtain the bound

$$O\left(\frac{R_{\text{I}}^2 \|c_\phi\|^2 m^2 m^{s+q}}{\epsilon^2}\right) .$$

4.3.4 *Alternative MI Kernels*

We will now investigate another soft-maximal set kernel (Section 3.3.2) with respect to these two criteria — separation and convergence. In particular, we now consider the kernel

$$k_{\mathrm{MI}}^*(X, X') = \sum_{x \in X, x' \in X'} \exp\left[\gamma k_{\mathrm{I}}(x, x')\right] . \qquad (4.4)$$

Actually, this kernel is a special case of (4.2) (replace $k_{\mathrm{I}}(\cdot, \cdot)$ there by $\exp\left[k_{\mathrm{I}}(\cdot, \cdot)\right]$). However, separation and convergence with this kernel is not a special case of the above theorem. We will assume that the underlying problem is separable with $k_{\mathrm{I}}(\cdot, \cdot)$ and not necessarily with $\exp\left[k_{\mathrm{I}}(\cdot, \cdot)\right]$.

Similar to Section 4.3.2 we can now show that this kernel separates MI problems.

Lemma 4.3. *Let m be a bound on the cardinality of the bags X. Assume the underlying problem can be separated with $k_{\mathrm{I}}(x, x') = \langle \phi(x), \phi(x') \rangle$ such that for some c_ϕ it holds for all x that $\nu_{\mathrm{I}}(x) \langle \phi(x), c_\phi \rangle \geq \epsilon > 0$. Then the corresponding MI concept ν_{MI} is separable with the kernel k_{MI}^*, as defined in (4.4), for $\gamma > \frac{\ln m}{2\epsilon}$.*

Proof. Let the function f be defined as:

$$f(X) = \sum_{x \in X} \exp\left[\gamma \langle \phi^*(x), c_\phi \rangle\right] .$$

If $\nu_{\mathrm{MI}}(X) = +1$ then

$$f(X) \geq \exp\left[\gamma\epsilon\right] > \exp\left[\frac{\ln m}{2}\right] = \sqrt{m} .$$

If $\nu_{\mathrm{MI}}(X) = -1$ then

$$f(X) \leq m \exp\left[-\gamma\epsilon\right] < m \exp\left[-\frac{\ln m}{2}\right] = \sqrt{m} .$$

$\square$

Next we investigate the convergence of the kernel perceptron with the alternative MI kernel.

Theorem 4.3. *The number of mistakes made by the kernel perceptron with the MI kernel as defined in (4.4) can be bounded by a function that is polynomial in the size m of the bags but exponential in the parameters $R_{\mathrm{I}}, \epsilon, \|c_\phi\|$ of the underlying concept.*

Proof. Let all variables and functions be defined as in the proof of Lemma 4.3. Let Φ be such that $k_{\mathrm{MI}}^*(X, X') = \langle \Phi(X), \Phi(X') \rangle$ and c_Φ such that $f(X) = \langle \Phi(X), c_\Phi \rangle$. Let R_{I} be such that $k_{\mathrm{I}}(x, x) \leq R_{\mathrm{I}}^2$ and let $(X_1, Y_1), \ldots (X_n, Y_n); X \subseteq \mathcal{X}; Y_i \in \{-1, +1\}$ be a sequence of labelled bags. With $\gamma = \frac{\ln m}{\epsilon}$ we have:
If $\nu_{\mathrm{MI}}(X) = +1$ then

$$f(X) \geq \exp[\gamma \epsilon] = \exp[\ln m] = m \ .$$

If $\nu_{\mathrm{MI}}(X) = -1$ then

$$f(X) \leq m \exp[-\gamma \epsilon] = m \exp[-\ln m] = 1 \ .$$

To apply Novikoff's theorem, we consider

$$Y_i \left\langle \left(\Phi(X_i), -1 \right), \left(c_\Phi, \frac{m+1}{2} \right) \right\rangle \geq \frac{m-1}{2} = \xi_{\mathrm{MI}} \ .$$

Next, we need to find $\|(c_\Phi, \frac{m+1}{2})\|^2$ and R_{MI} such that $\|(\Phi(X_i), -1)\|^2 \leq R_{\mathrm{MI}}^2$ for all X_i. Using again $2|k_{\mathrm{I}}(x, x')| \leq k_{\mathrm{I}}(x, x) + k_{\mathrm{I}}(x', x') \leq 2R_{\mathrm{I}}^2$, we obtain $R_{\mathrm{MI}}^2 = 1 + m^2 \exp[\gamma R_{\mathrm{I}}^2]$ as

$$\begin{aligned} \|(\Phi(X), -1)\|^2 &= 1 + k_{\mathrm{MI}}(X, X) \\ &= 1 + \sum_{x, x' \in X} \exp[\gamma k_{\mathrm{I}}(x, x')] \\ &\leq 1 + m^2 \exp[\gamma R_{\mathrm{I}}^2] \ . \end{aligned}$$

By construction of c_Φ we know that $\|c_\Phi\|^2 = \exp[\gamma \|c_\phi\|^2]$. Thus

$$\left\| \left(c_\Phi, \frac{m+1}{2} \right) \right\|^2 = \exp[\gamma \|c_\phi\|^2] + \left(\frac{m+1}{2} \right)^2 \ .$$

Then

$$\frac{R_{\mathrm{MI}}^2 \, \|(c_\Phi, \frac{m+1}{2})\|^2}{\xi_{\mathrm{MI}}^2} = \frac{\left(1 + m^2 \exp[\gamma R_{\mathrm{I}}^2] \right) \left(\exp[\gamma \|c_\phi\|^2] + \left(\frac{m+1}{2} \right)^2 \right)}{\left(\frac{m-1}{2} \right)^2} \ .$$

$\square$

Note that in the above proof we have quietly assumed $m > 1$. Otherwise, the margin would become zero and the bound infinite. This is due to our choice of γ.

We can simplify the above bound to

$$O \left(m^2 \exp[\gamma R_{\mathrm{I}}^2 + \gamma \|c_\phi\|^2] \right) = O \left(m^2 m^{\frac{R_{\mathrm{I}}^2}{\epsilon}} m^{\frac{\|c_\phi\|^2}{\epsilon}} \right) \ .$$

4.3.5 *Learning MI Ray Concepts*

Having shown in the previous section that MI problems can be separated with our MI kernel, we will now describe a simple approach that can be used to apply support vector machines as well as other propositional learning algorithms to MI problems. The motivation is based on some observations in the drug activity prediction domain. The advantage of this approach is the efficiency — in real world drug activity prediction problems bags can be huge which renders the computation of k_{MI} too expensive. In the empirical evaluation of this method (see Section 4.5.2) we will show that — in spite of the simplicity of this approach — an SVM using this kernel can outperform several other MI learning algorithms.

Statistics If we can make further assumptions on the properties of $\mathcal{X}$, such as being generated by a normal distribution, by a mixture thereof, or other properties that can be summarised in a compact fashion then computing statistics on $X, X' \in \mathcal{X}$ can be useful in defining kernels on sets.

Definition 4.6. Denote by $s : X \mapsto s(X)$ a map computing statistics on $X \subset \mathcal{X}$. Then we call

$$k_{\mathrm{stat}}(X, X') := k(s(X), s(X')) \tag{4.5}$$

the statistic kernel.

Here $s(X)$ is a collection of properties of the set, say the mean, median, maximum, minimum, etc. Typically, $s(X)$ will be a vector of real numbers. A similar approach has been used in the context of inductive logic programming [Krogel and Wrobel (2001)], where relational aggregations are used to compute statistics over a database.

As described above, it is not uncommon in drug activity prediction to represent a molecule by a bag of descriptions of its different conformations where each conformation is in turn described by a feature vector. It is often believed that the concept space of drug activity prediction can be described by putting upper and lower bounds on the components of these feature vectors. Consider MI rays, i.e., concepts on sets of reals such that

$$r_{\mathrm{MI}-\theta}(X) \Leftrightarrow \exists\, x \in X : x \geq \theta \ .$$

These concepts are the complement (negation) of upper bounds. Motivated by the observation that $r_{\mathrm{MI}-\theta}$ can be learnt using only the maximal element of the set, we find the following statistics kernel particularly interesting for drug activity prediction:

Example 4.6 (Minimax Kernel). *Define* s *to be the vector of the coordinate-wise maxima and minima of* X, *i.e.,*

$$s(X) = (\min_{x \in X} x_1, \ldots, \min_{x \in X} x_m, \max_{x \in X} x_1, \ldots, \max_{x \in X} x_m) \ .$$

In our experiments we used a polynomial modifier with $s(X)$, that is, $k(X, X') = (\langle s(X), s(X') \rangle + 1)^p$.

4.4   Related Work

In this section we briefly describe some work related to the results presented in this section. We begin with work on kernels for general data structures and proceed with work on multi-instance learning.

4.4.1   *Kernels for General Data Structures*

Using kernel methods for learning in propositional logic has been investigated by a number of researchers [Sadohara (2001); Kowalczyk *et al.* (2002); Khardon *et al.* (2002)]. Propositional and attribute-value logic, however, do not offer the flexibility in modelling that higher-order logic does.

Similarly, the kernels reviewed in Section 3.4 are also not as general as the kernels presented in this chapter, rather are they on particular data structures like strings and trees. Although our default kernel for basic terms also offers special case kernels for strings and trees, the general framework we propose is more flexible as it allows the user to incorporate also other kernel functions. The choice of the kernel function for a particular part of an object always depends on the knowledge about that part.

Kernel methods have been applied in inductive logic programming [Krogel and Wrobel (2001)] by exploiting the link structure in databases and using relational aggregations to compute statistics about the instance in the database. Approaches that transform instances represented by relational structures into a propositional or attribute-value representation are known as propositionalisation approaches. For an overview see Kramer *et al.* (2001b), Knobbe *et al.* (2002), and Perlich and Provost (2006). Like other learning algorithms, support vector machines can be applied to such propositionalised data. Most propositionalisation approaches share with the basic term kernel the problems of dealing with identifiers and links. Most propositionalisation approaches still try to exploit the link structure and overcome the convergence and computational problems by exploiting the links only until a given maximal depth is reached. Obviously, a similar technique could be used in our kernel function as this essentially means that a structure with links is viewed as a structure without links. We do deliberately not use this approach, rather will we consider truly exploiting link structure in Chapter 4.6 where we describe kernels for directed and undirected graphs. In Section 4.5 where we describe different applications of basic term kernels, we will compare them on one domain to the mini-max kernel (Section 4.3.5) which is a kind of propositionalisation approach. We will there show that this approach works well on domains with a simple relational structure but fails to work well on more complex structures, where the basic term kernels show superior performance. Other applications that we consider in Section 4.5 have a structure that is very difficult to be exploited by propositionalisation approaches and we do not know of any approaches to propositionalise these.

Mavroeidis and Flach (2003) proposed a kernel function on terms in a first order logic and suggested an extension to also handle sets and multisets. The kernel function can, however, not be applied to arbitrary abstractions like the ones considered in this chapter. Other kernel function for relational data have been proposed in [Cumby and Roth (2003); Landwehr *et al.* (2006); Passerini *et al.* (2006); Wachman and Khardon (2007)]. For other learning algorithms on basic terms see [Ng (2005); Ng and Lloyd (2008)].

4.4.2 *Multi-Instance Learning*

Apart from approaches that ignore the MI setting during training, two major categories of approaches can be distinguished: upgrading existing attribute-value learning algorithms, and designing a new learning algorithm specifically for MI problems. Algorithms that have specifically been designed for MI problems are: the axis-parallel rectangles (APR) algorithm and variants [Dietterich *et al.* (1997)], an algorithm based on simple statistics of the bags [Auer (1997)], and algorithms based on the diverse density approach [Maron and Lozano-Pérez (1998); Zhang and Goldman (2002)]. Algorithms that have been upgraded until now are: the lazy learning algorithms Bayesian-kNN and Citation-kNN [Wang and Zucker (2000)], the neural network MI-NN [Ramon and De Raedt (2000)], the decision tree learner RELIC [Ruffo (2001)], and the rule learner (Naive)RipperMI [Chevaleyre and Zucker (2001)]. Inductive logic programming algorithms have also been used, for instance, the first-order decision tree learner TILDE [Blockeel and De Raedt (1998)].

Novel kernels for multi-instance problems are proposed in [Blaschko and Hofmann (2006); Tao *et al.* (2007); Kwok and Cheung (2007)]. Andrews *et al.* (2003) describes, how the quadratic program underlying support vector machines can be reformulated to be applicable to MI problems. The two alternative algorithms presented in [Andrews *et al.* (2003)] can, however, only be formulated by mixed-integer programs. For that, heuristic solutions have to be used to make the algorithm feasible. A different adaption of support vector machines to multi-instance problems is proposed by Bunescu and Mooney (2007) which focusses on exploiting the sparsity of positive bags. These approaches are not only applied to classification of chemical compounds but also to image (region) classification. These algorithm and the algorithm presented in [Ramon and De Raedt (2000)] share with our approach that they are all based on well known learning algorithms for the standard classification setting.

Theoretical results on MI learning can be found, for example, in [Blum and Kalai (1998)] and [Auer *et al.* (1997)]. Both papers present PAC type sample complexity bounds. An empirical evaluation of the latter algorithm can be found in [Auer (1997)]. One disadvantage of these bounds is that the sample complexity there depends at least quadratically on the dimensionality of the instances. Furthermore, the learning algorithms considered in these papers are special purpose algorithms that are not based on well known learning algorithms for the standard classification setting.

4.5   Applications and Experiments

In this section, we empirically investigate the appropriateness of our kernel definitions on a variety of domains. The implementation and application of most algorithms mentioned below has been simplified by using the Weka data mining toolkit [Witten and Frank (2000)]. In the tables presented in this section we will use the acronym 'KeS' (kernel for structured data) to refer to a support vector machine using our kernel for basic terms, and the acronym 'DeS' (distance for structured data) to refer to a nearest neighbour algorithm using our distance for basic terms.

4.5.1   *East/West Challenge*

We performed some experiments with the East/West challenge dataset introduced earlier in Section 4.2.3. We used the default kernels for all types, i.e., the product kernel for all numbers, the matching kernel for all other atomic types, and no kernel modifiers. As this toy data set only contains 20 labelled instances, the aim of this experiment was not to achieve a high predictive accuracy but to check whether this problem can actually be separated using our default kernel. We applied a support vector machine and a 3-nearest neighbour classifier to the full data set. In both experiments, we achieved 100% training accuracy, verifying that the data is indeed separable with the default kernels.

4.5.2 *Drug Activity Prediction*

Often drug activity prediction problems are used to assess MI learning algorithms (Section 4.3). The musk domain, introduced by Dietterich *et al.* (1997), involves predicting the strength of synthetic musk molecules. The class labels have been found by human domain experts. Two overlapping data sets are available. Musk1 contains 47 molecules labelled as 'Musk' (if the molecule is known to smell musky) and 45 labelled as 'Non-Musk'. The 92 molecules are altogether described by 476 conformations. Musk2 contains 39 'Musk' molecules and 63 'Non-Musk' molecules, described by 6598 conformations altogether. 162 uniformly distributed rays have been chosen to represent each conformation. Additionally, four further features are used that describe the position of an oxygen atom in the conformation.

The formal specification of the structure of the musk data set along with the kernel applied in [Gärtner *et al.* (2002a)] is as follows:

```
type Molecule = Con -> Bool with modifier normalised
type Con = (Rays,Distance,Offset) with modifier gaussian 10^-5.5
type Rays = (Real,Real,...,Real)
type Offset = (Real,Real,Real)
type Distance = Real
```

Several empirical results on these two data sets have been achieved and reported the in literature. The results in Table 4.1 are in alphabetical order. They have either been obtained by multiple tenfold cross-validation runs (10CV) or by leave-one-out estimation (LOO). The best classification results from each section are marked in boldface. The table is organised as follows: The first section contains algorithms specifically designed for MI learning. The second one contains algorithms that are designed as general purpose learning algorithms, but have been adapted to learn MI problems. The results reported in this table are of the algorithms mentioned in Section

Table 4.1   Classification errors of other algorithms (in %) on Musk1 and Musk2.

ALGORITHM	MUSK1	MUSK2	EVAL.
EM-DD	15.2	15.1	10CV
GFS KDE APR	8.7	19.6	10CV
ITERATIVE APR	**7.6**	**10.8**	10CV
MAXDD	12.0	16.0	10CV
MULTINST	23.3	16.0	10CV
BAYESIAN-KNN	9.8	17.6	LOO
CITATION-KNN	**7.6**	13.7	LOO
MI-NN	11.1	17.5	10CV
MI-SVM	16.0	21.1	10CV
MI-SVM	11.0	14.7	10CV
NAIVERIPPERMI	12.0	23.0	?
RELIC	16.3	**12.7**	10CV
RIPPERMI	12.0	23.0	?
TILDE	13.0	20.6	10CV

Table 4.2   Classification errors of some learning algorithms (in %) on Musk1 and Musk2 in very simple feature spaces.

ALGORITHM	MUSK1		MUSK2	
	LOO	10-OUT	LOO	10-OUT
MINIMAX FEATURE SPACE				
DECISION TREE	19.6	18.5	19.6	17.6
BOOSTED DT	**14.1**	**12.0**	20.6	20.6
BOOSTED NB	**14.1**	**12.0**	16.7	**16.7**
IGNORING THE MI SETTING WHILE TRAINING				
DECISION TREE		28.3		43.1
BOOSTED DT		18.5		28.4
BOOSTED NB		20.3		36.7
SVM		**13.0**		**18.6**

4.3.1. Where applicable we report those results that have been reported in [Andrews *et al.* (2003)]. Table 4.2 contains algorithms that have been run on the musk data using the minimax feature space described above, and by ignoring the MI setting while learning but obeying it when testing. That is, we viewed the training data as the union over all training instances and labelled each element of a set with the label of the set. That way we can learn a function that classifies the elements of the test instances. A test instance is then labelled positive if one of its elements is classified positive by the hypothesis function. For the SVM, an RBF kernel was used with $\gamma = 10^{-6}$. Boosted NB (DT) refers to a boosted naïve Bayes (decision tree) classifier.

Table 4.3 contains results from using SVMs with a polynomial version

Table 4.3 Classification errors for SVMs with the minimax kernel and the MI kernel (in %) on Musk1 and Musk2.

KERNEL	MUSK1		MUSK2	
	LOO	10-OUT	LOO	10-OUT
POLYNOMIAL MINIMAX KERNEL				
$p = 5$	**7.6**	**8.4 ± 0.7**	13.7	13.7 ± 1.2
LOO		15.5 ± 2.2		17.5 ± 2.1
LOO, NORMALISED		17.5 ± 2.1		18.5 ± 1.9
MI KERNEL $(k_I(x, x') = \exp(-\gamma\|x - x'\|^2))$				
$\gamma = 10^{-5.5}$	13.0	13.6 ± 1.1	**7.8**	12.0 ± 1.0
LOO		15.0 ± 1.9		19.0 ± 2.2
LOO, NORMALISED		19.0 ± 2.7		14.5 ± 2.4

of the minimax kernel and using MI kernels. Due to the extremely small sample size (MUSK1 contains only 96 bags and Musk2 only 104) which is furthermore not divisible by 10, 10-fold cross-validation is a very noisy and unreliable process. To address this problem, we opted to compute an error estimate by averaging over 1000 trials of randomly leaving out 10 instances. The advantage of this approach is that in addition to the error estimates we also obtain confidence intervals, which allows us to compare our results with the ones obtained in the literature. Finally, for the sake of comparability, also the leave-one-out error was computed.

We chose a Gaussian modifier for the elements of the bag, using the rule of thumb that σ^2 should be in the order of magnitude of $2d^2 \approx 10^5$ or lower, where d is the dimensionality of the data[1]. This led to an almost optimal choice of parameters (the optimum lay within an order of magnitude of the initial estimate). As for preprocessing, the data was rescaled to zero mean and unit variance on a per coordinate basis. In the ray-kernel case, we simply used a polynomial kernel on $s(X)$. In order to avoid adjusting too many parameters, we chose the ν-parameterised support vector machines (Section 2.4.2), with ν set to 0.075. The latter corresponds to an error level comparable to the ones in the published literature.

To assess the true performance of the estimation procedure, one must not, however, fix a set of parameters and only then use a cross-validation step to assess the error for the now *fixed* set of parameters. We therefore adjusted the parameters, such as kernel width and the value of ν and γ for each leave-10-out sample separately and computed the CV error for this procedure. 20 random leave-10-out samples were drawn. The corresponding results are reported in Table 4.3, denoted by LOO and LOO norm (the

---

[1]Note that the parameter p of MI kernels is chosen implicitly when choosing γ; as for Gaussian RBF kernels, k_1^p is a Gaussian RBF kernel itself.

latter refers to kernels with normalisation in feature space). It is rather obvious that the method degrades dramatically due to the small sample size effects (only 100 observations). Also, the choice of suitable normalisation in feature space yields only diminishing returns, given the high variance of the model selection procedure. It is well known [Cherkassky and Mulier (1998)] that the choice of model selection rules has a significant influence on the performance of the overall estimator, quite often more than the choice of the estimator itself.

The fact that polynomial minimax kernels outperformed the MI kernel (Gaussian RBF) on Musk1 can be explained by the fact that Musk1 contains much fewer conformations per bag than Musk2, hence the min and max statistic $s(X)$ is a quite adequate description of each bag. A small bag size is a major shortcoming also of other (synthetically generated) datasets, making them very unrealistic – as to our understanding real-world drug activity prediction problems usually involve big bags.

It has been mentioned in the literature that multi-instance problems capture most of the complexity of relational learning problems [Raedt (1998)]. This experiment demonstrates that our general approach is competitive with special-purpose algorithms applied to structured data. Furthermore, our kernel-based approach has the additional advantage that learning problems other than simple classification can also be tackled by simply changing to a different kernel method.

4.5.3 *Structure Elucidation from Spectroscopic Analyses*

The problem of diterpene structure elucidation from ^{13}C nuclear magnetic resonance (NMR) spectra was introduced to the machine learning community in [Džeroski *et al.* (1998b)]. There, different algorithms were compared on a dataset of 1503 diterpene ^{13}C NMR spectra. Diterpenes are compounds made up from 4 isoprene units and are thus terpenes – the general term used for oligomers of isoprene. Terpenes are the major component of essential oils found in many plants. Often these oils are biologically active or exhibit some medical properties most of which are due to the presence of terpenes.

NMR spectroscopy is one of the most important techniques in analytical chemistry. It is used as a tool in the search for new pharmaceutical products to help in determining the structure-activity relationships of biologically active compounds. Once these have been determined, it is clear which variations of the compound do not lose the biological activity. In NMR

Table 4.4   Classification accuracy (in %) on diterpene data

FOIL	ICL	TILDE	RIBL	KES	DES
46.5	65.3	81.6	86.5	94.7	97.1

experiments the sample is placed in an external magnetic field and the nuclei are excited by a pulse over a range of radio frequencies. The signal emitted by the nuclei as they return to equilibrium with their surrounding is analysed to obtain an NMR spectrum of radio frequencies.

In the dataset considered in [Džeroski *et al.* (1998b)], each spectrum is described by the frequency and multiplicity of all peaks. Depending on the number of protons connected to the carbon atom, the multiplicity of a peak is either a singlet (no proton), a doublet (one proton), a triplet (two protons), or a quartet (three protons). The formal specification of the data and the kernel is as follows:

```
type Spectrum = Frequency -> Multiplicity
type Frequency = Real with modifier gaussian 0.6
data Multiplicity = s | d | t | q | 0 with default 0
```

In addition to the multiplicities s(ingulet), d(oublet), t(riplet), and q(uartet) we introduced also the multiplicity 0 and declared it as the default data constructor of the type `Multiplicity`. The abstraction `Spectrum` then maps every frequency (every real number) that is not emitted by the molecule to 0 and every emitted frequency to the multiplicity of the corresponding carbon atom.

The dataset consists of 1503 spectra of diterpenes, classified into 23 different classes according to their skeleton structure as follows (number of examples per class in brackets): Trachyloban (9), Kauran (353), Beyeran (72), Atisiran (33), Ericacan (2), Gibban (13), Pimaran (155), 6,7-seco-Kauran (9), Erythoxilan (9), Spongian(10), Cassan (12), Labdan (448), Clerodan (356), Portulan (5), 5,10-seco-Clerodan (4), 8,9-seco-Labdan (6), and seven classes with only one example each.

The accuracies reported in literature range up to 86.5%, achieved by RIBL [Emde and Wettschereck (1996)]. Other results were reported for FOIL [Quinlan (1990)], TILDE [Blockeel and De Raedt (1998)], and ICL [De Raedt and Van Laer (1995)]. See Table 4.4 for details. After including some manually constructed features, 91.2% accuracy has been achieved by the best system – a 1-nearest neighbour classifier using a first-order distance (RIBL).

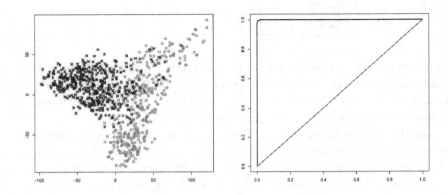

Figure 4.1   Left: Projection of the diterpenes with structure type Labdan and Clerodan onto their first two principal directions. Right: ROC curve for the binary classification problem of separating Labdan and Clerodan diterpenes using a 1-nearest neighbour algorithm.

We applied a support vector machine (see column 'KeS') using the above presented kernel function to the diterpene dataset without the manually constructed features and achieved results between 94.74% and 95.48% accuracy over a range of parameters (the parameter of the Gaussian modifier was chosen such that $\frac{1}{\sigma^2} \in \{0.6, 0.06, 0.006\}$ and the default $C = 1$ complexity parameter of the SVM was used). We also applied a 1-nearest neighbour algorithm (see column 'DeS') to this domain and achieved accuracies between 97.07% and 98.07% on the same set of parameters. For the overview in Table 4.4 and for the following experiments, the parameter of the Gaussian modifier was fixed to 0.6.

To further strengthen our results, we performed kernel PCA of the diterpene data and plotted a ROC curve. To allow for a useful illustration we restricted the data to molecules with structure classes Labdan and Clerodan. Figure 4.1 (left) shows the projection of molecules of these two classes onto the first two principal components (Section 2.4.5). It can be seen that already the first two principal directions separate the classes Labdan and Clerodan quite well. Figure 4.1 (right) shows the ROC curve (Section 2.2.3) obtained for a 1-nearest neighbour algorithm on Labdan and Clerodan diterpenes in a leave-one-out experiment. The area under this curve is 0.9998. This is very close to the optimal area under the ROC curve of 1.0.

4.5.4 *Spatial Clustering*

The problem of clustering spatially close and thematically similar data points occurs, for example, when given demographic data about households in a city and trying to optimise facility locations given this demographic data. The location planning algorithms can usually only deal with a fairly small number of customers (less than 1000) and even for small cities the number of households easily exceeds 10000. Therefore, several households have to be aggregated so that as little information as possible is lost. Thus the households that are aggregated have to be spatially close (so that little geographic information is lost) and similar in their demographic description (so that little demographic information is lost). The problem is to automatically find such an aggregation using an unsupervised learning algorithm.

Due to the difficulty in obtaining suitable data, we investigated this problem on a slightly smaller scale. The demographic data was already aggregated for data protection and anonymity reasons such that information is given not on a household level but on a (part of) street level. The data set describes roughly 500 points in a small German city by its geographic coordinates and 76 statistics, e.g., the number of people above or below certain age levels, the number of people above or below certain income levels, and the number of males or females living in a small area around the data point.

The simplest way to represent this data is a feature vector with 78 entries (2 for the x, y coordinates and 76 for the statistics). Drawing the results of a simple k-means algorithm on this representation clearly shows that although the spatial coordinates are taken into account, spatially compact clusters cannot be achieved. This is due to the fact that the semantics of the coordinates and the demographic statistics are different.

A better representation along with the kernel specification is as follows.

```
type Neighbourhood = Coords -> Statistics
type Coords=(Real,Real) with modifier gaussian 0.1
type Statistics = (Real,Real,...,Real) with modifier normalised
```

Here, the type Coords is used for the geographical coordinates and the type Statistics is used for the statistics of a neighbourhood of households. A neighbourhood is represented by an abstraction of type Coords -> Statistics that maps the coordinates of that neighbourhood to its statistics and the coordinates of all other neighbourhoods to the default term (0,0,...,0). Thus each abstraction is a lookup table with a single

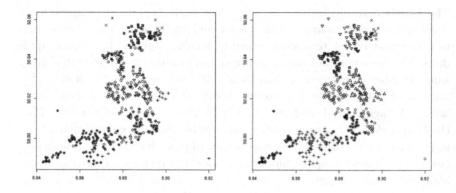

Figure 4.2   Plots of households spatially clustered with different parameters (left: 0.1, right: 0.02). Spatial compactness increases as the parameter is decreased.

entry corresponding to the neighbourhood represented by the abstraction. These abstractions capture the functional dependency that the coordinates determine the statistics of the neighbourhoods. It also means that the kernel on neighbourhoods multiplies the kernel on the coordinates with the kernel on the statistics. (See Part 2 of Definition 4.3.)

It is worth noting that this use of abstractions is a convenient method for getting background knowledge into a kernel. Generally, each abstraction has a single entry consisting of an individual as the item and the features of that individual as the value of that item. The features, represented as a feature vector of booleans, for example, would be constructed from the background knowledge for the application. In the application of this section, the individuals are the coordinates of neighbourhoods and the features are their statistics.

Using this representation and applying a version of the k-means algorithm (Section 2.4.6) with the given kernel shows that the clusters are spatially compact (compactness depending on the choice of the kernel parameter). Two sample illustrations can be found in Figure 4.2. Instances belonging to the same cluster are represented by the same symbol.

4.6 Summary

Representation is a key issue in bringing together kernel methods and learning from structured data. In this chapter we defined a kernel for structured data, proved that it is positive definite, and showed that it works well in practise. Our kernel definition follows a 'syntax-driven' approach making use of a knowledge representation formalism that is able to accurately and naturally model the underlying semantics of structured data. It is based on the principles of using a typed syntax and representing individuals as (closed) terms. The typed syntax is important for pruning search spaces and for modelling as closely as possible the semantics of the data in a human- and machine-readable form. The individuals-as-terms representation is a simple and natural generalisation of the attribute-value representation and collects all information about an individual in a single term. In spite of this simplicity, the knowledge representation formalism is still powerful enough to accurately model highly structured data.

The definition of our kernel, along with the example applications presented, show that structured data can reasonably be embedded in inner product spaces. The main theoretical contribution of this section is the proof that the kernel is positive definite on all basic terms (of the same type), and that the kernel perceptron converges to a consistent hypothesis function on multi-instance problems.

Empirical results have been provided on some real-world domains. For instance, on the diterpene dataset a support vector machine and a 1-nearest neighbour classifier using a kernel function from the framework presented in this paper improved over the best accuracy published in literature by more than 8% and 10%, respectively. This corresponds to making less than a third of the errors of the best algorithm applied to this problem so far.

Chapter 5

Graph Kernels

A perturbation in the reality field in which a spontaneous self-monitoring negentropic vortex is formed, tending progressively to subsume and incorporate its environment into arrangements of information.

(Philip K. Dick, VALIS)

In the previous chapter we showed how kernel functions can be defined for instances that have a natural representation as terms in a higher order logic. Although this representation is very general and can even be used to represent graphs, in this case one needs to introduce identifiers (see the end of Section 4.1). These identifiers are hard to take care of in a general framework as they might introduce recursion, giving rise to convergence and computational complexity issues. In contrast, ignoring these identifiers — as done in the previous chapter — leads to a loss of information. Though basic term kernels can take into account the information in the vertices and edges of a graph, they can not take into account the structure of graphs.

One line of research on kernels for graphs has concentrated on special types of graphs, for example strings and trees (see Sections 3.4.3 and 3.4.4). In this chapter we present work on data represented by general graphs. We will answer two important questions: is it possible to define graph kernels that distinguish between all (non-isomorphic) graphs and, if not, how can efficient graph kernels be defined that capture most of the structure of the graphs. Firstly, we prove that for any kernel function that is capable of fully recognising the structure of graphs, it is unlikely that there exists an efficient way to compute it. Secondly, we present a family of graph kernels based on walks which can be computed in polynomial time. Thirdly, we introduce a kernel function based on cycles in a graph that can not be

127

computed in polynomial time in general; that proofs, however, empirically very effective for classifying a large dataset of molecules. Last but not least, we show that real-world problems can be solved with these graph kernels and that for real-world datasets there exist more efficient graph kernels exploiting special properties of these domains.

The outline of this chapter is as follows: Section 5.1 first gives an intuitive overview over the important results of this chapter. Section 5.2 gives then a brief overview of graph theoretic concepts. Section 5.3 defines what might be the ideal graph kernel but also shows that such kernels cannot be computed in polynomial time. Section 5.4 introduces graph kernels based on common walks in the graphs and Section 5.5 introduces cyclic pattern kernels on graphs. Section 5.6 briefly surveys related work. Section 5.7 describes an application of these graph kernels in a relational reinforcement learning setting and Section 5.8 describes an application to molecule classification. Finally, Section 5.9 concludes with future work.

5.1   Motivation and Approach

Consider a graph kernel in the spirit of intersection and decomposition kernels (Section 3.3.1) — similar to kernels on special graphs (Sections 3.4.3 and 3.4.4) — that decomposes a graph into the set of its subgraphs. Alternatively, one could consider the map Φ that has one feature Φ_H for each possible graph H, each feature $\Phi_H(G)$ measuring how many subgraphs of G have the same structure as graph H (that is, are isomorphic to H).

Using the inner product in this feature space, graphs satisfying certain properties can be identified. In particular, one could decide whether a graph has a Hamiltonian path, i.e., a sequence of adjacent vertices and edges that contains every vertex and edge exactly once. Now this problem is known to be *NP*-complete; therefore we strongly believe that such kernels can not be computed in polynomial time. We thus consider alternative graph kernels.

In Section 5.4 we investigate an alternative approach based on measuring the number of walks with common label sequence. Although the set of common walks can be infinite, the inner product in this feature space can be computed in polynomial time by first building the product graph and then computing the limit of a matrix power series of the adjacency matrix. An alternative walk-based kernel function exploits only the length of all walks between all pairs of vertices with given label.

To illustrate these kernels, consider a simple graph with four vertices

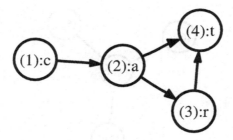

Figure 5.1   A directed graph with four vertices. We show the vertex identifiers (unique within each graph) in brackets and the vertex labels after the colon.

$1, 2, 3, 4$ labelled 'c', 'a', 'r', and 't', respectively. We also have four edges in this graph: one from the vertex labelled 'c' to the vertex labelled 'a', one from 'a' to 'r', one from 'r' to 't', and one from 'a' to 't'. Figure 5.1 illustrates this graph. The non-zero features in the label pair feature space are $\phi_{c,c} = \phi_{a,a} = \phi_{r,r} = \phi_{t,t} = \lambda_0$, $\phi_{c,a} = \phi_{a,r} = \phi_{r,t} = \lambda_1$, $\phi_{a,t} = \lambda_1 + \lambda_2$, $\phi_{c,r} = \lambda_2$, and $\phi_{c,t} = \lambda_2 + \lambda_3$. The non-zero features in the label sequence feature space are $\phi_c = \phi_a = \phi_r = \phi_t = \sqrt{\lambda_0}$, $\phi_{ca} = \phi_{ar} = \phi_{at} = \phi_{rt} = \sqrt{\lambda_1}$, $\phi_{car} = \phi_{cat} = \sqrt{\lambda_2}$, and $\phi_{cart} = \sqrt{\lambda_3}$. The λ_i are user defined weights and the square-roots appear only to make the computation of the kernel more elegant. In particular, we show how closed forms of the inner products in this feature space can be computed for exponential and geometric choices of λ_i.

The above kernels can be applied to directed as well as undirected graphs. For undirected graphs we derive a polynomial time algorithm to compute these graph kernels. In Section 5.5 we consider the class of undirected graphs which contain few cycles. For this class of graphs we propose a kernel function with time complexity polynomial in the number of vertices and cycles in the graph. For a real-world dataset of molecules, this kernel function can be computed much faster than the walk-based graph kernels described above.

The key idea of cyclic pattern kernels is to decompose every undirected graph into the set of cyclic and tree patterns in the graph. A cyclic pattern is a unique representation of the label sequence corresponding to a simple cycle in the graph. A tree pattern in the graph is a unique representation of the label sequence corresponding to a tree in the forest made up by the edges of the graph that do not belong to any cycle. The cyclic-pattern

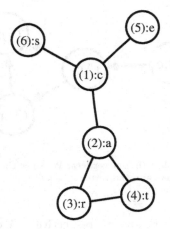

Figure 5.2 An undirected graph with a cyclic and a tree pattern. We show the vertex identifiers (unique within each graph) in brackets and the vertex labels after the colon.

kernel between two graphs is defined by the cardinality of the intersection of the pattern sets associated with each graph.

Consider a graph with vertices $1, \ldots, 6$ and labels (in the order of vertices) 'c', 'a', 'r', 't', 'e', and 's'. Let the edges be the set

$$\{\{1,2\}, \{2,3\}, \{3,4\}, \{2,4\}, \{1,5\}, \{1,6\}\}.$$

Figure 5.2 illustrates this graph. This graph has one simple cycle, and the lexicographically smallest representation of the labels along this cycle is the string 'art'. The bridges of the graph are $\{1,2\}, \{1,5\}, \{1,6\}$ and the bridges form a forest consisting of a single tree. The lexicographically smallest representation of the labels of this tree (in pre-order notation) is the string 'aces'.

5.2 Labelled Directed Graphs

This section gives a brief overview of labelled directed graphs. For a more in-depth discussion of these and related concepts the reader is referred to [Diestel (2000); Korte and Vygen (2002)].

5.2.1 *Basic Terminology and Notation*

Generally, a *graph* G is described by a finite set of *vertices* $\mathcal{V}$, a finite set of *edges* $\mathcal{E}$, and a function Ψ. For *hypergraphs* this function maps each edge to a set of vertices $\Psi : \mathcal{E} \to \{X \subseteq \mathcal{V}\}$. For *undirected* graphs the codomain of the function is restricted to sets of vertices with two elements only $\Psi : \mathcal{E} \to \{X \subseteq \mathcal{V} : |X| = 2\}$. For *directed* graphs the function maps each edge to the tuple consisting of its initial and terminal node $\Psi : \mathcal{E} \to \{(u, v) \in \mathcal{V} \times \mathcal{V}\}$. Edges e in a directed graph for which $\Psi(e) = (v, v)$ are called *loops*. Two edges e, e' are *parallel* if $\Psi(e) = \Psi(e')$. We will sometimes assume some enumeration of the vertices in a graph, i.e., $\mathcal{V} = \{\nu_i\}_{i=1}^n$ where $n = |\mathcal{V}|$.

For *labelled* graphs there is additionally a set of labels Σ along with a function *label* assigning a label to each edge and/or vertex. In *edge-labelled* graphs, labels are assigned to edges only; in *vertex-labelled* graphs, labels are assigned to vertices only; and in *fully-labelled* graphs, labels are assigned to edges and vertices. Note that there are trivial maps between the three kinds of labelled graphs but concentrating on one or other kind simplifies the presentation in some of the following sections considerably. Graphs without labels can be seen as a special case of labelled graphs where the same label is assigned to each edge and/or vertex. For labelled graphs it is useful to have some enumeration of all possible labels at hand, i.e., $\Sigma = \{\ell_r\}_{r \in \mathbb{N}}$.[1]

The directed graphs we are mostly concerned with in this chapter are labelled directed graphs without parallel edges. In this case we can – for simplicity of notation – identify an edge with its image under the map Ψ. In Sections 5.5 and 5.8 we consider undirected graphs. In Section 5.7 we consider directed graphs with parallel edges. In Section 5.3 we consider directed graphs without labels. Everywhere else 'graph' will always refer to labelled directed graphs without parallel edges and each graph will be described by a pair $G = (\mathcal{V}, \mathcal{E})$ such that $\mathcal{E} \subseteq \mathcal{V} \times \mathcal{V}$. Note that undirected graphs can be seen as directed graphs where $(v_i, v_j) \in \mathcal{E} \Leftrightarrow (v_j, v_i) \in \mathcal{E}$.

To refer to the vertex and edge set of a specific graph we will use the notation $\mathcal{V}(G), \mathcal{E}(G)$. Wherever we distinguish two graphs by their subscript (G_i) or some other symbol (G', G^*) the same notation will be used to distinguish their vertex and edge sets.

Last but not least we need to define some special graphs. A *walk* w in a directed graph $G = (\mathcal{V}, \mathcal{E})$ is a sequence of vertices $w = v_1, v_2, \ldots v_{n+1}$; $v_i \in \mathcal{V}$ such that $(v_i, v_{i+1}) \in \mathcal{E}$. The *length* of the walk is equal to the

---

[1]While ℓ_1 will be used to always denote the same label, l_1 is a variable that can take different values, e.g., $\ell_1, \ell_2, \ldots$. The same holds for vertex ν_1 and variable v_1.

number of edges in this sequence, i.e., n in the above case. A *path* in a directed graph is a walk in which $v_i \neq v_j \Leftrightarrow i \neq j$. A *cycle* in a directed graph is a path with $(v_{n+1}, v_1) \in \mathcal{E}$. A *path- (cycle-) graph* is a graph for which a sequence containing all vertices exists that forms a path (cycle) and that does not contain any edges except the ones making up the path (cycle).

A graph $G = (\mathcal{V}, \mathcal{E})$ is called *connected* if there is a walk between any two vertices in the following graph: $(\mathcal{V}, \ \mathcal{E} \cup \{(u,v) : (v,u) \in \mathcal{E}\})$. For a graph $G = (\mathcal{V}(G), \mathcal{E}(G))$, we denote by $G[\mathcal{V}^*]$ the subgraph *induced* by the set of vertices $\mathcal{V}^* \subseteq \mathcal{V}(G)$, that is $G[\mathcal{V}^*] = (\mathcal{V}^*, \{(u,v) \in \mathcal{E}(G) : u,v \in \mathcal{V}^*\})$. A *subgraph* of G is a graph $H = (\mathcal{V}(H), \mathcal{E}(H))$ with $\mathcal{V}(H) \subseteq \mathcal{V}(G)$ and $\mathcal{E}(H) \subseteq \mathcal{E}(G[\mathcal{V}(H)])$. A subgraph H of G is *proper* if $\mathcal{V}(H) \subset \mathcal{V}(G)$; it is *spanning* if $\mathcal{V}(H) = \mathcal{V}(G)$. If a path or a cycle is a subgraph of a graph G, it is often called a walk or cycle in G. A spanning path in G is called a *Hamiltonian path*; a spanning cycle in G is called a *Hamiltonian cycle*.

5.2.2   *Matrix Notation and some Functions*

For the description of our graph kernels it turns out to be useful to have a matrix representation for (labelled directed) graphs. For two matrices A, B of the same dimensionality, the inner product is defined as $\langle A, B \rangle = \sum_{i,j} [A]_{ij} [B]_{ij}$.

A graph G can uniquely be described by its label and adjacency matrices. The label matrix L is defined by $[L]_{ri} = 1 \Leftrightarrow \ell_r = label(\nu_i)$, $[L]_{ri} = 0 \Leftrightarrow \ell_r \neq label(\nu_i)$. The adjacency matrix E is defined by $[E]_{ij} = 1 \Leftrightarrow (\nu_i, \nu_j) \in \mathcal{E}$, $[E]_{ij} = 0 \Leftrightarrow (\nu_i, \nu_j) \notin \mathcal{E}$. We also need to define some functions describing the neighbourhood of a vertex v in a graph G: $\delta^+(v) = \{(v,u) \in \mathcal{E}\}$ and $\delta^-(v) = \{(u,v) \in \mathcal{E}\}$. Here, $|\delta^+(v)|$ is called the *outdegree* of a vertex and $|\delta^-(v)|$ the *indegree*. Furthermore, the maximal indegree and outdegree are denoted by $\Delta^-(G) = max\{|\delta^-(v)|, v \in \mathcal{V}\}$ and $\Delta^+(G) = max\{|\delta^+(v)|, v \in \mathcal{V}\}$, respectively. It is clear that the maximal indegree equals the maximal column sum of the adjacency matrix and that the maximal outdegree equals the maximal row sum of the adjacency matrix.

Interpretation of Matrix Powers   First consider the diagonal matrix $LL^\top$. The i-th element of the diagonal of this matrix, i.e. $[LL^\top]_{ii}$, corresponds to the number of times label ℓ_i is assigned to a vertex in the graph. Now consider the matrix E. The component $[E]_{ij}$ describes whether there is an edge between vertex ν_i and ν_j. Now we combine the label and adjacency matrix as $LEL^\top$. Each component $[LEL^\top]_{ij}$ corresponds to the number of edges between vertices labelled ℓ_i and vertices labelled ℓ_j.

Replacing the adjacency matrix E by its n-th power ($n \in \mathbb{N}, n \geq 0$), the interpretation is quite similar. Each component $[E^n]_{ij}$ of this matrix gives the number of walks of length n from vertex ν_i to ν_j. Multiplying this with the label matrix, we obtain the matrix $LE^n L^\top$. Each component $[LE^n L^\top]_{ij}$ now corresponds to the number of walks of length n between vertices labelled ℓ_i and vertices labelled ℓ_j.

5.2.3 *Product Graphs*

Product graphs [Imrich and Klavžar (2000)] are a very interesting tool in discrete mathematics. The four most important graph products are the Cartesian, the strong, the direct, and the lexicographic product. While the most fundamental one is the Cartesian graph product, in our context the direct graph product is the most important one.

Usually, graph products are defined on unlabelled graphs. However, in many real-world machine learning problems it could be important to be able to deal with labelled graphs. We extend the definition of graph products to labelled graphs, as follows.

Definition 5.1. We denote the *direct product* of two graphs $G_1 = (\mathcal{V}_1, \mathcal{E}_1)$ and $G_2 = (\mathcal{V}_2, \mathcal{E}_2)$ by $G_1 \times G_2$. The vertex and edge set of the direct product are respectively defined as:

$$\mathcal{V}(G_1 \times G_2) = \{(v_1, v_2) \in \mathcal{V}_1 \times \mathcal{V}_2 : (label(v_1) = label(v_2))\}$$
$$\mathcal{E}(G_1 \times G_2) = \{((u_1, u_2), (v_1, v_2)) \in (\mathcal{V}(G_1 \times G_2))^2 :$$
$$(u_1, v_1) \in \mathcal{E}_1 \wedge (u_2, v_2) \in \mathcal{E}_2 \wedge (label(u_1, v_1) = label(u_2, v_2))\} .$$

A vertex (edge) in the graph $G_1 \times G_2$ has the same label as the corresponding vertices (edges) in G_1 and G_2.

Figure 5.3 illustrates two graphs along with their direct product.

5.2.4 *Limits of Matrix Power Series*

In Section 3.2.1 we already briefly discussed limits of matrix power series of the form $\lim_{n \to \infty} \sum_{i=0}^{n} \lambda_i E^i$. For symmetric matrices (i.e., undirected graphs), these limits can be computed by means of the limits of eigenvalues of E.

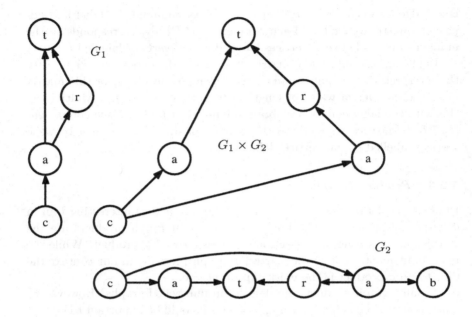

Figure 5.3   Two directed graphs and their direct product graph.

In this context it is important to note that for undirected graphs $\Delta^+(G) = \Delta^-(G)$ is greater than the largest eigenvalue of the adjacency matrix of G. We now review the relevant results from Section 3.2.1.

If the matrix E can be diagonalised such that $E = T^{-1}DT$ with a diagonal matrix D and a regular matrix T then arbitrary powers of the matrix E can easily be computed as $E^n = (T^{-1}DT)^n = T^{-1}D^nT$ and for the diagonal matrix D arbitrary powers can be computed component-wise ($[D^n]_{jj} = (D_{jj})^n$). These results carry over to the limit and

$$\lim_{n\to\infty} \sum_{i=0}^{n} \lambda_i E^i = T^{-1} \left(\lim_{n\to\infty} \sum_{i=0}^{n} \lambda_i D^i \right) T$$

with

$$\left[\lim_{n\to\infty} \sum_{i=0}^{n} \lambda_i D^i \right]_{jj} = \lim_{n\to\infty} \sum_{i=0}^{n} \lambda_i [D_{jj}]^i$$

if E can be diagonalised as above. Such a decomposition is always possible if E is symmetric (Section 2.1.7). Matrix diagonalisation is then a matrix eigenvalue problem and such methods have roughly cubic time complexity.

Two important special cases are now considered.

Exponential Series Similar to the exponential of a scalar value ($e^b = 1 + b/1! + b^2/2! + b^3/3! + \ldots$) the exponential of the square matrix E is defined as

$$e^{\beta E} = \lim_{n \to \infty} \sum_{i=0}^{n} \frac{(\beta E)^i}{i!}$$

where we use $\frac{\beta^0}{0!} = 1$ and $E^0 = \mathbf{I}$.

Once the matrix is diagonalised, computing the exponential matrix can be done in linear time.

Geometric Series The geometric series $\sum_i \gamma^i$ is known to converge if and only if $|\gamma| < 1$. In this case the limit is given by $\lim_{n \to \infty} \sum_{i=0}^{n} \gamma^i = \frac{1}{1-\gamma}$. Similarly, we define the geometric series of a matrix as

$$\lim_{n \to \infty} \sum_{i=0}^{n} \gamma^i E^i \ .$$

Feasible computation of the limit of a geometric series is possible by inverting the matrix $\mathbf{I} - \gamma E$. To see this, let $(\mathbf{I} - \gamma E)x = 0$, thus $\gamma E x = x$ and $(\gamma E)^i x = x$. Now, note that $(\gamma E)^i \to 0$ as $i \to \infty$. Therefore $x = 0$ and $\mathbf{I} - \gamma E$ is regular. Then $(\mathbf{I} - \gamma E)(\mathbf{I} + \gamma E + \gamma^2 E^2 + \cdots) = \mathbf{I}$ and $(\mathbf{I} - \gamma E)^{-1} = (\mathbf{I} + \gamma E + \gamma^2 E^2 + \cdots)$ is obvious. Like matrix diagonalisation, matrix inversion is roughly of cubic time complexity.

5.3 Complete Graph Kernels

In this section, all vertices and edges are assumed to have the same label. If there is no polynomial time algorithm for this special case then there is obviously no polynomial time algorithm for the general case.

When considering the set of all graphs $\mathcal{G}$, many graphs in this set differ only in the enumeration of vertices, and thus edges, and not in their structure: these graphs are *isomorphic*. Since usually in learning, the names (identifiers) given to vertices in different graphs have no meaning, we want kernels not to distinguish between isomorphic graphs. Formally, two graphs G, H are isomorphic if there is a bijection $\psi : \mathcal{V}(G) \to \mathcal{V}(H)$ such that for all $u, v \in \mathcal{V}(G) : (u, v) \in \mathcal{E}(G) \Leftrightarrow (\psi(u), \psi(v)) \in \mathcal{E}(H)$. We denote that G, H are isomorphic by $G \simeq H$. Whenever we say that two graphs have some or all subgraphs in common this will be with respect to isomorphism.

In the remainder of this chapter we define all kernels and maps on the quotient set of the set of all graphs with respect to isomorphism, i.e., the set

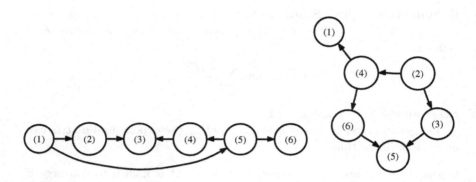

Figure 5.4   Two directed graphs without labels on the same set of vertices $\{1,\ldots,6\}$ that are isomorphic. The numbers in brackets denote the vertices.

of equivalence classes. To keep the notation simple, we will continue to refer to this set as $\mathcal{G}$, and also refer to each equivalence class simply by one of its representative graphs. Figure 5.4 shows a simple example of two directed, unlabelled graphs on the same set of vertices, that are isomorphic. Figure 5.5 shows the same two graphs (drawn slightly differently) and illustrates the isomorphism between them.

While it is easy to see that graph isomorphism is in NP it is — in spite of a lot of research devoted to this question — still not known whether graph isomorphism is in P or if it is NP-complete. It is believed that graph isomorphism lies between P and NP-complete [Köbler *et al.* (1993)].

The first class of graph kernels we are going to consider is those kernels that allow to distinguish between all (non-isomorphic) graphs in feature space. If a kernel does not allow us to distinguish between two graphs then there is no way any learning machine based on this kernel function can separate these two graphs. Investigating the complexity of graph kernels that distinguish between all graphs is thus an interesting problem.

The following definition is in line with the definition of complete kernels for objects other than graphs given in Section 3.1.2, except that equality of the objects is replaced by isomorphism of the graphs.

Definition 5.2. Let $\mathcal{G}$ denote the set of all graphs and let $\Phi : \mathcal{G} \to \mathcal{H}$ be a map from this set into a Hilbert space $\mathcal{H}$. Furthermore, let $k : \mathcal{G} \times \mathcal{G} \to \mathbb{R}$ be such that $\langle \Phi(G), \Phi(G') \rangle = k(G, G')$. If $\Phi(G) = \Phi(G')$ implies $G \simeq G'$ for all graphs G, G', k is called a *complete* graph kernel.

As we define all kernels and maps on the quotient set of the set of all graphs

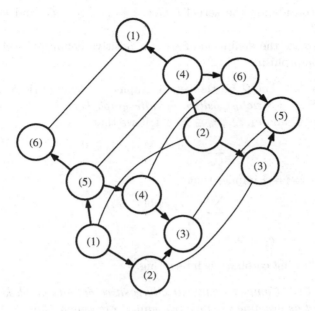

Figure 5.5 The graphs from Figure 5.4 drawn slightly differently. The thin lines now illustrate the isomorphism between both graphs

with respect to isomorphism $\Phi(G) = \Phi(G') \Leftarrow G \simeq G'$ holds always and for complete graph kernels $\Phi(G) = \Phi(G') \Leftrightarrow G \simeq G'$.

Proposition 5.1. *Computing any complete graph kernel is at least as hard as deciding whether two graphs are isomorphic.*

Proof. Let all functions be as in Definition 5.2. We need to show that if $k(\cdot, \cdot)$ could be computed in polynomial time, we could decide in polynomial time whether $\Phi(G) = \Phi(G')$ for all graphs G, G'. This can be seen as

$$k(G, G) - 2k(G, G') + k(G', G') = \langle \Phi(G) - \Phi(G'), \Phi(G) - \Phi(G') \rangle = 0$$

if and only if $\Phi(G) = \Phi(G')$. □

It is well known that there are polynomial time algorithms to decide isomorphism for several restricted graph classes [Köbler *et al.* (1993)], for example, planar graphs. However, considering kernels on restricted graph classes is beyond the scope of this book. The remaining question for us is whether the above complexity result is tight, i.e., if there is a complete graph kernel that is (exactly) as hard as deciding graph isomorphism. This is obvious considering the kernel $k(G, G') = 1 \Leftrightarrow G \simeq G'$ and $k(G, G') = 0 \Leftrightarrow G \not\simeq G'$.

Let us revise the definition of strictly positive definite kernels with respect to isomorphism:

Definition 5.3. Let $\mathcal{G}$ be the set of graphs. A symmetric function $k : \mathcal{G} \times \mathcal{G} \to \mathbb{R}$ is a *strictly positive definite graph kernel* if, for all $n \in \mathbb{N}$, $x_1, \ldots, x_n \in \mathcal{G}$, and $c_1, \ldots, c_n \in \mathbb{R}$, it follows that

$$\sum_{i,j \in \{1,\ldots,n\}} c_i \, c_j \, k(x_i, x_j) \geq 0$$

and $x_i \simeq x_j \Leftrightarrow i = j$ implies that

$$\sum_{i,j \in \{1,\ldots,n\}} c_i \, c_j \, k(x_i, x_j) = 0$$

only if $c_1 = \cdots = c_n = 0$.

Now the following corollary is interesting.

Corollary 5.1. *Computing any strictly positive definite graph kernel is at least as hard as deciding whether two graphs are isomorphic.*

Proof.   This follows directly from Proposition 5.1 and strictly positive definite graph kernels being complete. ☐

We will now look at another interesting class of graph kernels. Intuitively, it is useful to base the similarity of two graphs on their common subgraphs.

Definition 5.4. Let $\mathcal{G}$ denote the set of all graphs and let λ be a sequence $\lambda_1, \lambda_2, \ldots$ of weights ($\lambda_n \in \mathbb{R}; \lambda_n > 0$ for all $n \in \mathbb{N}$). The *subgraph feature space* is defined by the map $\Phi : \mathcal{G} \to \mathcal{H}$ into the Hilbert space $\mathcal{H}$ with one feature Φ_H for each connected graph $H \in \mathcal{G}$, such that for every graph $G \in \mathcal{G}$

$$\Phi_H(G) = \lambda_{|\mathcal{E}(H)|} \left| \{G' \text{ is subgraph of } G : G' \simeq H\} \right| \ .$$

Clearly, the inner product in the above feature space is a complete graph kernel and thus computing the inner product is at least as hard as solving the graph isomorphism problem. However, we are able to show an even stronger result.

Proposition 5.2. *Unless $P = NP$, there is no general, polynomial time algorithm for computing the inner product in the subgraph feature space.*

Proof. Let $P_n = (\{0, 1, \ldots, n\}, \{(i, i+1) : 0 \leq i < n\})$, i.e., the path-graph with n edges, and let $\mathbf{e}_H$ be a vector in the subgraph feature space such that the feature corresponding to graph H equals 1 and all other features equal 0. Let G be any graph with m vertices. As $\{\Phi(P_n)\}_{n \in \mathbb{N}}$ is linearly independent, there are $\alpha_1, \ldots, \alpha_m$ such that $\alpha_1 \Phi(P_1) + \ldots + \alpha_m \Phi(P_m) = \mathbf{e}_{P_m}$. These $\alpha_1, \ldots, \alpha_m$ can be found in polynomial time, as in each image of a path P_n under the map Φ only n features are different from 0. Then,

$$\alpha_1 \langle \Phi(P_1), \Phi(G) \rangle + \ldots + \alpha_m \langle \Phi(P_m), \Phi(G) \rangle = \langle \mathbf{e}_{P_m}, \Phi(G) \rangle > 0$$

if and only if G has a Hamiltonian path. It is well known that the decision problem whether a graph has a Hamiltonian path is NP-complete. $\square$

Note that the same result holds if we restrict the codomain of Φ_H to $\{0, 1\}$, that is we consider the set of subgraphs instead of the multiset. A first approach to defining graph kernels for which there is a polynomial time algorithm might be to restrict the feature space of Φ to features Φ_H where H is a member of a restricted class of graphs. However, even if H is restricted to paths the above proof still applies. Closely related to the Hamiltonian path problem is the problem of finding the longest path in a graph. This problem is known to be NP-complete even on many restricted graph classes [Skiena (1997)].

The results shown in this section indicate that it is intractable to compute complete graph kernels and inner products in feature spaces made up by graphs isomorphic to subgraphs. Our approach to define polynomial time computable graph kernels is to have the feature space be made up by graphs homomorphic to subgraphs. In the following section we will thus concentrate on walks instead of paths in graphs.

5.4 Walk Kernels

Clearly, we do not want to distinguish between isomorphic graphs. Thus our kernel function should be such that all isomorphic graphs are mapped to the same point in feature space. This is the case if we describe a graph by all subgraphs or by all walks in the graph.

Above we then showed that for kernel functions which are such that only isomorphic graphs are mapped to the same point, it is unlikely we will find a way to compute it in polynomial time. We furthermore showed a similar result for kernels based on common subgraphs, for example common paths,

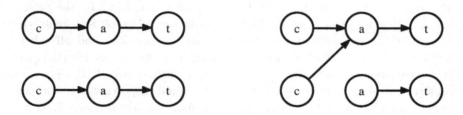

Figure 5.6   Two non-isomorphic directed graphs that have all paths and walks in common.

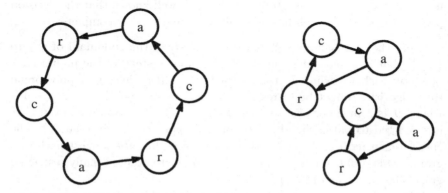

Figure 5.7   Two non-isomorphic directed graphs that do not have all paths in common but that have all walks in common.

in graphs. In this section we now propose kernels based on common walks in graphs. Considering such kernels is only reasonable if they do not fall in any of the above negative results. Figure 5.6 illustrates two graphs that have the same paths and walks but are not isomorphic. Figure 5.7 then motivates that there is still hope that kernels based on common walks in graphs might be computed in polynomial time, as there are graphs with the same walks that do not have the same paths.

5.4.1   *Kernels Based on Label Pairs*

In this section we consider vertex-labelled graphs only. In applications where there is reason to suppose that only the distance between (all) pairs of vertices of some label has an impact on the classification of the graph, we suggest the following feature space.

Definition 5.5. Let $\mathcal{W}_n(G)$ denote the set of all possible walks with n edges in G and let λ be a sequence $\lambda_0, \lambda_1, \ldots$ of weights ($\lambda_n \in \mathbb{R}; \lambda_n \geq 0$ for all $n \in \mathbb{N}$). For a given walk $w \in \mathcal{W}_n(G)$ let $l_1(w)$ denote the label of the first vertex of the walk and $l_{n+1}(w)$ denote the label of the last vertex of the walk.

The label pair feature space is defined by one feature ϕ_{ℓ_i, ℓ_j} for each pair of labels ℓ_i, ℓ_j:

$$\phi_{\ell_i, \ell_j}(G) = \sum_{n=0}^{\infty} \lambda_n \left| \{ w \in \mathcal{W}_n(G) : l_1(w) = \ell_i \wedge l_{n+1}(w) = \ell_j \} \right|$$

Let all functions and variables be defined as in Definition 5.5. The key to an efficient computation of the kernel corresponding to the above feature map is the following equation:

$$\langle \phi(G), \phi(G') \rangle = \left\langle L \left(\sum_{i=0}^{\infty} \lambda_i E^i \right) L^{\top}, L' \left(\sum_{j=0}^{\infty} \lambda_j E'^j \right) L'^{\top} \right\rangle$$

To compute this graph kernel, it is then necessary to compute the above matrix power series. See Section 5.2.4 for more details.

Although the map ϕ_{ℓ_i, ℓ_j} is injective if the function *label* is injective, the dimensionality of the label pair feature space is low if the number of different labels is small. In particular the dimensionality of the label pair feature space equals the number of different labels squared (that is $|\Sigma|^2$). In domains in which only few labels occur, we might thus not be able to discriminate enough graphs in the feature space. be a feature space of too low dimension.

One obvious way to achieve a higher dimensional — and thus more expressive — feature space is to use a more expressive label set including, for example, some information about the neighbourhood of the vertices. Still, this manual enrichment of the feature space might not be sufficient in all cases. For that reason, in the next section we describe a kernel function that operates in a more expressive feature space. The key idea of the kernel is to have each dimension of the feature space correspond to one particular label sequence. Thus even with very few — and even with a single — labels, the feature space will already be of infinite dimension.

5.4.2   Kernels Based on Contiguous Label Sequences

In this section we consider graphs with labels on vertices and/or edges. In the presence of few labels, the kernel described in the previous section suffers from too little expressivity. The kernel described in this section overcomes this by defining one feature for every possible label sequence and then counting how many walks in a graph match this label sequence. In order not to have to distinguish all three cases of edge-labelled, vertex-labelled, and fully-labelled graphs explicitly, we extend the domain of the function *label* to include all vertices and edges. In edge-labelled graphs we define $label(v) = \#$ for all vertices v and in vertex-labelled graphs we define $label(u, v) = \#$ for all edges (u, v).

We begin by defining the feature space of contiguous (or unbroken) label sequences.

Definition 5.6. Let $\mathcal{S}_n$ denote the set of all possible label sequences of walks with n edges and let λ be a sequence $\lambda_0, \lambda_1, \ldots$ of weights ($\lambda_i \in \mathbb{R}; \lambda_i \geq 0$ for all $i \in \mathbb{N}$). Furthermore, let $\mathcal{W}_n(G)$ denote the set of all possible walks with n edges in graph G. For a given walk $w \in \mathcal{W}_n(G)$ let $l_i(w)$ denote the i-th label of the walk.

The sequence feature space is defined by one feature for each possible label sequence. In particular, for any given length n and label sequence $s = s_1, \ldots, s_{2n+1}; s \in \mathcal{S}_n$, the corresponding feature value for every graph G is:

$$\phi_s(G) = \sqrt{\lambda_n} \left| \{ w \in \mathcal{W}_n(G), \forall\, i : s_i = l_i(w) \} \right| .$$

Before showing how to compute the inner product under this map we first describe and interpret some properties of the product graph. The following proposition relates the number of times a label sequence occurs in the product graph to the number of times it occurs in each factor.

Proposition 5.3. *Let all variables and functions be defined as in Definitions 5.6 and 5.1. Furthermore, let G, G' be two graphs. Then*

$$\left| \{ w \in \mathcal{W}_n(G \times G'), \forall i : s_i = l_i(w) \} \right|$$
$$= \left| \{ w \in \mathcal{W}_n(G), \forall i : s_i = l_i(w) \} \right| \cdot \left| \{ w \in \mathcal{W}_n(G'), \forall i : s_i = l_i(w) \} \right|$$

Proof.   It is sufficient to show a bijection between every walk in the product graph and one walk in both graphs such that their label sequences match.

Consider first a walk in the product graph $w^* \in \mathcal{W}_n(G \times G')$:

$$w^* = (v_1, v_1'), (v_2, v_2'), \ldots, (v_n, v_n')$$

with $(v_i, v_i') \in \mathcal{V}(G \times G')$. Now let $w = v_1, v_2, \ldots, v_n$ and $w' = v_1', v_2', \ldots, v_n'$. Clearly $w \in \mathcal{W}_n(G)$, $w' \in \mathcal{W}_n(G')$, and

$$\forall i : l_i(w^*) = l_i(w) = l_i(w')$$

The opposite holds as well: For every two walks $w \in \mathcal{W}_n(G)$, $w' \in \mathcal{W}_n(G')$ with matching label sequences, there is a walk $w^* \in \mathcal{W}_n(G \times G')$ with a label sequence that matches the label sequences of w and w'. $\square$

Having introduced product graphs and having shown how these can be interpreted, we are now able to define the direct product kernel.

Definition 5.7. Let G_1, G_2 be two graphs, let $E_\times$ denote the adjacency matrix of their direct product $G_1 \times G_2$, and let $\mathcal{V}_\times$ denote the vertex set of the direct product $\mathcal{V}_\times = \mathcal{V}(G_1 \times G_2)$. With a sequence of weights $\lambda = \lambda_0, \lambda_1, \ldots$ ($\lambda_i \in \mathbb{R}; \lambda_i \geq 0$ for all $i \in \mathbb{N}$) the direct product kernel is defined as

$$k_\times(G_1, G_2) = \sum_{i,j=1}^{|\mathcal{V}_\times|} \left[\sum_{n=0}^{\infty} \lambda_n E_\times^n \right]_{ij}$$

if the limit exists.

Proposition 5.4. *Let ϕ be as in Definition 5.6 and $k_\times$ as in Definition 5.7. For any two graphs G, G', $k_\times(G, G') = \langle \phi(G), \phi(G') \rangle$*

Proof. This follows directly from Proposition 5.3. $\square$

To compute this graph kernel, it is then necessary to compute the above matrix power series. See Section 5.2.4 for more details on how this can be accomplished.

5.4.3 *Transition Graphs*

In some cases graphs are employed to model discrete random processes such as Markov chains [Gray (1987)]. In these cases a *transition probability* is assigned to each edge. We only consider the case that the transition probability does not change over time. Such graphs will be called *transition graphs*. In transition graphs vertices are often called *states*. We denote the probability of going from vertex u to v by $p_{(u,v)}$. More precisely this denotes the probability of the process being in state v at time $t + 1$ given that it was in state u at time t. Usually, transitions are without loss, i.e., $\forall u \in \mathcal{V} : \sum_{(u,v) \in \mathcal{E}} p_{(u,v)} = 1$. In some cases, there is a probability p_{stop} that the process stops at any time.

In order to deal with graphs modelling random processes, we replace the adjacency matrix E of a graph by the transition matrix R with $[R]_{ij} = p_{(\nu_i,\nu_j)}(1 - p_{\text{stop}})$ if $(\nu_i, \nu_j) \in \mathcal{E}$ and $[R]_{ij} = 0$ otherwise. Without loss of generality we assume $p_{(\nu_i,\nu_j)} > 0 \Leftrightarrow (\nu_i, \nu_j) \in \mathcal{E}$. Before we can apply the kernel introduced in the previous section to transition graphs we have to redefine the functions $\Delta^+(G), \Delta^-(G)$ (from Section 5.2.2) to be the maximal row and column sum of the matrix R of a graph G, respectively. Clearly $\Delta^+(G), \Delta^-(G) \leq 1$.

If we use the transition matrix R instead of the adjacency matrix, we get to a similar interpretation. $[R^n]_{ij}$ determines then the probability of getting from vertex ν_i to vertex ν_j in n steps. The interpretation of $[LR^n L^\top]_{ij}$ is a bit more complicated. If we divide by the number of times label ℓ_i occurs, however, an interpretation becomes easy again: $[LR^n L^\top]_{ij}/[LL^\top]_{ii}$ is the probability that having started at any vertex labelled ℓ_i and taking n steps, we arrive at any vertex labelled ℓ_j. The division by $[LL^\top]_{ii}$ can be justified by assuming a uniform distribution for starting at a particular vertex with label ℓ_i.

A graph with some transition matrix R and stopping probability $p_{\text{stop}} = 0$ can be interpreted as a *Markov chain*. A vertex v with a transition probability $p_{(v,v)} = 1$ in a Markov chain is called *absorbing*. An absorbing Markov chain is a Markov chain with a vertex v such that v is absorbing and there is a walk from any vertex u to the absorbing vertex v. It is known [Gray (1987)] that in absorbing Markov chains the limit of R^n for $n \to \infty$ is $\mathbf{0}$. If we define $N = \mathbf{I} + R + R^2 + \cdots$ then $[N]_{ij}$ is the expected number of times the chain is in vertex ν_j given that it starts in vertex ν_i. N can be computed as the inverse of the matrix $\mathbf{I} - R$.

In the case of graphs with transition probabilities on the edges, the edges in the product graph have probability $p_{(u_{12},v_{12})} = p_{(u_1,v_1)} p_{(u_2,v_2)}$ where $u_{12} = (u_1, u_2) \in \mathcal{V}(G_1 \times G_2)$ and $v_{12} = (v_1, v_2) \in \mathcal{V}(G_1 \times G_2)$. Let p_1, p_2 denote the stopping probability in graphs G_1, G_2 respectively. The stopping probability p_{12} in the product graph is then given by $p_{12} = 1 - (1 - p_1)(1 - p_2)$. A similar interpretation to Proposition 5.3 can be given for graphs with transition probabilities by replacing the cardinality of the sets of walks with the sum over the probabilities of the walks.

5.4.4 *Non-Contiguous Label Sequences*

The (implicit) representation of a graph by a set of walks through the graph suggests a strong relation to string kernels (Section 3.4.3). There, the similarity of two strings is based on the number of common substrings. In contrast to the direct product kernel suggested in Section 5.4.2, however, the substrings need not be contiguous.

In this section we will describe a graph kernel such that the similarity of two graphs is based on common non-contiguous label sequences. We will consider only edge-labelled graphs in this section. A similar technique can be used for fully-labelled graphs, however, its presentation becomes more lengthy.

Before defining the desired feature space we need to introduce the wild-card symbol '?' and the function $match(l, l') \Leftrightarrow (l = l') \vee (l =?) \vee (l' =?)$. In the following 'label' will refer to an element of the set $\Sigma \cup \{?\}$.

Definition 5.8. Let $\mathcal{S}_{n,m}$ denote the set of all possible label sequences of length n containing $m \geq 0$ wildcards. Let λ be a sequence $\lambda_0, \lambda_1, \ldots$ of weights $(\lambda_n \in \mathbb{R}; \lambda_n \geq 0$ for all $n \in \mathbb{N})$ and let $0 \leq \alpha \leq 1$ be a parameter for penalising gaps. Furthermore, let $\mathcal{W}_n(G)$ denote the set of all possible walks with n edges in graph G and let $\mathcal{W}(G) = \bigcup_{i=0}^{n} \mathcal{W}_i(G)$. For a given walk $w \in \mathcal{W}(G)$ let $l_i(w)$ denote the label of the i-th edge in this walk.

The sequence feature space is defined by one feature for each possible label sequence. In particular, for any given n, m and label sequence $s = s_1, \ldots, s_n \in \mathcal{S}_{n,m}$, the corresponding feature value is

$$\phi_s(G) = \sqrt{\lambda_n \alpha^m} \, |\{w \in \mathcal{W}(G), \forall i : \, match(s_i, l_i(w))\}|$$

We proceed directly with the definition of the non-contiguous sequence kernel.

Definition 5.9. Let G_1, G_2 be two graphs, let $G_\times = G_1 \times G_2$ be their direct product, and let G_o be their direct product when ignoring the labels in G_1 and G_2. With a sequence of weights $\lambda = \lambda_0, \lambda_1, \ldots (\lambda_i \in \mathbb{R}; \lambda_i \geq 0$ for all $i \in \mathbb{N})$ and a factor $0 \leq \alpha \leq 1$ penalising gaps, the non-contiguous sequence kernel is defined as

$$k_*(G_1, G_2) = \sum_{i,j=1}^{|\mathcal{V}_\times|} \left[\sum_{n=0}^{\infty} \lambda_n \left((1 - \alpha)E_\times + \alpha E_o\right)^n \right]_{ij}$$

if the limit exists.

This kernel is very similar to the direct product kernel. The only difference is that instead of the adjacency matrix of the direct product graph, the matrix $(1-\alpha)E_\times + \alpha E_o$ is used. The relationship can be seen by adding

— parallel to each edge — a new edge labelled # with weight $\sqrt{\alpha}$ in both factor graphs.

Note, that the above defined feature space contains features for 'trivial label sequences', i.e., label sequences that consist only of wildcard symbols. This can be corrected by using the kernel $k_*(G_1, G_2) - \sum_n \lambda_n \alpha^n E_o^n$ instead.

5.5 Cyclic Pattern Kernels

The walk-based graph kernels that we described above can be computed in polynomial time on graphs where the adjacency matrix is symmetric. These are undirected graphs. One possible application area of learning algorithms on undirected graphs is the classification of molecules as represented by their chemical structure graphs. In Section 5.8 we will consider one such real-world application with more than 40000 molecules, including molecules with more that 200 atoms (not counting hydrogens). It will there turn out that the exact computation of walk-based kernels on this domain is not feasible. We will thus have to resort to alternative approaches. Alternatives are approximation of walk-based kernels or exploiting special properties of this domain. In this section we will propose a graph kernel that can be computed efficiently only if the set of labelled undirected graphs they are applied to contains few cycles. The kernel function we propose can be computed in polynomial time in the number of vertices and simple cycles of the graph. We will show in Section 5.8 that the molecules in this domain indeed contain only few simple cycles. Cyclic pattern kernels can be computed much faster on this domain than walk-based kernels.

The graphs we consider in this section are always labelled undirected graphs, introduced in Section 5.5.1. Section 5.5.2 defines cyclic pattern kernels and Section 5.5.3 shows how to compute these in time polynomial in the number of simple cycles of the graphs.

5.5.1 *Undirected Graphs*

Recall that the edges $\mathcal{E}$ of undirected graphs without parallel edges are represented by a subset of the vertex set with cardinality two. A path in an undirected graph is a sequence $v_1, \ldots, v_n$ of distinct vertices $v_i \in \mathcal{V}$ where $\{v_i, v_{i+1}\} \in \mathcal{E}$. A simple cycle in an undirected graph is a path, where also $\{v_1, v_n\} \in \mathcal{E}$. A bridge is an edge not part of any simple cycle; the graph made up by all bridges is a forest, i.e., a set of trees.

Let $G = (\mathcal{V}, \mathcal{E}, label)$ and $G' = (\mathcal{V}', \mathcal{E}', label')$ be labelled undirected graphs. G' is a *subgraph* of G, if $\mathcal{V}' \subseteq \mathcal{V}$, $\mathcal{E}' \subseteq \mathcal{E} \cap 2^{\mathcal{V}}$, and $label'(x) = label(x)$ for every $x \in \mathcal{V}' \cup \mathcal{E}'$. A graph is *connected* if there is a path between any pair of its vertices. A *connected component* of a graph G is a maximal subgraph of G that is connected. Given a forest (a set of pairwise disjoint trees), we call the connected components of the forest the (maximal) trees of the forest. A vertex v of a graph G is an *articulation* (also called *cut*) vertex, if its removal disconnects G (i.e., the subgraph obtained from G by removing v and all edges containing v has more connected components than G). A graph is *biconnected* if it contains no articulation vertex.

A *biconnected component* (or *block*) of a graph is a maximal subgraph that is biconnected. It holds that biconnected components of a graph G are pairwise edge disjoint and thus form a partition on the set of G's edges. This partition, in turn, corresponds to the following equivalence relation on the set of edges: two edges are equivalent if and only if they belong to a common simple cycle. This property of biconnected components implies that an edge of a graph belongs to a simple cycle if and only if its biconnected component contains more than one edge. Edges not belonging to simple cycles are called *bridges*. The subgraph of a graph G formed by the bridges of G is denoted by $\mathcal{B}(G)$. Clearly, $\mathcal{B}(G)$ is a forest.

5.5.2 *Kernel Definition*

We denote by $\mathcal{S}(G)$ the set of simple cycles of a graph G. Two simple cycles C and C' in G are considered to be the same if and only if C or its reverse is a cyclic permutation of C'. We start by defining the set of cyclic patterns induced by the set of simple cycles of a graph. Let $G = (\mathcal{V}, \mathcal{E}, label)$ be a graph and

$$C = \{v_0, v_1\}, \{v_1, v_2\}, \ldots, \{v_{k-1}, v_0\}$$

be a sequence of edges that forms a simple cycle in G. The *canonical representation* of C is the lexicographically smallest string $\pi(C) \in \Sigma^*$ among the strings obtained by concatenating the labels along the vertices and edges of the cyclic permutations of C and its reverse. More precisely, denoting by $\rho(s)$ the set of cyclic permutations of a sequence s and its reverse, we define $\pi(C)$ by

$$\pi(C) = \min\{\sigma(w) : w \in \rho(v_0 v_1 \ldots v_{k-1})\},$$

where for $w = w_0 w_1 \ldots w_{k-1}$,

$$\sigma(w) = label(w_0) label(\{w_0, w_1\}) label(w_1) \ldots label(w_{k-1}) label(\{w_{k-1}, w_0\}).$$

Clearly, π is unique up to isomorphism, and hence, it indeed provides a canonical string representation of simple cycles. The set of *cyclic patterns* of a graph G, denoted by $\mathcal{C}(G)$, is then defined by

$$\mathcal{C}(G) = \{\pi(C) : C \in \mathcal{S}(G)\} \ .$$

To assign a set of cyclic patterns to a graph G, above we have used its set of simple cycles. To add more information to the kernel, we also consider the graph obtained by removing the edges of all simple cycles. As discussed before, the resulting graph is a forest consisting of the set of bridges of the graph. To assign a set of tree patterns to G, we associate each (maximal) tree T in the forest formed by the set $\mathcal{B}(G)$ of bridges of G with a pattern $\pi(T) \in \Sigma^*$ that is unique up to isomorphism [Asai *et al.* (2003); Zaki (2002)], and define the set of *tree patterns* $\mathcal{T}(G)$ assigned to G by

$$\mathcal{T}(G) = \{\pi(T) : \ T \text{ is a connected component of } \mathcal{B}(G)\} \ .$$

We are now ready to define cyclic pattern kernels for graphs. In the definition below, we assume without loss of generality that $\mathcal{C}(G) \cap \mathcal{T}(G) = \emptyset$ for every G in the database. Using the intersection kernel given in Equation (3.1) on the sets defined by

$$\Phi_{\text{CP}}(G) = \mathcal{C}(G) \cup \mathcal{T}(G) \tag{5.1}$$

for every G we define *cyclic pattern kernels* by

$$\begin{aligned}
k_{\text{CP}}(G_i, G_j) &= k_\cap(\Phi_{\text{CP}}(G_i), \Phi_{\text{CP}}(G_j)) \\
&= |\mathcal{C}(G_i) \cap \mathcal{C}(G_j)| + |\mathcal{T}(G_i) \cap \mathcal{T}(G_j)| \tag{5.2}
\end{aligned}$$

for every G_i, G_j in a graph database $\mathcal{G}$.

5.5.3 *Kernel Computation*

Cyclic pattern kernels are essentially a special case of subgraph kernels (Definition 5.4) that can not be computed in polynomial time. The proof of Proposition 5.2 can, however, only be applied with some modifications. Indeed, we can give a simpler proof for this special case:

Proposition 5.5. *Unless P=NP, cyclic pattern kernels can not be computed in time polynomial in the number of vertices in the graphs.*

Proof. Let G and C_n be a graph and a simple cycle, respectively, such that both G and C_n consist of n vertices that are all mapped to the same label. Applying the cyclic pattern kernel to G and C_n, it holds that $k_{\text{CP}}(G, C_n) = 1$ if and only if G has a Hamiltonian cycle. $\qquad\square$

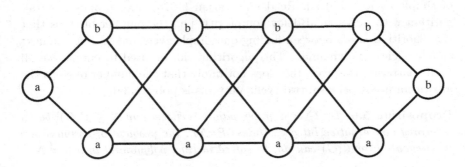

Figure 5.8 An example of a graph with $2n+2$ vertices (n=4), two labels, and a number of cyclic patterns exponential in n.

Furthermore, the set of simple cycles in a graph can not be computed in polynomial time – even worse – the number of simple cycles in a graph can be exponential in the number of vertices of the graph. For an example just consider a complete graph. In fact, the number of simple cycles in a graph can grow *faster* with n than 2^n, and remains exponential even for many restricted graph classes in the worst case. For instance, Alt *et al.* (1999) investigate simple cycles of *planar* graphs, and show that there are planar graphs with lower bound 2.28^n on the number of simple cycles. For us it is more interesting to determine the number of cyclic patterns in a graph. Again, the complete graph with all vertices labelled differently is an example of a graph where the number of cyclic patterns grows exponentially with the number of vertices, however, if we restrict the alphabet (the label set) to cardinality 1, the number of cyclic patterns is linear in the number of vertices. To see that the number of cyclic patterns can even grow exponentially if the alphabet is restricted to cardinality 2, consider a graph with $2n+2$ vertices, consisting of two paths $v_0, \ldots v_n$ and $u_0, \ldots u_n$ and additional edges $\{\{v_i, u_i\} : 0 \leq i \leq n\} \cup \{\{v_i, u_{i-2}\} : 2 \leq i \leq n\}$. The number of Hamiltonian cycles of this graph is 2^n. The vertex sequence of each Hamiltonian cycle has $2(2n+2)$ cyclic permutations. If we assign the label 'a' to all vertices u_i and the label 'b' to all vertices v_i, the number of cyclic patterns of this graph is still greater than $2^n/(4n+4)$. Figure 5.8 illustrates this graph for $n = 4$.

The only remaining hope for a practically feasible algorithm is that the number of simple cycles in each graph can be bound by a small polynomial and that we can find an algorithm that is polynomial in the number of simple cycles. Indeed, Read and Tarjan (1975) have proposed an algorithm with polynomial delay complexity, i.e., the number of steps that the algorithm needs between finding one simple cycle and finding the next simple cycle is polynomial. This algorithm can be used to enumerate all cyclic patterns. However, this does not imply that the number of steps the algorithm needs between two cyclic patterns is polynomial.

Proposition 5.6. *Let G be a graph with n vertices, and $N \leq |\mathcal{C}(G)|$ be an arbitrary non-negative integer. Unless P=NP, the problem of enumerating N elements from $\mathcal{C}(G)$ can not be solved in time polynomial in n and N.*

Proof.   We show that the NP-complete Hamiltonian cycle problem is polynomial-time reducible to the above enumeration problem. Let G be an ordinary undirected graph (i.e., a graph without labels) with n vertices. We assign a (labelled undirected) graph G' to G such that G' has the same sets of vertices and edges as G, and each vertex and edge of G' is labelled by the same symbol, say 0. Since simple cycles of the same length in G' are mapped to the same pattern (i.e., simple cycles of length ℓ are associated with the pattern $0^{2\ell}$), $|\mathcal{C}(G')| < n$. Applying the enumeration algorithm with $N = n - 1$, we obtain a set S containing at most $n - 1$ elements of $\mathcal{C}(G')$. Clearly, 0^{2n} is in S if and only if G has a Hamiltonian cycle.   □

This shows that we can not enumerate the cyclic patterns of a graph in polynomial time but it does not yet imply that cyclic pattern kernels can not be computed in time polynomial in N, however, this can be seen directly from the above proof.

Corollary 5.2. *Let G, G' be two graphs with n, n' vertices, respectively. Let $N \leq |\mathcal{C}(G)|$ be an arbitrary non-negative integer. Unless P=NP, cyclic pattern kernels can not be computed in time polynomial in n, n', and N.*

Proof.   In the proof of Proposition 5.6 we showed that for graphs where all vertices have equal label, the number of cyclic patterns is linear in the number of vertices. The corollary follows then directly from Proposition 5.5.   □

In order to overcome the negative complexity results above, we consider a restriction that yields an effective *practical* problem class. In contrast to the case of cyclic patterns, the set $\mathcal{S}(G)$ of simple cycles of a graph G can be listed in polynomial output complexity by the algorithm of Read and Tarjan (1975). Their depth-first search algorithm computes $N \leq |\mathcal{S}(G)|$ simple cycles of a graph G in time $\mathcal{O}\left((N + 1)n + m\right)$ where m is the number of edges. From their result it also follows that, for a given graph G and $M \geq 0$, one can decide in time polynomial in n and M, whether or not the number of simple cycles in G is bounded by M. Thus, we only consider cyclic pattern kernels on sets of graphs where the number of simple cycles is bounded by a small number for every graph. To sum up, cyclic pattern kernels are applied as follows:

- Check whether the graph database is well-behaved, i.e., the number of simple cycles of every graph is bound by a small (user-defined) constant.
- Partition the edges of each graph into bridges and non-bridges.
- Consider only the edges of each graph that are not bridges:
    - Enumerate the simple cycles of each biconnected component.
    - Convert each simple cycle into a cyclic pattern (unique up to isomorphism).
- Consider only the bridges of each graph:
    - Enumerate the connected components of the forest formed by the bridges.
    - Convert each of these trees into a tree pattern (unique up to isomorphism).
- Given two graphs, compute the cyclic pattern kernel as the cardinality of the intersection of the pattern sets of each graph.

In Section 5.8 we will compare walk and cycle based graph kernels in the context of drug design and prediction of properties of molecules. It is illustrated there that indeed for the application considered, only few molecules exist that have a large number of simple cycles. Before that, we describe an application of walk based graph kernels in a relational reinforcement learning setting.

5.6 Related Work

The obvious approach to define kernels on objects that have a natural representation as a graph is to decompose each graph into a set of subgraphs and measure the intersection of two decompositions. As we have seen, with such a graph kernel, one could decide whether a graph has a Hamiltonian path or not. As this problem is known to be NP-hard, it is strongly believed that the obvious graph kernel can not be computed in polynomial time. This holds even if the decomposition is restricted to paths only.

In literature different approaches have been tried to overcome this problem. Graepel (2002) restricted the decomposition to paths up to a given size, and Deshpande *et al.* (2002) only consider the set of connected graphs that occur frequently as subgraphs in the graph database. The approach taken there to compute the decomposition of each graph is an iterative one [Kuramochi and Karypis (2001)]. The algorithm starts with a frequent set of subgraphs with one or two edges only. Then, in each step, from the set of frequent subgraphs of size l, a set of candidate graphs of size $l + 1$ is generated by joining those graphs of size l that have a subgraph of size $l - 1$ in common. Of the candidate graphs only those satisfying a frequency threshold are retained for the next step. The iteration stops when the set of frequent subgraphs of size l is empty.

The walk-based graph kernels we introduced above, though computable in polynomial time, still have a high computational complexity. Novel graph kernels or modifications of known graph kernels have been proposed to speed up their computation, increase their expressiveness, or to adapt them to particular application domains.

A walk-based kernel function on transition graphs has independently been proposed by Kashima *et al.* (2003). In the feature space considered there, each feature corresponds to the probability with which a label sequence is generated by a random walk on the direct product graph. There, transition graphs with a uniform distribution over all edges leaving the same vertex are considered and convergence is guaranteed by assuming a high halting probability. In Section 5.4.3 we showed how our graph kernels can be extended to cover general transition graphs. The kernel proposed by Kashima *et al.* (2003) is a special case of this extended kernel.

The first approach to increase the expressiveness is based on the idea of using tree patterns instead of walks on the graphs [Ramon and Gärtner (2003)]. Tree patterns are similar to the image of a tree on a graph under homomorphism. This approach has later been refined and applied to discriminate toxic from non-toxic molecules [Mahe *et al.* (2006)]. Another approach is to remove tottering walks and use the Morgan algorithm to increase the number of different labels [Mahé *et al.* (2004)]. A graph kernel based on comparing local neighbourhoods of atoms has been proposed by Menchetti *et al.* (2005) and a graph kernel based on comparing the set of shortest paths in two graphs has been proposed by Borgwardt and Kriegel (2005). Cyclic pattern kernels have been revisited by Horváth (2005) who shows that for graphs of bounded treewidth, cyclic pattern kernels can be computed in time polynomial in the number of cyclic patterns, which in turn can be exponentially smaller than that of simple cycles. Furthermore Horváth (2005) proposed an alternative to cyclic pattern kernels based on the set of relevant cycles which is known to be enumerable with polynomial delay and its cardinality is typically only cubic in the number of vertices.

Another approach to define kernel function on graphs is to employ the empirical kernel map, i.e., to represent an instance as a vector of the (dis)similarities to some prototypes, together with, e.g., a set distance measure [Woznica *et al.* (2006)] or a graph edit distance [Bunke and Riesen (2007)]. Kernels defined by the empirical kernel map are per definition positive definite. Distances can, however, also be incorporated in the definition of the kernel function directly, e.g., in convolution kernels [Neuhaus and Bunke (2006a)] or in walk kernels [Neuhaus and Bunke (2006b)]. The latter approach restricts the walk kernels to vertices that play a role in optimal matchings. Somewhat related, based on matching atoms, (Frohlich *et al.*, 2005) proposed a similarity function for which, however, indefiniteness can been shown. Other indefinite similarity measures have been proposed in [Jain *et al.* (2004, 2005)] based on the Schur-Hadamard inner product. As computing these kernels has prohibitive complexity, a neural network based non-exact computation is used.

Vishwanathan *et al.* (2007a) employ fast methods for solving Sylvester equations as well as conjugate gradient and fixed point iteration methods to speed up walk based kernels. The thus obtained kernels have been adapted to handle missing values and applied on co-integrated gene expression/protein-protein interaction data [Borgwardt *et al.* (2006b)]. A java package implementing these and other algorithms can be found in [Borgwardt *et al.* (2006a)]. A generalisation of graph kernels to dynamical systems is proposed in [Vishwanathan and Smola (2004)] and applied to analysis of dynamic scenes [Vishwanathan *et al.* (2007b)]. Motivated by the matrix reconstruction theorem, Borgwardt *et al.* (2007) propose a graph kernel based on counting common graphlets. Further speedup is achieved by sampling graphlets, in which case the thus introduced error can be bound as a function of the sample size. An initial effort to investigate the expressiveness of graph kernels is made by Florencio (2007).

As for applications of graph kernels, Aldea *et al.* (2007a,b) modeled images as graphs and applied graph kernels for medical image analysis. Tree pattern based graph kernels are used for image classification based on segmentation graphs [Harchaoui and Bach (2007)]. Borgwardt *et al.* (2005) combined walk based graph kernels with different other kernels and applied them for the prediction of functional class membership of enzymes and non-enzymes. Jacob *et al.* (2007) combined graph kernels for ligands with kernels on targets and improved results for ligand prediction on enzymes, GPCR, and ion channels are achieved. A graph kernel based on the decomposition of graphs into canonical subgraphs is used by Faulon *et al.* (2008) for the task of predicting whether proteins can catalyse some reactions and whether drugs can bind to some target. Pahikkala *et al.* (2006) propose a graph representation for dependency parses and apply it with modified graph kernels to parse ranking biomedical texts.

For classifying chemical compounds, recently it has also been proposed to make use of the 3D structure [Mahé *et al.* (2006); Swamidass *et al.* (2005)], e.g., by making use of pharmacophore information, as well as to incorporate the feature (substructure) computation and the minimisation of the learning risk more tightly [Saigo *et al.* (2006)].

More efficient kernels can be obtained for subclasses of the set of all graphs such as the set of sequences (see Section 3.4.3) and trees (see Section 3.4.4).

5.7   Relational Reinforcement Learning

Reinforcement learning [Sutton and Barto (1998)], in a nutshell, is about controlling an autonomous agent in an unknown environment — often called the state space. The agent has no prior knowledge about the environment and can only obtain some knowledge by acting in that environment. The only information the agent can get about the environment is the state in which it currently is and whether it received a reward. The aim of reinforcement learning is to act such that this reward is maximised.

Q-learning [Watkins (1989)] — one particular form of reinforcement learning — tries to map every state-action-pair to a real number (Q-value) reflecting the quality of that action in that state, based on the experience so far. While in small state-action spaces it is possible to represent this mapping extensionally, in large state-action spaces this is not feasible for two reasons: On the one hand, one can not store the full state-action space; on the other hand the larger the state-action space gets, the smaller becomes the probability of ever getting back into the same state. For this reason, the extensional representation of the quality mapping is often substituted with an intensional mapping found by a learning algorithm that is able to generalise to unseen states. Ideally, an incrementally learnable regression algorithm is used to learn this mapping.

Relational reinforcement learning [Džeroski *et al.* (1998a); Driessens *et al.* (2001)] (RRL) is a Q-learning technique that can be applied whenever the state-action space can not easily be represented by tuples of constants but has an inherently relational representation instead. In this case explicitly representing the mapping from state-action-pairs to Q-values is — in general — not feasible. So far first-order distance-based algorithms as well as first-order regression trees have been used as learning algorithms to approximate the mapping between state-action pairs and their Q-value.

In this section we use Gaussian processes with a slightly modified version of the graph kernels introduced earlier in this chapter to learn the mapping from relational state-action spaces to Q-values. Related work on reinforcement learning with kernel methods is very limited so far[2]. In order to employ Gaussian processes in a relational setting we use graph kernels as the covariance function between state-action pairs. One advantage of using Gaussian processes in RRL is that rather than predicting a single Q-value, they actually return a probability distribution over Q-values. Experiments conducted in the blocks world show that Gaussian processes with graph kernels can compete with, and often improve on, regression trees and instance based regression as a generalisation algorithm for relational reinforcement learning.

The outline of this Section is as follows Subsection 5.7.1 briefly presents the relational reinforcement learning framework and discusses some previous implementations of the RRL-system. Subsection 5.7.2 extends graph kernels such that they are able to deal with the structural nature of state-action pairs in RRL. Subsection 5.7.3 shows how states and actions in the blocks world can be represented by graphs. Subsection 5.7.4 presents some experimental results that compare Gaussian processes with other regression algorithms in RRL.

5.7.1 *Relational Reinforcement Learning*

Relational reinforcement learning (RRL) [Džeroski *et al.* (1998a); Driessens (2004)] is a Q-learning technique that allows structural representations for states and actions.

The RRL-system learns through exploration of the state-space in a way that is very similar to normal Q-learning algorithms. It starts with run-

---

[2]In [Ormoneit and Sen (2002)] the term 'kernel' is not used to refer to a positive definite function but to a probability density function.

Figure 5.9 The RRL-algorithm. In the case of the algorithm proposed in this paper updating $\hat{Q}_e$ means computing the inverse of the covariance matrix of the examples. This can be done incrementally using partitioned inverse equations.

Initialise the Q-function hypothesis $\hat{Q}_0$
$e \leftarrow 0$
repeat (for each episode)
    Examples $\leftarrow \phi$
    Generate a starting state s_0
    $i \leftarrow 0$
    repeat (for each step of episode)
        Choose a_i for s_i using the policy derived from the current hypothesis $\hat{Q}_e$
        Take action a_i, observe r_i and s_{i+1}
        $i \leftarrow i+1$
    until s_i is terminal
    for j=i-1 to 0 **do**
        Generate example $x = (s_j, a_j, \hat{q}_j)$, where $\hat{q}_j \leftarrow r_j + \gamma max_a \hat{Q}_e(s_{j+1}, a)$
        and add x to Examples
    Update $\hat{Q}_e$ using Examples and an incremental relational regression
    algorithm to produce $\hat{Q}_{e+1}$.
    $e \leftarrow e+1$
until no more episodes

ning an episode[3] just like table-based Q-learning, but uses the encountered states, chosen actions and the received rewards to generate a set of examples that can then be used to build a Q-function generalisation. These examples use a structural representation of states and actions.

To build this generalised Q-function, RRL applies an incremental relational regression engine that can exploit the structural representation of the constructed example set. The resulting Q-function is then used to decide which actions to take in the following episodes. Every new episode can be seen as new experience and is thus used to updated the Q-function generalisation. A more formal description of the RRL-algorithm is given in figure 5.9.

---

[3]An 'episode' is a sequence of states and actions from an initial state to a terminal state. In each state, the current Q-function is used to decide which action to take.

Previous implementations of the RRL-system have used first order regression trees and relational instance based regression to build a generalised Q-function. Here, we suggest using Gaussian processes as a generalisation algorithm for RRL. Gaussian processes not only provide a prediction for unseen examples but can also determine a probability distribution over Q-values. In reinforcement learning, this probability distribution can, for example, very easily be used to determine the exploration strategy. We will compare our new approach with both previous implementations of RRL.

RRL-TG [Driessens *et al.* (2001)] uses an incremental first order regression tree algorithm TG to construct the Q-function. Although the TG -algorithm is very fast compared to other approaches, the performance of this algorithm depends greatly on the language definition that is used by the TG -algorithm to construct possible tree refinements. Also, TG has shown itself to be sensitive with respect to the order in which the (state, action, qvalue)-examples are presented and often needs more training episodes to find a competitive policy.

RRL-RIB [Driessens and Ramon (2003)] uses relational instance based regression for Q-function generalisation. The instance based regression offers a robustness to RRL not found in RRL-TG but requires a first order distance to be defined between (state, action)-pairs. The definition of a meaningful first order distance is seldom trivial.

5.7.2 *Kernels for Graphs with Parallel Edges*

So far, we only considered graphs without parallel edges in this chapter, however, in this application it is important to consider digraphs with parallel edges. In this case we can not identify edges with their image under Ψ. A *graph* G is now described by a finite set of *vertices* $\mathcal{V}$, a finite set of *edges* $\mathcal{E}$, and a function Ψ. We also have to adapt some definitions given in the previous sections. We summarise these now.

First, a walk w in a directed graph with parallel edges is a sequence of vertices $v_i \in \mathcal{V}$ and edges $e_i \in \mathcal{E}$ with $w = v_1, e_1, v_2, e_2, \ldots e_n, v_{n+1}$ and $\Psi(e_i) = (v_i, v_{i+1})$. We also need to change the definition of the functions describing the neighbourhood of vertex v in a graph G: $\delta^+(v) = \{e \in \mathcal{E} \mid \Psi(e) = (v, u)\}$ and $\delta^-(v) = \{e \in \mathcal{E} \mid \Psi(e) = (u, v)\}$.

The component $[E]_{ij}$ of the adjacency matrix now corresponds to the number of edges between vertex ν_i and ν_j. Replacing the adjacency matrix E by its n-th power ($n \in \mathbb{N}, n \geq 0$), the interpretation is still the same: Each component $[E^n]_{ij}$ of this matrix gives the number of walks of length

n from vertex ν_i to ν_j.

Also the definition of the direct product becomes somewhat more complicated due to the parallel edges that have to be considered now.

Definition 5.10. We denote the direct product of two graphs $G_1 = (\mathcal{V}_1, \mathcal{E}_1, \Psi_1)$ and $G_2 = (\mathcal{V}_2, \mathcal{E}_2, \Psi_2)$ by $G_1 \times G_2$. The vertex set of the direct product is defined as:

$$\mathcal{V}(G_1 \times G_2) = \{(v_1, v_2) \in \mathcal{V}_1 \times \mathcal{V}_2 : label(v_1) = label(v_2)\} \, .$$

The edge set is then defined as:

$$\mathcal{E}(G_1 \times G_2) = \{(e_1, e_2) \in \mathcal{E}_1 \times \mathcal{E}_2 \; : \exists \, (u_1, u_2), (v_1, v_2) \in \mathcal{V}(G_1 \times G_2)$$
$$\wedge \, \Psi_1(e_1) = (u_1, v_1) \wedge \Psi_2(e_2) = (u_2, v_2)$$
$$\wedge \, label(e_1) = label(e_2)\} \, .$$

Given an edge $(e_1, e_2) \in \mathcal{E}(G_1 \times G_2)$ with $\Psi_1(e_1) = (u_1, v_1)$ and $\Psi_2(e_2) = (u_2, v_2)$ the value of $\Psi_{G_1 \times G_2}$ is:

$$\Psi_{G_1 \times G_2}((e_1, e_2)) = ((u_1, u_2), (v_1, v_2)) \, .$$

The labels of the vertices and edges in graph $G_1 \times G_2$ correspond to the labels in the factors. The graphs G_1, G_2 are called the factors of graph $G_1 \times G_2$.

Modulo the above changed definitions, the definition of the product graph kernel remains

$$k_\times(G_1, G_2) = \sum_{i,j=1}^{|\mathcal{V}_\times|} \left[\sum_{n=0}^{\infty} \lambda_n E_\times^n \right]_{ij} \, .$$

5.7.3 *Kernel Based RRL in the Blocks World*

In this subsection we first show how the states and actions in the blocks world can be represented as a graph. Then we discuss which kernel is used as the covariance function between blocks worlds.

5.7.3.1 *State and Action Representation*

A blocks world consists of a constant number of identical blocks. Each block is put either on the floor or on another block. On top of each block is either another block, or 'no block'. Figure 5.10 illustrates a (state,action)-pair in a blocks world with four blocks in two stacks. The right side of Figure

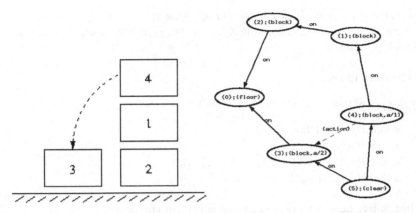

Figure 5.10 Simple example of a blocks world state and action (left) and its representation as a graph (right). The vertex number is in brackets before the colon and the label is after the colon.

5.10 shows the graph representation of this blocks world. The vertices of the graph correspond either to a block, the floor, or 'clear'; where 'clear' basically denotes 'no block'. This is reflected in the labels of the vertices. Each edge labelled 'on' (solid arrows) denotes that the block corresponding to its initial vertex is on top of the block corresponding to its terminal vertex. The edge labelled 'action' (dashed arrow) denotes the action of putting the block corresponding to its initial vertex on top of the block corresponding to its terminal vertex; in the example "put block 4 on block 3". The labels 'a/1' and 'a/2' denote the initial and terminal vertex of the action, respectively.

To represent an arbitrary blocks world as a labelled directed graph we proceed as follows. Given the set of blocks numbered $1, \ldots, n$ and the set of stacks $1, \ldots, m$:

(1) The vertex set $\mathcal{V}$ of the graph is $\{\nu_0, \ldots, \nu_{n+1}\}$.
(2) The edge set $\mathcal{E}$ of the graph is $\{e_1, \ldots, e_{n+m+1}\}$.

The node ν_0 will be used to represent the floor, ν_{n+1} will indicate which blocks are clear. Since each block is on top of something and each stack has one clear block, we need $n + m$ edges to represent the blocks world state. Finally, one extra edge is needed to represent the action.
For the representation of a state it remains to define the function Ψ:

(3) For $1 \leq i \leq n$, we define $\Psi(e_i) = (\nu_i, \nu_0)$ if block i is on the floor, and

$\Psi(e_i) = (\nu_i, \nu_j)$ if block i is on top of block j.

(4) For $n < i \leq n + m$, we define $\Psi(e_i) = (\nu_{n+1}, \nu_j)$ if block j is the top block of stack $i - n$.

And the function *label*:

(5) Let $\Sigma = 2^{\{\{\text{'floor'}\},\{\text{'clear'}\},\{\text{'block'}\},\{\text{'on'}\},\{\text{'a/1'}\},\{\text{'a/2'}\}\}}$ and define

- $label(\nu_0) = \{\text{'floor'}\}$,
- $label(\nu_{n+1}) = \{\text{'clear'}\}$,
- $label(\nu_i) = \{\text{'block'}\}$ $(1 \leq i \leq n)$, and
- $label(e_i) = \{\text{'on'}\}$ $(1 \leq i \leq n + m)$.

All that is left now is to represent the action in the graph

(6) We define:

- $\Psi(e_{n+m+1}) = (\nu_i, \nu_j)$ if block i is moved to block $j(j > 0)$ or on the floor $(j = 0)$,
- $label(\nu_i) \leftarrow label(\nu_i) \cup \{\text{'a/1'}\}$,
- $label(\nu_j) \leftarrow label(\nu_j) \cup \{\text{'a/2'}\}$, and
- $label(e_{n+m+1}) = \{\text{'action'}\}$.

It is clear that this mapping from blocks worlds to graphs is injective.

In some cases the 'goal' of a blocks world problem is to stack blocks in a given configuration (e.g. "put block 3 on top of block 4"). We then need to represent this in the graph. This is handled in the same way as the action representation, i.e. by an extra edge along with an extra 'g/1', 'g/2', and 'goal' labels for initial and terminal blocks, and the new edge, respectively. Note that by using more than one 'goal' edge, we can model arbitrary goal configurations, e.g., "put block 3 on top of block 4 and block 2 on top of block 1".

5.7.3.2 *Blocks World Kernels*

In finite state-action spaces Q-learning is guaranteed to converge if the mapping between state-action pairs and Q-values is represented explicitly. One advantage of Gaussian processes is that for particular choices of the covariance function, the representation is explicit.

To see this we use the matching kernel k_δ as the covariance function between examples ($k_\delta : \mathcal{X} \times \mathcal{X} \to \mathbb{R}$ is defined as $k_\delta(x, x') = 1$ if $x = x'$ and $k_\delta(x, x') = 0$ if $x \neq x'$). Let the predicted Q-value be the mean of the distribution over target values, i.e., $\hat{t}_{n+1} = \mathbf{c}^\top \mathbf{C}^{-1} \mathbf{t}$ where the variables are used as defined in Section 2.4.3. Assume the training examples are distinct and the test example is equal to the j-th training example. It then turns out that $\mathbf{C} = \mathbf{I} = \mathbf{C}^{-1}$ where $\mathbf{I}$ denotes the identity matrix. As furthermore $\mathbf{c}$ is then the vector with all components equal to 0 except the j-th which is equal to 1, it is obvious that $\hat{t}_{n+1} = t_j$ and the representation is thus explicit.

A frequently used kernel function for instances that can be represented by vectors is the Gaussian radial basis function kernel (RBF). Given the bandwidth parameter σ the RBF kernel is defined as: $k_{\mathrm{rbf}}(x, x') = \exp(-||x - x'||^2/\sigma^2)$. For small enough σ the RBF kernel behaves like the matching kernel. In other words, the parameter σ can be used to regulate the amount of generalisation performed in the Gaussian process algorithm: For very small σ all instances are very different and the Q-function is represented explicitly; for large enough σ all examples are considered very similar and the resulting function is very smooth.

In order to have a similar means to regulate the amount of generalisation in the blocks world setting, we do not use the graph kernel proposed in Section 5.7.2 directly, but use a Gaussian modifier with it. Let k be the graph kernel with exponential weights, then the kernel used in the blocks world is given by

$$k^*(x, x') = \exp\left[-(k(x.x) - 2k(x, x') + k(x', x'))/\sigma^2\right] \ .$$

5.7.4 *Experiments*

In this section we describe the tests used to investigate the utility of Gaussian processes and graph kernels as a regression algorithm for RRL. We use the graph-representation of the encountered (state,action)-pairs and the blocks world kernel as described in the previous section,

The RRL-system was trained in worlds where the number of blocks varied between 3 and 5, and given "guided" traces [Driessens and Džeroski (2002)] in a world with 10 blocks. The Q-function and the related policy were tested at regular intervals on 100 randomly generated starting states in worlds where the number of blocks varied from 3 to 10 blocks.

We evaluated RRL with Gaussian processes on three different goals: stacking all blocks, unstacking all blocks and putting two specific blocks on each other. For each goal we ran five times 1000 episodes with different parameter settings to evaluate their influence on the performance of RRL.

After that we chose the best parameter setting and ran another ten times 1000 episodes with different random initialisations. For the "stack-goal" only 500 episodes are shown, as nothing interesting happens thereafter. The results obtained by this procedure are then used to compare the algorithm proposed in this paper with previous versions of RRL.

5.7.4.1 *Parameter Influence*

The used kernel has two parameters that need to be chosen: the exponential weight β (which we shall refer to as *exp* in the graphs) and the radial base function parameter $\gamma = 1/\sigma^2$ (which we shall refer to as *rbf*).

The *exp*-parameter gives an indication of the importance of long walks in the product graph. Higher *exp*-values place means a higher weight for long walks. The *rbf*-parameter gives an indication of the amount of generalisation that should be done. Higher *rbf*-values means lower σ-values for the radial base functions and thus less generalisation.

We tested the behaviour of RRL with Gaussian processes on the "stack-goal" with a range of different values for the two parameters. The experiments were all repeated five times with different random seeds. The results are summarised in Figure 5.11. The graph on the left shows that for a small *exp*-values RRL can not learn the task of stacking all blocks. This makes sense, since we are trying to create a blocks-world-graph which has the longest walk possible, given a certain amount of blocks. However, for very large values of *exp* we have to use equally small values of *rbf* to avoid numeric overflows in our calculations, which in turn results in non-optimal behaviour. The right side of Figure 5.11 shows the influence of the *rbf*-parameter. As expected, smaller values result in faster learning, but when choosing too small *rbf*-values, RRL can not learn the correct Q-function and does not learn an optimal strategy.

For the "unstack-" and "on(A,B)-goal", the influence of the *exp*-parameter is smaller as shown in the left sides of Figure 5.12 and Figure 5.13 respectively. For the "unstack-goal" there is even little influence from the *rbf*-parameter as shown in the right side of Figure 5.12 although it seems that average values work best here as well.

The results for the "on(A,B)-goal" however, show a large influence of the *rbf*-parameter (right side of Figure 5.13). In previous work we have always noticed that "on(A,B)" is a hard problem for RRL to solve [Driessens *et al.* (2001); Driessens and Džeroski (2002)]. The results we obtained with RRL-KBR give an indication why. The learning-curves show that the performance

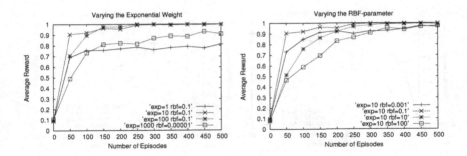

Figure 5.11 Comparing parameter influences for the stack goal

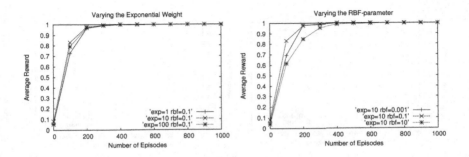

Figure 5.12 Comparing parameter influences for the unstack goal

of the resulting policy is very sensitive to the amount of generalisation that is used. The performance of RRL drops rapidly as a result of over- or under-generalisation.

5.7.4.2 *Comparison with previous RRL-implementations*

Figure 5.14 shows the results of RRL-KBR on the three blocks world problems in relation to the two previous implementations of RRL, i.e. RRL-TG and RRL-RIB. For each goal we chose the best parameter settings from the experiments described above and ran another ten times 1000 episodes. These ten runs were initialised with different random seeds than the experiments used to choose the parameters.

RRL-KBR clearly outperforms RRL-TG with respect to the number of episodes needed to reach a certain level of performance. Note that the

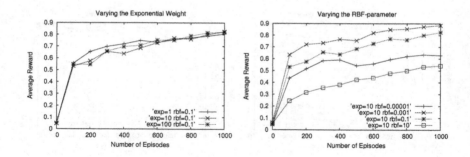

Figure 5.13   Comparing parameter influences for the on(A,B) goal

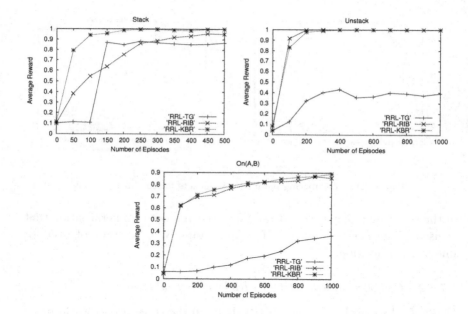

Figure 5.14   Comparing Kernel Based RRL with previous versions

comparison as given in Figure 5.14 is not entirely fair with RRL-TG. Although RRL-TG does need a lot more episodes to reach a given level of performance, it processes these episodes much faster. This advantage is, however, lost when acting in expensive or slow environments.

RRL-KBR performs better than RRL-RIB on the "stack-goal" and obtains comparable results on the "unstack-goal" and on the "on(A,B)-goal". Our current implementation of RRL-KBR is competitive with RRL-RIB in computation times and performance. However, a big advantage of RRL-KBR is the possibility to achieve further improvements with fairly simple modifications, as we will outline in the next section .

5.7.5 *Future Work*

Future work will investigate how reinforcement techniques such as local linear models [Schaal *et al.* (2000)] and the use of convex hulls to make safe predictions [Smart and Kaelbling (2000)] can be applied in RRL.

A promising direction for future work is also to exploit the probabilistic predictions made available in RRL by the algorithm suggested in this paper. The obvious use of these probabilities is to exploit them during exploration. Actions or even entire state-space regions with low confidence on their Q-value predictions could be given a higher exploration priority. This approach is similar to interval based exploration techniques [Kaelbling *et al.* (1996)] where the upper bound of an estimation interval is used to guide the exploration into high promising regions of the state-action space. In the case of RRL-KBR these upper bounds could be replaced with the upper bound of a 90% or 95% confidence interval.

So far, we have not put any selection procedures on the $(state, action, qvalue)$ examples that are passed to the Gaussian processes algorithm by RRL. Another use of the prediction probabilities would be to use them as a filter to limit the examples that need to be processed. This would cause a significant speedup of the regression engine. Other instance selection strategies that might be useful are suggested in [Driessens and Ramon (2003)] and have there successfully been applied in instance based RRL.

Many interesting reinforcement learning problems apart from the blocks world also have an inherently structural nature. To apply Gaussian processes and graph kernels to these problems, the state-action pairs just need to be represented by graphs. Future work will explore such applications.

The performance of the algorithm presented here could be improved by using only an approximate inverse in the Gaussian process. The size of the kernel matrix could be reduced by so called instance averaging techniques [Forbes and Andre (2002)]. While the explicit construction of average instances is far from being trivial, still the kernel between such average instances and test instances can be computed easily without ever constructing average instances.

In our empirical evaluation, the algorithm presented in this paper proved competitive or better than the previous implementations of RRL. From our point of view, however, this is not the biggest advantage of using graph kernels and Gaussian processes in RRL. The biggest advantages are the elegance and potential of our approach. Very good results could be achieved without sophisticated instance selection or averaging strategies. The generalisation ability can be tuned by a single parameter. Probabilistic predictions can be used to guide exploration of the state-action space.

5.8 Molecule Classification

One of the most interesting application areas for predictive graph mining algorithms is the classification of molecules—known as virtual ligand screening. An alternative to docking based approaches [Klebe (2006)] are similarity based approaches [Eckert and Bajorath (2007)] on which we focus our attention here. It has been shown, that kernel methods such as the support vector machines with standard sets of molecular descriptors used in chemoinformatics have competitive or better performance than other similarity based virtual ligand screening methods [Müller *et al.* (2005); Jorissen and Gilson (2005); Geppert *et al.* (2008)]. In this section we investigate the performance of kernel methods with graph kernels and compare it to other state-of-the-art machine learning techniques.

5.8.1 *Mutagenicity*

We consider now the drug activity prediction problem of predicting the mutagenicity of molecules. A molecule is considered active if it is able to cause DNA to mutate. The original dataset [Srinivasan *et al.* (1996)], described by a set of Prolog predicates, has widely been used in the inductive logic programming community.

Srinivasan *et al.* (1999) consider different types of information. The basic data is described by two relations, the atoms of the molecule and the bonds between the atoms, other representations include global molecular descriptors. In the simplest representation, each atom of a molecule is described by the tuple of element, atom-type, and atom-charge; each bond is described by its adjacent atoms and its bond-type. Other representations contain indicator as well as numeric variables that simplify the learning

Table 5.1   Mutagenesis: Best results on atom and bond data from [Flach and Lachiche (2004)].

dataset	Acc	AUC
friendly	0.82	0.83
unfriendly	0.79	0.73

task.

Though incorporating the additional attributes in our kernel function would be very easy, here we consider each molecule as a graph only. A vertex label in this graph is the element of the corresponding atom and all edges have the same label. This representation contains less (explicit) information than the representations considered in the literature, which (at least) also make use of atom-type, bond-type, and charge. Additional features such as the above mentioned indicator and numeric variables have been shown to significantly improve the results achieved by many learning algorithms.

Two sets of instances are frequently used, the so called 'regression-friendly' dataset containing 125 active and 63 inactive instances, and the 'regression-unfriendly' dataset containing 13 active and 29 inactive instances. Usually, algorithms are evaluated using leave-one-out on the unfriendly dataset, and 10-fold crossvalidation on the friendly dataset. The best results reported in literature are accuracy 0.89 [Srinivasan *et al.* (1999)] and area under the ROC curve of 0.91 [Flach and Lachiche (2004)] on the friendly data; and accuracy 0.83 [King *et al.* (1995)] and area under the ROC curve of 0.73 [Flach and Lachiche (2004)] on the unfriendly data. Often worse results have been reported. With only the atom and bond information, however, worse results are reported in literature. The best results then have then been achieved by Flach and Lachiche (2004) with 1BC(2). Their results are summarised in Table 5.1.

By applying a one-nearest-neighbour algorithm with graph kernels to the graph representation of the mutagenesis dataset, we were able to achieve results similar to those obtained with more expressive representations and superior to those with the basic representation. Note that even the basic representation used in literature makes use of more information (e.g., atom-charge) than we do with our merely graph based representation. Our results over a variety of parameters are reported in Table 5.2.

Table 5.2   Mutagenesis: leave-one-out with 1-nearest neighbour.

	regression-unfriendly (13/26)		regression-friendly (125/63)	
exp-weight	Acc	AUC	Acc	AUC
0.02	0.83	0.83	0.88($\pm$0.08)	0.84($\pm$0.12)
0.04	0.83	0.84	0.88($\pm$0.08)	0.84($\pm$0.12)
0.06	0.83	0.84	0.88($\pm$0.07)	0.85($\pm$0.10)
0.08	0.83	0.84	0.89($\pm$0.07)	0.85($\pm$0.10)
0.10	0.83	0.84	0.89($\pm$0.07)	0.85($\pm$0.10)
0.20	0.81	0.86	0.89($\pm$0.07)	0.87($\pm$0.09)
0.40	0.83	0.87	0.89($\pm$0.07)	0.86($\pm$0.08)
0.60	0.81	0.91	0.88($\pm$0.08)	0.86($\pm$0.10)
0.80	0.79	0.91	0.88($\pm$0.08)	0.85($\pm$0.09)
1.00	0.81	0.93	0.88($\pm$0.07)	0.85($\pm$0.09)
2.00	0.71	0.74	0.89($\pm$0.07)	0.87($\pm$0.10)

5.8.2 *HIV Data*

Here, we use the HIV dataset of chemical compounds to evaluate the predictive power of walk- and cycle-based graph kernels. The HIV database
is maintained by the U.S. National Cancer Institute (NCI)[4] and describes
information of the compounds capability to inhibit the HIV virus. This
database has been used frequently in the empirical evaluation of graph
mining approaches (for example [Borgelt and Berthold (2002); Deshpande
et al. (2003); Kramer *et al.* (2001a)]). However, the only approaches to
predictive graph mining on this dataset are described in [Deshpande *et al.*
(2003, 2002)]. There, a support vector machine was used with the frequent
subgraph kernel mentioned in Section 5.6.

Figure 5.15 shows the number of molecules with a given number of
simple cycles. This illustrates that in the HIV domain the assumption
made in the development of cyclic pattern kernels holds.

Dataset   In the NCI-HIV database, each compound is described by its
chemical structure and classified into one of three categories: confirmed
inactive (CI), moderately active (CM), or active (CA). A compound is
inactive if a test showed less than 50% protection of human CEM cells.
All other compounds were re-tested. Compounds showing less than 50%
protection (in the second test) are also classified inactive. The other compounds are classified active, if they provided 100% protection in both tests,
and moderately active, otherwise. The NCI-HIV dataset we used[5] contains
42689 molecules, 423 of which are active, 1081 are moderately active, and
41185 are inactive.

---

[4]http://cactus.nci.nih.gov
[5]http://cactus.nci.nih.gov/ncidb/download.html

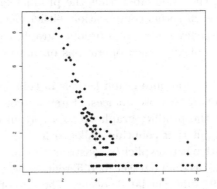

Figure 5.15   Log-log plot of the number of molecules (y) versus the number of simple cycles (x)

Vertex Colouring Though the number of molecules and thus atoms in this dataset is rather large, the number of vertex labels is limited by the number of elements occurring in natural compounds. For that, it is reasonable to not just use the element of the atom as its label. Instead, we use the pair consisting of the atom's element and the multiset of all neighbours' elements as the label. In the HIV dataset this increases the number of different labels from 62 to 1391.

More sophisticated vertex colouring algorithms are used in isomorphism tests. There, one would like two vertices to be coloured differently iff they do not lie on the same orbit of the automorphism group [Fürer (1995)]. As no efficient algorithm for the ideal case is known, one often resorts to colourings such that two differently coloured vertices can not lie on the same orbit. One possibility there is to apply the above simple vertex colouring recursively. This is guaranteed to converge to a "stable colouring".

Implementation Issues The size of this dataset, in particular the size of the graphs in this dataset, hinders the computation of walk-based graph kernels by means of eigendecompositions on the product graphs. The largest graph contains 214 atoms (not counting hydrogen atoms). If all had the same label, the product graph would have 45796 vertices. As different elements occur in this molecule, the product graph has less vertices. However, it turns out that the largest product graph (without the vertex colouring step) still has 34645 vertices. The vertex colouring above changes the number of vertices with the same label, thus the product graph is reduced to 12293 vertices. For each kernel computation, either eigendecomposition or inversion of the adjacency matrix of a product graph has to be performed. With cubic time complexity, such operations on matrices of this size are not feasible.

The only chance to compute graph kernels in this application is to approximate them. There are two choices. First we consider counting the number of walks in the product graph up to a certain depth. In our experiments it turned out that counting walks with 13 or less vertices is still feasible. An alternative is to explicitly construct the image of each graph in feature space. In the original dataset 62 different labels occur and after the vertex colouring 1391 different labels occur. The size of the feature space of label sequences of length 13 is then $62^{13} > 10^{23}$ for the original dataset and $1391^{13} > 10^{40}$ with the vertex colouring. We would also have to take into account walks with less than 13 vertices but at the same time not all walks will occur in at least one graph. The size of this feature space hinders explicit computation. We thus resorted to counting walks with 13 or less vertices in the product graph.

Experimental Methodology   We compare our approach to the results presented in [Deshpande *et al.* (2002)] and [Deshpande *et al.* (2003)]. The classification problems considered there were: (1) distinguish CA from CM, (2) distinguish CA and CM from CI, and (3) distinguish CA from CI. Additionally, we will consider (4) distinguish CA from CM and CI. For each problem, the area under the ROC curve (AUC), averaged over a 5-fold crossvalidation, is given for different misclassification cost settings.

In order to choose the parameters of the walk-based graph kernel we proceeded as follows. We split the smallest problem (1) into 10% for parameter tuning and 90% for evaluation. First we tried different parameters for the exponential weight $(10^{-3}, 10^{-2}, 10^{-1}, 1, 10)$ in a single nearest neighbour algorithm (leading to an average AUC of $0.660, 0.660, 0.674, 0.759, 0.338$) and decided to use 1 from now. Next we needed to choose the complexity (regularisation) parameter of the SVM. Here we tried different parameters $(10^{-3}, 10^{-2}, 10^{-1}$ leading to an average AUC of $0.694, 0.716, 0.708)$ and found the parameter 10^{-2} to work best. Evaluating with a SVM and these parameters on the remaining 90% of the data, we achieved an average AUC of 0.820 and standard deviation 0.024.

For cyclic pattern kernels, only the complexity constant of the support

Table 5.3   Area under the ROC curve for different costs and problems (•: significant loss against walk-based kernels at 10% / ••: significant loss against walk-based kernels at 1% / ∘: significant loss against cyclic pattern kernels at 10% / ∘ ∘: significant loss against cyclic pattern kernels at 1%)

task	cost	walk-based kernels	cyclic pattern kernels	FSG	FSG*
(1)	1	0.818(±0.024)	0.813(±0.014)	0.774 ••∘∘	0.810
(1)	5/2	0.825(±0.032)	0.827(±0.013)	0.782 • ∘∘	0.792 • ∘∘
(2)	1	0.815(±0.015)	0.775(±0.017) ••	0.742 ••∘∘	0.765 ••
(2)	35	0.799(±0.011)	0.801(±0.017)	0.778 ••∘	0.794
(3)	1	0.942(±0.015)	0.919(±0.011) •	0.868 ••∘∘	0.839 ••∘∘
(3)	100	0.944(±0.015)	0.929(±0.01) •	0.914 •• ∘	0.908 ••∘∘
(4)	1	0.926(±0.015)	0.908(±0.024) •	—	—
(4)	100	0.928(±0.013)	0.921(±0.026)	—	—

vector machine has to be chosen. Here, the heuristic as implemented in SVM-light [Joachims (1999)] is used. Also, we did not use any vertex colouring with cyclic pattern kernels.

Results of Experimental Evaluation   To compare our results to those achieved in previous work, we fixed these parameters and rerun the experiments on the full data of all three problems. Table 5.3 summarises these results and the results reported in [Deshpande *et al.* (2002)]. In [Deshpande *et al.* (2003)] the authors of [Deshpande *et al.* (2002)] describe improved results (FSG*). There, the authors report results obtained with an optimised threshold on the frequency of patterns[6]. Clearly, the graph kernels proposed here outperform FSG and FSG* over all problems and misclassification cost settings

To evaluate the significance of our results we proceeded as follows: As we did not know the variance of the area under the ROC curve for FSG, we assumed the same variance as obtained with graph kernels. Thus, to test the hypothesis that graph kernels significantly outperform FSG, we used a pooled sample variance equal to the variance exhibited by graph kernels. As FSG and graph kernels were applied in a 5-fold crossvalidation, the estimated standard error of the average difference is the pooled sample variance times $\sqrt{\frac{2}{5}}$. The test statistic is then the average difference divided by its estimated standard error. This statistic follows a t distribution. The null hypothesis — graph kernels perform no better than FSG — can be

---

[6] In [Deshpande *et al.* (2003)] also including a description of the three dimensional shape of each molecule is considered. We do not compare our results to those obtained using the three dimensional information. We are considering to also include three dimensional information in our future work and expect similar improvements.

rejected at the significance level α if the test statistic is greater than $t_8(\alpha)$, the corresponding percentile of the t distribution.

Table 5.3 shows the detailed results of this comparison. Walk-based graph kernels perform always better or at least not significantly worse than any other kernel. Cyclic pattern kernels are sometimes outperformed by walk-based graph kernels but can be computed much more efficiently. For example, in the classification problem where we tried to distinguish active compounds from moderately active compounds and inactive compounds, five-fold crossvalidation with walk-based graph kernels finished in about eight hours, while changing to cyclic pattern kernels reduced the runtime to about twenty minutes.

5.9 Summary

In this chapter we showed that computing a complete graph kernel is at least as hard as deciding whether two graphs are isomorphic, and that the problem of computing a graph kernel based on common (isomorphic) subgraphs is *NP*-hard. Therefore, we presented alternative graph kernels that are conceptually based on the label sequences of all possible walks in the graph. Efficient computation of these kernels is made possible by the use of product graphs and by choosing the weights such that a closed form of the resulting matrix power series exists.

The advantage of the label pair graph kernel is that the feature space can be computed explicitly and thus linear optimisation methods for support vector machines can be applied. Therefore, learning with this kernel can be very efficient. The advantage of the direct product kernel and the non-contiguous graph kernel is the expressivity of their feature spaces. Both definitions are based on the concept of graph products. We have shown that the direct graph product can be employed to count the number of contiguous label sequences occurring in two graphs and that it can be to extended to count the number of non-contiguous label sequences occurring in two graphs.

A problem with walk based kernels is that we are not able to distinguish between cyclic and acyclic subgraphs. An alternative graph kernel, the cyclic pattern kernel, can however only be computed in polynomial time on graphs for which the number of simple cycles can be bound by a polynomial in the number of vertices.

To empirically evaluate our approach, in Section 5.7 we proposed Gaussian processes and graph kernels as a new regression algorithm in relational reinforcement learning. Gaussian processes have been chosen as they are able to make probabilistic predictions and can be learnt incrementally. The use of graph kernels as the covariance functions allows for a structural representation of states and actions. Experiments in the blocks world show comparable and even better performance for RRL using Gaussian processes when compared to previous implementations: decision tree based RRL and instance based RRL. With graph kernels it is not only possible to apply Gaussian processes in RRL but also other regression algorithms can be used.

To further strengthen these empirical results, we also applied graph kernels to the problem of molecule classification. One of the databases considered contains more than 40000 molecules described by their chemical structure graph. Using a support vector machine and graph kernels on the undirected graphs describing the molecules, we were able to obtain substantial improvements over previous results. It turns out that though walk-based graph kernels are able to achieve somewhat better predictive performance, cyclic pattern kernels can be computed in much less time on this domain.

Chapter 6

Conclusions

*"And that's why I so violently objected to the business of having me
boiled. I could see the image in your mind—most of me in the frozen
food locket, some of me in the kettle, a bit for your pet cat—"*

*"So you read minds?" the Captain said. "How interesting. Anything
else? I mean, what else can you do along these lines?"*

"A few odds and ends," the wub said absently, staring around the room.

(Philip K. Dick, Beyond Lies the Wub)

In this book we investigated how to apply kernel methods to structured data. Before, kernel methods had very successfully been applied to
real-world machine learning problems in which the instances can easily be
embedded in a Euclidean space. This is the case, for example, for instances
represented by a single row in a single table.

By structured data we mean any kind of data for which this embedding
is not obvious or for which obvious embeddings are not meaningful. In particular we investigated two representations: basic terms and graphs. Basic
terms are ground terms in a typed higher-order logic and can be used as
a very general modelling tool for instances. Although this representation
is sufficiently powerful to also represent general graphs, for the representation of general graphs we need to introduce identifiers linking one part
of an instance to another. As exploiting these identifiers causes convergence and computational issues, we ignored them when considering kernels
for basic terms. Exploiting this kind of identifiers is essential, however,
when investigating graphs. We thus considered graph kernels in a separate
chapter.

A theoretical investigation of basic term kernels for multi-instance con-

175

cepts showed some nice properties of basic term kernels on this kind of problems. An empirical investigation of basic term kernels in different real-world applications showed that basic term kernels perform competitive or better than other algorithms proposed for these problems.

Classifying graphs is a problem that—when solved—could help speed up the development of new drugs, for example. We first showed that graph kernels that are able to distinguish two graphs if and only if they are not isomorphic, can not be computed in polynomial time. We then proposed alternative kernels that are based on the label sequences of walks or simple cycles in the graphs. While walk-based graph kernels can be computed in polynomial time for general undirected graphs, cyclic pattern kernels can only be computed in polynomial time in the number of simple cycles of the graphs. We evaluated walk-based graph kernels in a relational reinforcement learning setting and compared them with cyclic pattern kernels on a molecule classification problem. Both walk- and cycle-based kernels performed better or at least competitive with earlier proposed learning algorithms over all learning tasks we considered.

We end this book with a brief overview of some related research ideas that can be investigated in future work.

Separation and convergence Similar to the investigation of separation and convergence properties of basic term kernels for multi-instance concepts, it would be very interesting and important to investigate these issues for other concept classes. As a first step, concept classes that occur frequently in real world problems have to be identified.

Unifying graph kernels We described a number of different kernels between instances represented by graphs. A related problem is the definition of kernels between the vertices of the same graph. Unifying these two types of graph kernels would enable the transfer of theoretical results from one area to the other.

Polynomial fragments of cyclic pattern kernels We showed that cyclic pattern kernels can in general not be computed in polynomial time. However, it would be interesting to investigate whether the restriction to cycles with particular properties only can lead to polynomial time algorithms.

Application of graph kernels in games In board games like for example go each board state can be described by a graph. By using graph kernels it could be possible to achieve better computer opponents for this kind of board games.

Learning with structured output spaces Recently more and more researchers are interested in learning tasks where the set of labels is infinite and structured, for example, one wants to predict a tree structure from a sequence. Using graph kernels on output spaces could be one step towards the prediction of graph structures.

Using graph kernels with spatial data Spatial data can not only be modelled using spatial coordinates, but also using spatial relations. Special graph kernels for spatial relations could be used in location planning problems.

Bibliography

Buying books would be a good thing if one could also buy the time to read them in: but as a rule the purchase of books is mistaken for the appreciation of their contents.

(Arthur Schopenhauer, Parerga and Paralipomena)

Aldea, E., Atif, J. and Bloch, I. (2007a). Image classification using marginalized kernels for graphs, in *Graph Based Representation for Pattern Recognition*, pp. 103–113.

Aldea, E., Fouquier, G., Atif, J. and Bloch, I. (2007b). Kernel fusion for image classification using fuzzy structural information, in *Advances in Visual Computing*, pp. II: 307–317.

Alt, H., Fuchs, U. and Kriegel, K. (1999). On the number of simple cycles in planar graphs, *Combinatorics, Probability & Computing* **8**, 5, pp. 397–405.

Andrews, S., Tsochantaridis, I. and Hofmann, T. (2003). Support vector machines for multiple-instance learning, in *Advances in Neural Information Processing Systems*, Vol. 15 (MIT Press).

Aronszajn, N. (1950). Theory of reproducing kernels, *Transactions of the American Mathematical Society* **68**.

Asai, T., Arimura, H., Uno, T. and Nakano, S. (2003). Discovering frequent substructures in large unordered trees, in *ICDS: International Conference on Data Discovery, DS* (LNCS).

Auer, P. (1997). On learning from multi-instance examples: Empirical evalutaion of a theoretical approach, in *Proceedings of the 14th International Conference on Machine Learning* (Morgan Kaufmann), pp. 21–29.

Auer, P., Long, P. and Srinivasan, A. (1997). Approximating hyper-rectangles: learning and pseudo-random sets, in *Proceedings of the twenty-ninth annual ACM symposium on Theory of computing* (ACM Press), pp. 314–323.

Baldi, P. and Ralaivola, L. (2004). Graph kernels for molecular classification and prediction of mutagenicity, toxicity, and anti-cancer activity, Presented at the Computational Biology Workshop of NIPS.

Barnett, S. (1979). *Matrix Methods for Engineers and Scientists* (MacGraw-Hill).

Bennett, K. and Campbell, C. (2000). Support vector machines: Hype or hallelujah? *SIGKDD Explorations* **2**, 2.

Blaschko, M. B. and Hofmann, T. (2006). Conformal multi-instance kernels, in *NIPS 2006 Workshop on Learning to Compare Examples*.

Blockeel, H. and De Raedt, L. (1998). Top-down induction of first order logical decision trees, *Artificial Intelligence* **101**, 1-2, pp. 285–297.

Blum, A. and Kalai, A. (1998). A note on learning from multiple-instance examples, *Machine Learning* **30**, 1, pp. 23–29.

Borgelt, C. and Berthold, M. R. (2002). Mining molecular fragments: Finding relevant substructures of molecules, in *Proc. of the 2002 IEEE International Conference on Data Mining* (IEEE Computer Society).

Borgwardt, K., Böttger, S. and Kriegel, H. P. (2006a). Vgm: visual graph mining, in *Proceedings of the 2006 ACM SIGMOD international conference on Management of data*, pp. 733–735.

Borgwardt, K. M. and Kriegel, H. P. (2005). Shortest-path kernels on graphs, in *Int. Conf on Data Mining, 0*, Vol. 7481.

Borgwardt, K. M., Kriegel, H.-P., Vishwanathan, S. V. N. and Schraudolph, N. (2006b). Graph kernels for disease outcome prediction from protein-protein interaction networks, in *Biocomputing 2007-Proceedings of the Pacific Symposium*.

Borgwardt, K. M., Ong, C. S., Schonauer, S., Vishwanathan, S. V. N., Smola, A. J. and Kriegel, H. P. (2005). Protein function prediction via graph kernels, *Bioinformatics* **21**, pp. i47–i56.

Borgwardt, K. M., Petri, T., Vishwanathan, S. V. N. and Kriegel, H.-P. (2007). An efficient sampling scheme for comparison of large graphs, in P. Frasconi, K. Kersting and K. Tsuda (eds.), *Mining and Learning with Graphs, MLG 2007, Firence, Italy, August 1-3, 2007, Proceedings*.

Boser, B. E., Guyon, I. M. and Vapnik, V. N. (1992). A training algorithm for optimal margin classifiers, in D. Haussler (ed.), *Proceedings of the 5th Annual ACM Workshop on Computational Learning Theory* (ACM Press), ISBN 0-89791-498-8, pp. 144–152.

Bunescu, R. C. and Mooney, R. J. (2007). Multiple instance learning for sparse positive bags, in *Proceedings of the 24th international conference on Machine learning*, pp. 105–112.

Bunke, H. and Allerman, G. (1983). Inexact graph matching for structural pattern recognition, *Pattern Recognition Letters* **4**.

Bunke, H. and Riesen, K. (2007). A family of novel graph kernels for structural pattern recognition, in *Iberoamerican Congress on Pattern Recognition*, pp. 20–31.

Cantor, G. (1895). Beiträge zur Begründung der transfiniten Mengelehre, *Mathematische Annalen* **XLVI**.

Cherkassky, V. and Mulier, F. (1998). *Learning from Data — Concepts, Theory and Methods* (John Wiley & Sons, New York).

Chevaleyre, Y. and Zucker, J.-D. (2001). A framework for learning rules from multiple instance data, in L. De Raedt and P. Flach (eds.), *Proceedings of the 12th European Conference on Machine Learning* (Springer-Verlag).

Collins, M. and Duffy, N. (2002). Convolution kernels for natural language, in T. G. Dietterich, S. Becker and Z. Ghahramani (eds.), *Advances in Neural Information Processing Systems*, Vol. 14 (MIT Press).

Cristianini, N. and Shawe-Taylor, J. (2000). *An Introduction to Support Vector Machines (and Other Kernel-Based Learning Methods)*. (Cambridge University Press).

Cumby, C. and Roth, D. (2003). On kernel methods for relational learning, in *Proceedings of ICML03*.

De Raedt, L. and Van Laer, W. (1995). Inductive constraint logic, in K. Jantke, T. Shinohara and T. Zeugmann (eds.), *Proceedings of the 6th International Workshop on Algorithmic Learning Theory, LNAI*, Vol. 997 (Springer Verlag), ISBN 3-540-60454-5, pp. 80–94.

Deshpande, M., Kuramochi, M. and Karypis, G. (2002). Automated approaches for classifying structures, in *Proceedings of the 2nd ACM SIGKDD Workshop on Data Mining in Bioinformatics*.

Deshpande, M., Kuramochi, M. and Karypis, G. (2003). Frequent sub-structure based approaches for classifying chemical compounds, in *Proc. of the 2003 IEEE International Conference on Data Mining* (IEEE Computer Society).

Diestel, R. (2000). *Graph Theory* (Springer-Verlag).

Dietterich, T. G., Lathrop, R. H. and Lozano-Pérez, T. (1997). Solving the multiple instance problem with axis-parallel rectangles, *Artificial Intelligence* **89**, 1–2, pp. 31–71.

Driessens, K. (2004). *Relational Reinforcement Learning*, Ph.D. thesis, K. U. Leuven.

Driessens, K. and Džeroski, S. (2002). Integrating experimentation and guidance in relational reinforcement learning, in C. Sammut and A. Hoffmann (eds.), *Proceedings of the Nineteenth International Conference on Machine Learning* (Morgan Kaufmann Publishers, Inc), pp. 115–122, URL http://www.cs.kuleuven.ac.be/cgi-bin-dtai/publ_info.pl?id=38%637.

Driessens, K. and Ramon, J. (2003). Relational instance based regression for relational reinforcement learning, in *Proceedings of the 20th International Conference on Machine Learning (to be published)*.

Driessens, K., Ramon, J. and Blockeel, H. (2001). Speeding up relational reinforcement learning through the use of an incremental first order decision tree learner, in L. De Raedt and P. Flach (eds.), *Proceedings of the 13th European Conference on Machine Learning, Lecture Notes in Artificial Intelligence*, Vol. 2167 (Springer-Verlag), pp. 97–108.

Durbin, R., Eddy, S., Krogh, A. and Mitchison, G. (1998). *Biological Sequence Analysis: Probabilistic Models of Proteins and Nucleic Acids.* (Cambridge University Press).

Džeroski, S., De Raedt, L. and Blockeel, H. (1998a). Relational reinforcement learning, in *Proceedings of the 15th International Conference on Machine Learning* (Morgan Kaufmann), pp. 136–143.

Džeroski, S., Schulze-Kremer, S., Heidtke, K. R., Siems, K., Wettschereck, D. and Blockeel, H. (1998b). Diterpene structure elucidation from ^{13}C NMR spectra with inductive logic programming, *Applied Artificial Intelligence* **12**, 5, pp. 363–383, special Issue on First-Order Knowledge Discovery in Databases.

Eckert, H. and Bajorath, J. (2007). Molecular similarity analysis in virtual screening: foundations, limitations and novel approaches, *Drug discovery today* **12**, pp. 225–33, pMID: 17331887.

Eiter, T. and Mannila, H. (1997). Distance measures for point sets and their computation, *Acta Informatica* **34**.

Emde, W. and Wettschereck, D. (1996). Relational instance-based learning, in *Proceedings of the 13th International Conference on Machine Learning* (Morgan Kaufmann), pp. 122–130.

Faulon, J. L., Misra, M., Martin, S., Sale, K. and Sapra, R. (2008). Genome scale enzyme metabolite and drug target interaction predictions using the signature molecular descriptor, *Bioinformatics* **24**, p. 225.

Fayyad, U., Haussler, D. and Stolorz, P. (1996). Mining scientific data, *Communications of the ACM* **39**, 11, pp. 51–57.

Fischer, R. A. and Fischer, M. J. (1974). The string-to-string correction problem, *Journal of the Association for Computing Machinery* **21**, 1.

Flach, P. A. (2003). The geometry of ROC space: understanding machine learning metrics through ROC isometrics, in *Proc. 20th International Conference on Machine Learning* (AAAI Press).

Flach, P. A. and Lachiche, N. (2004). Naïve bayesian classification of structured data, *Machine Learning* Submitted.

Florencio, C. C. (2007). Unsupervised learning of graph languages using kernels: New results, in *LNVD*.

Forbes, J. and Andre, D. (2002). Representations for learning control policies, in E. de Jong and T. Oates (eds.), *Proceedings of the ICML-2002 Workshop on Development of Representations* (The University of New South Wales, Sydney), pp. 7–14.

Frohlich, H., Wegner, J. K., Sieker, F. and Zell, A. (2005). Optimal assignment kernels for attributed molecular graphs, pp. 225–232.

Fung, G. and Mangasarian, O. L. (2001). Proximal support vector machines, in *Proceedings of the 7th ACM SIGKDD International Conference on Knowledge Discovery and Data Mining* (ACM).

Fürer, M. (1995). Graph isomorphism testing without numberics for graphs of bounded eigenvalue multiplicity, in *Proceedings of the Sixth Annual ACM-SIAM Symposium on Discrete Algorithms*.

Gärtner, T., Flach, P. A., Kowalczyk, A. and Smola, A. J. (2002a). Multi-instance kernels, in *Proceedings of the 19th International Conference on Machine Learning* (Morgan Kaufmann).

Gärtner, T., Lloyd, J. W. and Flach, P. A. (2002b). Kernels for structured data, in *Proceedings of the 12th International Conference on Inductive Logic Programming* (Springer-Verlag).

Gauss, C. F. (1880). Theoria combinationis observationum erroribus minimis obnoxiae, pars prior, in *Werke, IV* (Königlichen Gesellschaft der Wissenschaften zu Göttingen), pp. 1–26, first published in 1821.

Geppert, H., Horváth, T., Gärtner, T., Wrobel, S. and Bajorath, J. (2008). Support-vector-machine-based ranking significantly improves the effectiveness of similarity searching using 2d fingerprints and multiple reference compounds, *Journal of Chemical Information and Modeling* .

Gower, J. C. (1971). A general coefficient of similarity and some of its properties, *Biometrics* **27**, pp. 857–871.

Graepel, T. (2002). *PAC-Bayesian Pattern Classification with Kernels*, Ph.D. thesis, TU Berlin.

Graettinger, T. (1999). Digging up dollars with data mining, *The Data Administration Newsletter* **10**.

Gray, R. M. (1987). *Probability, Random Processes, and Ergodic Properties* (Springer-Verlag).

Harchaoui, Z. and Bach, F. (2007). Image classification with segmentation graph kernels, in *IEEE Computer Society Conference on Computer Vision and Pattern Recognition (CVPR)*.

Haussler, D. (1999). Convolution kernels on discrete structures, Tech. rep., Department of Computer Science, University of California at Santa Cruz.

Horváth, T. (2005). Cyclic pattern kernels revisited, in *Proc. of Advances in Knowledge Discovery and Data Mining, 9th Pacific-Asia Conference, PAKDD 2005, LNAI*, Vol. 3518 (Springer Verlag), pp. 791–801.

Imrich, W. and Klavžar, S. (2000). *Product Graphs: Structure and Recognition* (John Wiley).

Jaakkola, T. S., Diekhans, M. and Haussler, D. (2000). A discriminative framework for detecting remote protein homologies, *Journal of Computational Biology* **7**, 1,2.

Jaakkola, T. S. and Haussler, D. (1999a). Exploiting generative models in discriminative classifiers, in *Advances in Neural Information Processing Systems*, Vol. 10.

Jaakkola, T. S. and Haussler, D. (1999b). Probabilistic kernel regression models, in *Proceedings of the 1999 Conference on AI and Statistics*.

Jacob, L., de Paris, E. M. and Vert, J. P. (2007). Kernel methods for in silico chemogenomics, eprint arXiv: 0709.3931.

Jain, B. J., Geibel, P. and Wysotzki, F. (2004). Combining recurrent neural networks and support vector machines for structural pattern recognition, in *KI 2004: 27th Annual German Conference on AI, KI 2004, Ulm, Germany, September 20-24, 2004: Proceedings*.

Jain, B. J., Geibel, P. and Wysotzki, F. (2005). Svm learning with the schur–hadamard inner product for graphs, *Neurocomputing* **64**, pp. 93–105.

Joachims, T. (1999). Making large–scale SVM learning practical, in B. Schölkopf, C. J. C. Burges and A. J. Smola (eds.), *Advances in Kernel Methods — Support Vector Learning* (MIT Press).

Joachims, T. (2002). *Learning to Classify Text using Support Vector Machines* (Kluwer Academic Publishers).

Jones, S. P. and Hughes, J. (eds.) (1998). *Haskell98: A Non-Strict Purely Functional Language*, URL http://haskell.org/.

Jorissen, R. N. and Gilson, M. K. (2005). Virtual screening of molecular databases using a support vector machine, *Journal of Chemical Information and Modeling* **45**, 3, pp. 549–561.

Kaelbling, L., Littman, M. and Moore, A. (1996). Reinforcement learning: A survey. *Journal of Artificial Intelligence Research* **4**, pp. 237–285.

Kandola, J., Shawe-Taylor, J. and Christianini, N. (2003). Learning semantic similarity, in S. Becker, S. Thrun and K. Obermayer (eds.), *Advances in Neural Information Processing Systems*, Vol. 15 (MIT Press).

Karchin, R., Karplus, K. and Haussler, D. (2002). Classifying g-protein coupled receptors with support vector machines, *Bioinformatics* **18**, 1, pp. 147–159.

Kashima, H. and Koyanagi, T. (2002). Kernels for semi-structured data, in C. Sammut and A. Hoffmann (eds.), *Proceedings of the 19th International Conference on Machine Learning* (Morgan Kaufmann).

Kashima, H., Tsuda, K. and Inokuchi, A. (2003). Marginalized kernels between labeled graphs, in T. Fawcett and N. Mishra (eds.), *Machine Learning, Proceedings of the Twentieth International Conference (ICML 2003), August 21-24, 2003, Washington, DC, USA* (AAAI Press), pp. 321–328.

Keeler, J. D., Rumelhart, D. E. and Leow, W.-K. (1991). Integrated segmentation and recognition of hand-printed numerals, in R. Lippmann, J. Moody and D. Touretzky (eds.), *Advances in Neural Information Processing Systems*, Vol. 3 (Morgan Kaufmann), pp. 557–563.

Khardon, R., Roth, D. and Servedio, R. (2002). Efficiency versus convergence of boolean kernels for on-line learning algorithms, in T. Dietterich, S. Becker and Z. Ghahramani (eds.), *Advances in Neural Information Processing Systems*, Vol. 14 (MIT Press).

King, R. D., Srinivasan, A. and Sternberg, M. J. E. (1995). Relating chemical activity to structure: an examination of ilp successes, *New Gen. Comput.* .

Klebe, G. (2006). Virtual ligand screening: strategies, perspectives and limitations, *Drug discovery today* **11**, pp. 580–94, pMID: 16793526.

Knobbe, A., Siebes, A. and Marseille, B. (2002). *Involving Aggregate Functions in Multi-relational Search*, pp. 145–168, URL http://dx.doi.org/10.1007/3-540-45681-3_24.

Köbler, J., Schöning, U. and Toràn, J. (1993). *The Graph Isomorphism Problem: Its Structural Complexity*, Progress in Theoretical Computer Science (Birkhäuser).

Kolmogorov, A. N. and Fomin, S. V. (1960a). *Elements of the Theory of Functions and Functional Analysis: Measure, Lebesgue Integrals, and Hilbert Space*, Vol. 2 (Academic Press).

Kolmogorov, A. N. and Fomin, S. V. (1960b). *Elements of the Theory of Functions and Functional Analysis: Metric and Normed Spaces*, Vol. 1 (Academic Press).

Kondor, R. I. and Lafferty, J. (2002). Diffusion kernels on graphs and other discrete input spaces, in C. Sammut and A. Hoffmann (eds.), *Proceedings of the 19th International Conference on Machine Learning* (Morgan Kaufmann), pp. 315–322.

Korte, B. and Vygen, J. (2002). *Combinatorial Optimization: Theory and Algorithms* (Springer-Verlag).

Kowalczyk, A., Smola, A. J. and Williamson, R. C. (2002). Kernel machines and boolean functions, in T. Dietterich, S. Becker and Z. Ghahramani (eds.), *Advances in Neural Information Processing Systems*, Vol. 14 (MIT Press).

Kramer, S., De Raedt, L. and Helma, C. (2001a). Molecular feature mining in HIV data, in F. Provost and R. Srikant (eds.), *Proceedings of the Seventh ACM SIGKDD International Conference on Knowledge Discovery and Data Mining*, pp. 136–143.

Kramer, S., Lavrač, N. and Flach, P. A. (2001b). Propositionalization approaches to relational data mining, in *Relational Data Mining*, chap. 11 (Springer-Verlag).

Krogel, M.-A. and Wrobel, S. (2001). Transformation-based learning using multirelational aggregation, in C. Rouveirol and M. Sebag (eds.), *Proceedings of the 11th International Conference on Inductive Logic Programming* (Springer-Verlag).

Kuramochi, M. and Karypis, G. (2001). Frequent subgraph discovery, in *Proceedings of the IEEE International Conference on Data Mining*.

Kwok, J. and Cheung, P. M. (2007). Marginalized multi-instance kernels, in *Proc. of Int. Joint Conf. on Aritificial Intelligence*, p. 901–906.

Landwehr, N., Passerini, A., Raedt, L. D. and Frasconi, P. (2006). kfoil: Learning simple relational kernels, in *Proceedings of the 21st National Conference on Artificial Intelligence*.

Leslie, C., Eskin, E. and Noble, W. (2002). The spectrum kernel: A string kernel for SVM protein classification, in *Proceedings of the Pacific Symposium on Biocomputing*, pp. 564–575.

Leslie, C., Eskin, E., Weston, J. and Noble, W. (2003). Mismatch string kernels for SVM protein classification, in S. Becker, S. Thrun and K. Obermayer (eds.), *Advances in Neural Information Processing Systems*, Vol. 15 (MIT Press).

Lloyd, J. W. (2003). *Logic for Learning* (Springer-Verlag).

Lodhi, H., Saunders, C., Shawe-Taylor, J., Cristianini, N. and Watkins, C. (2002). Text classification using string kernels, *Journal of Machine Learning Research* **2**.

Lodhi, H., Shawe-Taylor, J., Christianini, N. and Watkins, C. (2001). Text classification using string kernels, in T. Leen, T. Dietterich and V. Tresp (eds.), *Advances in Neural Information Processing Systems*, Vol. 13 (MIT Press).

MacKay, D. J. C. (1997). Introduction to Gaussian processes, Available at http://wol.ra.phy.cam.ac.uk/mackay.

Mahe, P., de Paris, E. M. and Vert, J. P. (2006). Graph kernels based on tree patterns for molecules, Arxiv preprint q-bio.QM/0609024.

Mahé, P., Ueda, N., Akutsu, T., Perret, J.-L. and Vert, J.-P. (2004). Extensions of marginalized graph kernels, in C. E. Brodley (ed.), *Machine Learning, Proceedings of the Twenty-first International Conference (ICML 2004), Banff, Alberta, Canada, July 4-8, 2004*, Vol. 69 (ACM).

Mahé, P., Ralaivola, L., Stoven, V. and Vert, J. P. (2006). The pharmacophore kernel for virtual screening with support vector machines, Arxiv preprint q-bio.QM/0603006.

Maron, O. and Lozano-Pérez, T. (1998). A framework for multiple-instance learning, in M. I. Jordan, M. J. Kearns and S. A. Solla (eds.), *Advances in Neural Information Processing Systems*, Vol. 10 (MIT Press).

Mavroeidis, D. and Flach, P. A. (2003). Improved distances for structured data, in *Proceedings of the 13th International Conference on Inductive Logic Programming* (Springer-Verlag).

Menchetti, S., Costa, F. and Frasconi, P. (2005). Weighted decomposition kernels, in *Proceedings of the 22nd international conference on Machine learning*, pp. 585–592.

Meschkowski, H. (1960). *Hilbertsche Räume mit Kernfunktion* (Springer Verlag).

Messmer, B. T. (1995). *Graph Matching Algorithms and Applications*, Ph.D. thesis, University of Bern.

Michie, D., Muggleton, S., Page, D. and Srinivasan, A. (1994). To the international computing community: A new eastwest challenge, Tech. rep., Oxford University Computing laboratory, Oxford,UK.

Mitchell, T. M. (1996). *Machine learning* (McGraw Hill, New York, US).

Müller, K.-R., Rätsch, G., Sonnenburg, S., Mika, S., Grimm, M. and Heinrich, N. (2005). Classifying 'drug-likeness' with kernel-based learning methods, *Journal of Chemical Information and Modeling* **45**, 2, pp. 249–253, URL http://dx.doi.org/10.1021/ci049737o.

Neuhaus, M. and Bunke, H. (2006a). A convolution edit kernel for error-tolerant graph matching, in *International Conference on Pattern Recognition*, pp. IV: 220–223.

Neuhaus, M. and Bunke, H. (2006b). A random walk kernel derived from graph edit distance, p. 191.

Neumaier, A. (1998). Solving ill-conditioned and singular linear systems: A tutorial on regularization, *SIAM Review* **40**, 3, pp. 636–666, URL http://dx.doi.org/10.1137/S0036144597321909.

Ng, K. (2005). *Learning Comprehensible Theories from Structured Data*, Ph.D. thesis, Australian National University.

Ng, K. and Lloyd, J. W. (2008). Probabilistic reasoning in a classical logic, *Journal of Applied Logic* To appear.

Novikoff, A. (1963). On convergence proofs for perceptrons, in *Proceedings of the Symposium on the Mathematical Theory of Automata*, Vol. 12, pp. 615–622.

Ormoneit, D. and Sen, S. (2002). Kernel-based reinforcement learning, *Machine Learning* **49**, pp. 161–178.

Paass, G., Leopold, E., Larson, M., Kindermann, J. and Eickeler, S. (2002). SVM classification using sequences of phonemes and syllables, in T. Elomaa, H. Mannila and H. Toivonen (eds.), *Proceedings of the 6th European Conference on Principles of Data Mining and Knowledge Discovery* (Springer-Verlag).

Pahikkala, T., Tsivtsivadze, E., Boberg, J. and Salakoski, T. (2006). Graph kernels versus graph representations: a case study in parse ranking, in *MLG*, Vol. 6.

Passerini, A., Frasconi, P. and Raedt, L. D. (2006). Kernels on prolog proof trees: Statistical learning in the ilp setting, *The Journal of Machine Learning*

Research **7**, pp. 307–342.

Pavlidis, P., Furey, T., Liberto, M., Haussler, D. and Grundy, W. (2001). Promoter region-based classification of genes, in *Proceedings of the Pacific Symposium on Biocomputing*, pp. 151–163.

Perlich, C. and Provost, F. (2006). Distribution-based aggregation for relational learning with identifier attributes, *Mach. Learn.* **62**, pp. 65–105, URL http://portal.acm.org/citation.cfm?id=1113913.

Platt, J. C. (1999). Fast training of support vector machines using sequential minimal optimization, in B. Schölkopf, C. J. C. Burges and A. J. Smola (eds.), *Advances in kernel methods: support vector learning* (MIT Press).

Poggio and Smale (2003). The mathematics of learning: Dealing with data, *Notices of the American Mathematical Society* **50**.

Provost, F. and Fawcett, T. (2000). Robust classification for imprecise environments, *Machine Learing* **42**, 3.

Provost, F., Fawcett, T. and Kohavi, R. (1998). The case against accuracy estimation for comparing induction algorithms, in *Proceedings of the 15th International Conf. on Machine Learning* (Morgan Kaufmann).

Quinlan, J. R. (1990). Learning logical definitions from relations. *Machine Learning* **5**, 3, pp. 239–266.

Rabiner, L. R. (1989). A tutorial on hidden Markov models and selected applications in speech recognition, *Proceedings of the IEEE* **77**, 2, pp. 257–285.

Raedt, L. D. (1998). Attribute value learning versus inductive logic programming: The missing links (extended abstract), in *Proceedings of the 8th International Conference on Inductive Logic Programming* (Springer-Verlag).

Ramon, J. and De Raedt, L. (2000). Multi instance neural networks, in *Attribute-Value and Relational Learning: Crossing the Boundaries. A Workshop at the Seventeenth International Conference on Machine Learning (ICML-2000)*.

Ramon, J. and Gärtner, T. (2003). Expressivity versus efficiency of graph kernels, in *First International Workshop on Mining Graphs, Trees and Sequences*.

Read, R. C. and Tarjan, R. E. (1975). Bounds on backtrack algorithms for listing cycles, paths, and spanning trees, *Networks* **5**, 3, pp. 237–252.

Rifkin, R. M. (2002). *Everything Old is new again: A fresh Look at Historical Approaches to Machine Learning*, Ph.D. thesis, MIT.

Rosenblatt, F. (1957). The perceptron: A perceiving and recognizing automaton, Tech. rep., Project PARA, Cornell Aeronautical Laboratory.

Ruffo, G. (2001). *Learning Single and Multiple Instance Decision Trees for Computer Securtity Applications*, Ph.D. thesis, Università di Torino.

Sadohara, K. (2001). Learning of boolean functions using support vector machines, in N. Abe, R. Khardon and T. Zeugmann (eds.), *Proceedings of the 12th Conference on Algorithmic Learning Theory* (Springer-Verlag), pp. 106–118.

Saigo, H., Kadowaki, T. and Tsuda, K. (2006). A linear programming approach for molecular qsar analysis, in *International Workshop on Mining and Learning with Graphs (MLG)*, p. 85–96.

Saunders, C., Gammerman, A. and Vovk, V. (1998). Ridge regression learning algorithm in dual variables, in *Proceedings of the Fifteenth International Conference on Machine Learning* (Morgan Kaufmann).

Saunders, C., Shawe-Taylor, J. and Vinokourov, A. (2003). String kernels, fisher kernels and finite state automata, in S. Becker, S. Thrun and K. Obermayer (eds.), *Advances in Neural Information Processing Systems*, Vol. 15 (MIT Press).

Schaal, S., Atkeson, C. G. and Vijayakumar, S. (2000). Real-time robot learning with locally weighted statistical learning, in *Proceedings of the IEEE International Conference on Robotics and Automation* (IEEE Press, Piscataway, N.J.), pp. 288–293.

Schoelkopf, B., Smola, A. J. and Mueller, K.-R. (1997). Kernel principal component analysis, *Lecture Notes in Computer Science* **1327**.

Schölkopf, B., Herbrich, R. and Smola, A. J. (2001). A generalized representer theorem, in *Proceedings of the 14th annual conference on learning theory*.

Schölkopf, B. and Smola, A. J. (2002). *Learning with Kernels* (MIT Press).

Skiena, S. (1997). *The Algorithm Design Manual* (Springer-Verlag).

Smart, W. D. and Kaelbling, L. P. (2000). Practical reinforcement learning in continuous spaces. in *Proceedings of the 17th International Conference on Machine Learning* (Morgan Kaufmann), pp. 903–910.

Smith, N. and Gales, M. (2002). Speech recognition using SVMs, in T. Dietterich, S. Becker and Z. Ghahramani (eds.), *Advances in Neural Information Processing Systems*, Vol. 14 (MIT Press).

Smola, A., Schölkopf, B., Williamson, R. and Bartlett, P. (2000). New support vector algorithms, *Neural Computation* **12**, 5.

Smola, A. J. and Kondor, R. (2003). Kernels and regularization on graphs, in *Proceedings of the 16th Annual Conference on Computational Learning Theory and the 7th Kernel Workshop*.

Srinivasan, A., King, R. D. and Muggleton, S. (1999). The role of background knowledge: using a problem from chemistry to examine the performance of an ilp program, Tech. rep., Oxford University Computing Laboratory.

Srinivasan, A., Muggleton, S. H., Sternberg, M. J. E. and King, R. (1996). Theories for mutagenicity: a study in first-order and feature-based induction, *Artificial Intelligence* **85**, pp. 277–299.

Sutton, R. and Barto, A. (1998). *Reinforcement Learning: an introduction* (The MIT Press, Cambridge, MA).

Suykens, J. A. K. (2000). Least squares support vector machines for classification and nonlinear modelling, *Neural Network World* **10**.

Swamidass, S. J., Chen, J., Bruand, J., Phung, P., Ralaivola, L. and Baldi, P. (2005). Kernels for small molecules and the prediction of mutagenicity, toxicity and anti-cancer activity, *Bioinformatics* **21**, pp. i359–i368.

Tan, S. M. and Fox, C. (2005). Inverse problems, University of Auckland Lecture Notes.

Tao, Q., Scott, S., Vinodchandran, N. V., Osugi, T. and Mueller, B. (2007). Kernels for generalized multiple-instance learning, *IEEE Transactions on Pattern Analysis and Machine Intelligence* **27**.

Tikhonov, A. N. (1963). Solution of incorrectly formulated problems and the regularization method, *Soviet Math. Dokl.* **4**, pp. 1035–1038.

Tikhonov, A. N. and Arsenin, V. Y. (1977). *Solutions of Ill-posed problems* (W.H. Winston).

Tsuda, K., Kawanabe, M., Rätsch, G., Sonnenburg, S. and Müller, K.-R. (2002a). A new discriminative kernel from probabilistic models, in T. Dietterich, S. Becker and Z. Ghahramani (eds.), *Advances in Neural Information Processing Systems*, Vol. 14 (MIT Press).

Tsuda, K., Kin, T. and Asai, K. (2002b). Marginalized kernels for biological sequences, in *ISMB (Supplement of Bioinformatics)*, pp. 268–275.

Vapnik, V. N. (1995). *The Nature of Statistical Learning Theory* (Springer-Verlag).

Vapnik, V. N. (1999). An overview of statistical learning theory, *IEEE Transaction on Neural Networks* **10**, 5, p. 988.

Vert, J.-P. (2002). A tree kernel to analyse phylogenetic profiles, in *ISMB (Supplement of Bioinformatics)*, pp. 276–284.

Vert, J.-P. and Kanehisa, M. (2003). Graph driven features extraction from microarray data using diffusion kernels and kernel CCA, in S. Becker, S. Thrun and K. Obermayer (eds.), *Advances in Neural Information Processing Systems*, Vol. 15 (MIT Press).

Vishwanathan, S. V. N., Borgwardt, K. and Schraudolph, N. N. (2007a). Fast computation of graph kernels, in *Advances in Neural Information Processing Systems*, Vol. 19.

Vishwanathan, S. V. N. and Smola, A. J. (2003). Fast kernels for string and tree matching, in S. Becker, S. Thrun and K. Obermayer (eds.), *Advances in Neural Information Processing Systems*, Vol. 15 (MIT Press).

Vishwanathan, S. V. N. and Smola, A. J. (2004). Binet-cauchy kernels, in *Advances in Neural Information Processing Systems*, Vol. 17.

Vishwanathan, S. V. N., Smola, A. J. and Vidal, R. (2007b). Binet-cauchy kernels on dynamical systems and its application to the analysis of dynamic scenes, *International Journal of Computer Vision* **73**, pp. 95–119.

Wachman, G. and Khardon, R. (2007). Learning from interpretations: a rooted kernel for ordered hypergraphs, *Proceedings of the 24th international conference on Machine learning* , pp. 943–950.

Wahba, G. (1990). *Spline Models for Observational Data, CBMS-NSF Regional Conference Series in Applied Mathematics*, Vol. 59 (SIAM, Philadelphia).

Wang, J. and Zucker, J.-D. (2000). Solving the multiple-instance problem: A lazy learning approach, in *Proceedings of the 17th International Conference on Machine Learning* (Morgan Kaufmann), pp. 1119–1125.

Watkins, C. (1989). *Learning from Delayed Rewards*, Ph.D. thesis, King's College, Cambridge.

Watkins, C. (1999a). Dynamic alignment kernels, Tech. rep., Department of Computer Science, Royal Holloway, University of London.

Watkins, C. (1999b). Kernels from matching operations, Tech. rep., Department of Computer Science, Royal Holloway, University of London.

Witten, I. H. and Frank, E. (2000). *Data Mining: Practical Machine Learning Tools and Techniques with Java implementations* (Morgan Kaufmann).

Wolpert, D. H. and Macready, W. G. (1995). No free lunch theorems for search, Tech. rep., Santa Fe Institute.

Wolpert, D. H. and Macready, W. G. (1997). No free lunch theorem for optimization, *IEEE Transactions on Evolutionary Computation* **1**, 1.

Woznica, A., Kalousis, A. and Hilario, M. (2006). Matching based kernels for labeled graphs, in *MLG*.

Zaki, M. (2002). Efficiently mining frequent trees in a forest, in *Proceedings of the Eighth ACM SIGKDD International Conference on Knowledge Discovery and Data Mining (KDD-02)* (ACM Press, New York), pp. 71–80.

Zhang, Q. and Goldman, S. (2002). EM-DD: An improved multiple-instance learning technique, in T. Dietterich, S. Becker and Z. Ghahramani (eds.), *Advances in Neural Information Processing Systems*, Vol. 14 (MIT Press).

Zien, A., Ratsch, G., Mika, S., Schölkopf, B., Lengauer, T. and Muller, K.-R. (2000). Engineering support vector machine kernels that recognize translation initiation sites, *Bioinformatics* **16**, 9, pp. 799–807.

Index